Brought together by two leading authorities in the field, this volume significantly advances our understanding of global retailing in both theoretical and empirical terms. Tightly edited around the notion of 'global portfolio strategies' and using seven rich corporate case studies, it successfully captures the dynamics of contemporary multi-country, multi-format retailing.

Neil M. Coe, *National University of Singapore, Singapore*

A serious book on the contemporary state of international retailing is long overdue. Dawson and Mukoyama combine their own extensive experience with those of authors from Europe and Asia to produce a book that is rich in both theoretical and practical insights.

Jonathan Reynolds, *Academic Director, Oxford Institute of Retail Management, University of Oxford, UK*

As internationalization activities of retailers continue to grow and become more complex, it is imperative that the theories and strategies of global retailing evolve. This book, an excellent resource for academics and students, provides research and case studies that examine emerging theoretical frameworks relative to the multi-format and multi-continent retail environment.

Ann E. Fairhurst, *Professor, University of Tennessee, USA*

John Dawson was 'ahead of the curve' in his recognition of the importance of retail internationalisation. Moreover, as appreciation of multinational retailers' role as 'Market makers' in the global economy spread across the social sciences, Dawson proved equally perceptive in his promotion of interdisciplinary approaches to the understanding of these developments. Writing with long-term collaborator Mukoyama, this book enhances Dawson's claims to thought leadership on the globalization of retailing. It is an essential read.

Neil Wrigley, *FBA, Professor, University of Southampton, UK*

Global Strategies in Retailing

Large- and medium-sized retailers have increased their international operations substantially over the last 25 years. This is evident in: the number of countries to which these retailers expand; the growing international sales of retailers; and the heightening of the level of commitment of retailers to their international activity – a trend that is likely to continue over the next decade as general globalization in the service industries increases.

The managerial implications of the moves to become global are considerable. Different retailers are pursuing different approaches, to varying degrees of success and are no longer simply multi-national, but are also multi-continental. Consequently, existing concepts and theories of international business fit uneasily in explanations of international retailing, so new corporate strategies need to be explored.

Featuring in-depth studies of seven retailers, by international scholars from Japan, the UK and Sweden, *Global Strategies in Retailing* explores recent developments in strategy that are related to international retailing and in particular, the emergence of a Global Portfolio Strategy. As such, this book will be important reading for all international business and retailing students and academics researching in these areas.

John Dawson is Emeritus Professor at the Universities of Edinburgh and Stirling, both in the UK. He has been researching issues in international retailing over the last 20 years and has supervised a number of doctoral students in the area. His recent visiting positions include Visiting Researcher at the University of Valencia, Spain and Distinguished Professor at UMDS, Japan. He has been author or editor of over 20 books and is the founding co-editor of *International Review of Retail, Distribution and Consumer Research.*

Masao Mukoyama is Professor of Retailing at the University of Marketing and Distribution Sciences, Japan. He has published many papers on international retailing, including 'Toward the Emergence of Pure Global' (in Japanese), and is one of pioneers in international retailing research in Asia.

Routledge studies in international business and the world economy

Global Strategies in Retailing

Asian and European experiences

**Edited by John Dawson and
Masao Mukoyama**

Routledge
Taylor & Francis Group

LONDON AND NEW YORK

First published 2014 by Routledge

2 Park Square, Milton Park, Abingdon, Oxfordshire OX14 4RN
52 Vanderbilt Avenue, New York, NY 10017

Routledge is an imprint of the Taylor & Francis Group, an informa business

First issued in paperback 2019

British Library Cataloguing in Publication Data
A catalogue record for this book is available from the British Library

Library of Congress Cataloging in Publication Data
Global strategies in retailing: Asian and European experiences / edited by
John Dawson and Masao Mukoyama.
    pages cm. – (Routledge studies in international business and the world
    economy)
    Includes bibliographical references and index.
    1. Retail trade–Europe. 2. Retail trade–Asia. 3. International trade.
    4. Strategic planning–Europe. 5. Strategic planning–Asia. I. Dawson,
    John A. II. Mukoyama, Masao.
    HF5429.G5436 2013
    658.8'7–dc23

                                                      2013013857

ISBN: 978-0-415-64429-7 (hbk)
ISBN: 978-0-367-86749-2 (pbk)

Typeset in Times New Roman
by Wearset Ltd, Boldon, Tyne and Wear

Contents

Figures

Tables

Contributors

Jung-Yim Baek is Associate Professor of International Retailing at University of Marketing and Distribution Sciences, Kobe, Japan. She has spent time as Visiting Researcher at Le Ceridice, EACP-EAP. She has researched issues in the growth and internationalization process of the largest retailers in Asian emerging markets and competition with multinationals from developed countries.

Steve Burt is Professor of Retail Marketing and Senior Deputy Principal at the University of Stirling. He is author of numerous papers on international retailing and has worked on consultancy projects with major retailers. He has been involved with research, teaching and consulting on international retail issues since the mid-1980s. He has co-edited *Consuming IKEA* with Ulf Johansson and Åsa Thelander.

Sang Chul Choi is Professor of Marketing and Retail Studies, University of Marketing and Distribution Sciences, Kobe, Japan. He has published extensively in both Japan and South Korea on Japanese retailing and distribution systems. He is author of *Winning Companies of Japanese Retailing* published in Korean in 2010.

John Dawson is Emeritus Professor at The Universities of Edinburgh and Stirling. He has been researching issues in international retailing over the last 20 years and has supervised a number of doctoral students in the area. His recent visiting positions include Visiting Researcher at the University of Valencia, and Distinguished Professor at UMDS, Kobe. He has been author or editor of over 20 books and was founding co-editor of *International Review of Retail, Distribution and Consumer Research*.

Ulf Johansson is Professor of Marketing at University of Lund. He has been leading a research project on international retailing and branding He has spent periods as Visiting Professor at the University of Stirling as well as Melbourne Business School. He is co-editor with Steve Burt and Åsa Thelander of *Consuming IKEA: Different perspectives on consumer images of a global retailer* (Lund University Press, 2011).

Masao Mukoyama is Professor of Retailing at the University of Marketing and Distribution Sciences in Kobe, Japan. He has published papers on international retailing including 'Toward the Emergence of Pure Global' (in Japanese), and is one of the pioneers in international retailing research in Asia.

Tatsuro Toba is Associate Professor of Marketing at the University of Toyama. His research interests cover marketing activity of international retailers in Japanese market, social marketing of retailers and history of innovative retail format development.

Introduction

The nature of international retailing has changed since the mid-1990s. Spatial scope has extended and organizational complexity has increased. Compared to the manufacturing sector's investment in international production, retailers have been relatively slow to invest in international distribution, despite their long history in sourcing goods for resale from foreign suppliers. Through the 2000s, however, the amounts of foreign retailer investment, around the world, have increased substantially. As part of the wider globalization of economic activity retailer internationalization is now widespread and the strategies involved have become accepted mechanisms to create competitive retail firms operating across many markets. The surge in international activity by retailers has generated many new questions for what was long a sector characterized by a conservative approach to research, development and strategy. Whilst retailers have been able to learn from and draw some parallels with the international activity of manufacturers, many differences in the internationalization process of retailers have become apparent as international activity has taken place. Retailers have found it necessary to develop new managerial capabilities in order to operate successfully in the new markets being entered. The modes of entry and subsequent post-entry activities have required intensive knowledge acquisition and application with the managerial capabilities changing as the retailers have implemented their internationalization strategies.

It is clear that there is a complex set of processes required in taking a retailer into new markets. The complexity has increased as retailers have increased the spatial scope of markets being entered and have increased the types of retailing they take international. Retailers have moved from border-hopping activity involving a single format of retailing to operating several different formats on a multi-continental basis. In making this transition many of the retailers involved have moved from their position of being relatively passive economic agents responding to consumer demands and acting as intermediaries between producers and consumers. The retailers have become more active in shaping consumer demand, determining the activity of producers and taking control of relationships within the overall economic value chain. Whilst this has happened in their home market it has happened to the same or even greater extent when the retailer moves into a foreign market. The power for retailers to influence the form and direction of economic and social development has increased as very large firms have emerged with multi-continental and multi-format network structures.

This phenomenon has not gone unnoticed by academics. The international-ization of retailing and the growth in economic and social power of the major retail firms has generated substantial research to gain an understanding of the processes involved. The research reported in the following chapters is in this tra-dition and builds on these earlier studies. Empirical studies of the activities of retailers have played an important role in monitoring and describing the inter-nationalization process. But, as international retailing has entered into new areas of multi-format multi-continent operation so the processes of development have become more complex and new conceptual and theoretical frameworks are required to provide a context for the overall process in which some retailers are at an advanced stage whilst others are still undertaking tentative moves into adja-cent countries. For the retailers involved in internationalization, the nature of the knowledge that is required for success is new and the interplay between the internationalizing firm and the culture it enters has become more mutually inter-active. The interactions between firms and the society have become more important to an understanding of the process than either the 'top-down' strategy of the firm or the 'bottom-up' tactics of consumers.

The characteristics of a conceptual and theoretical framework that could be used to explore the recent changes in the nature of international retailing need to address the following types of issue:

• the condition that retailer internationalization is a continuing process both for individual retailers and for the sector as a whole;
• the critical events, internal to the firm and from the commercial environ-ment, which result in changes in the intensity and direction of operation of this process;
• the nature of the impacts and effects of retailer internationalization inter-nally in the internationalizing firm, on the commercial environment being entered and on the domestic commercial environment of the firm involved;
• the role and nature of interplay between the manager, the firm, the market and society (as communicated through consumer culture);
• the presence of constraints and catalysts, and the nature of these, that the firm, though its managers, can respond to in order to implement inter-national activity;
• the embedding of the process in time and space;
• the presence of continuous feedbacks in the process that reflect the learning activities that take place amongst the various groups involved, including managers in the retailer, its competitors and its suppliers, public policy administrators, consumers and others in the commercial environment;
• the variety of organizational structures that can be used to facilitate entry and development in the foreign market.

What in effect is taking place is a change in the structure of the retail market that involves processes of learning, innovation, competition and cooperation. These processes form the basis of interaction between the internationalizing firm and the society which it enters.

In considering these requirements then several of the past theoretical approaches suffer from various deficiencies. Despite the empirical evidence from many studies, several of the theories can be criticized for one or more of the following reasons:

- They tend to focus on one-to-one (dyadic) relationships between the parent firm and the subsidiary in the host country.
- They only consider the process of development in the host country.
- They fail to address differences in the development process between countries and the conditions generating those differences.
- They do not enable a holistic view of the internationalization process of the retailer but focus on specific aspects. The accumulation of dyadic relationships is not the same as a holistic view.
- They are inadequate in consideration of the timing and sequencing of events.
- They fail to appreciate that the differences in format, and particularly multi-format operation, are important in the internationalization process of retailing.
- They do not take into account the move to 'aggressive' internationalization apparent since around 2000.

There is therefore a strong case to consider alternative approaches to developing theory.

We make no claims that the research reported in the following chapters address all these issues or provides an all-encompassing theory. Generating theoretical frameworks relevant to the internationalization processes in retailing is a slow process of the development of ideas and concepts – accepting some, rejecting others. The research reported here provides some of these ideas and concepts. The rapid rate of change and development of the internationalization process undertaken by retailers means that theory seems to fall ever more behind practice. The emergence of multi-format multi-continent networks of operation has emerged but discussion of relevant theory and concepts has yet to occur. The research reported here is an attempt to initiate this discussion with the concept of a Global Portfolio being managed by the retailers.

The studies in this book were supported by Japan Society for the Promotion of Science (KAKENHI Grant Number 19203023). The researchers, based in Japan, UK and Sweden, undertook interviews with retailers, some of which have resulted in the following chapters, in Europe and East Asia. The focus of inquiry was on the nature and activities associated with post-entry development of internationalizing retailers. The retailers selected for inclusion as case studies reflect four aspects of development towards a multi-format multi-continent position.

Nitori is a strong single-format retailer that remains in East Asia and has aspirations to expand into several countries in this region. IKEA and Muji have remained very largely true to their original format and have been successful in taking this to several continents where they operate in multiple countries. Uni-President and Lotte operate multiple formats and have so far largely limited their operations to East Asia but are aware that future growth may mean moves to another continent. Metro and Delhaize have a substantial history of international activity operating multi-format and multi-continent networks into which countries and formats are entered and exited.

The international activities of retailers have far-reaching implications for the markets they enter and those they leave. The extent and influence of international retailers continue to increase year on year. Their expansion into new markets presents not only challenges for the firm involved but also for the commercial environment and consumer culture of the new host country. The dynamics of the internationalization process, what constitutes success and failure, the effects on consumer culture all continue to challenge researchers as well as managers. The emergence of multi-format multi-continent network structured retailers generates new issues to be addressed by retail executives and academic researchers as they seek to understand these new retail structures.

Acknowledgements

The research undertaken in the preparation of the studies of retailers reported in this book was supported in part by a Grant-in-Aid for Scientific Research from Japan Society for the Promotion of Science (Term of Project: 2007–2010, Project Number: 19203023).

1 Recent developments in retail internationalization

John Dawson and Masao Mukoyama

> *Our reasons to expand were different for every country but the goal is common – growth.*
>
> Jose Gomez, Senior Vice-President Business Development,
> Mango NRF Conference, 2013

Retailing was, and often still is, seen to be a domestic economic activity. Reality is somewhat different. Although consumers usually buy locally, there is a long history of international sourcing of products by retailers, an equally long history of the international flow of retail entrepreneurs, and of retailers moving across country boundaries to sell products. Whilst present, these non-domestic activities were, for several centuries, generally marginal to the overall functioning of retailing. The dominant structure of retailing was one in which the local economy provided products, and local entrepreneurs created services for consumers who bought locally. Clearly this is no longer the case with large retailers now functioning as part of a global economy with individual firms operating sales outlets on a multi-continental basis and being responsible for large international flows of products. The international structure of retailing, which has emerged over the last 40 years, exists alongside the legacy of the domestic structure. This dichotomy of domestic and international dimensions is central to any current consideration of the management, functioning, structure and perceptions of the retail sector. The power of the international activities, however, is eroding steadily the established domestic hegemony in retailing. As the large international retailers become global organizations they are faced with strategic challenges very different from those associated with their historical domestic position.

The origins of significant international dimensions to retailing reside in the power of scale economies in the operations of retailers. The entrepreneurs who developed department stores in the nineteenth century sought scale-related cost economies through serving more customers per unit of infrastructure and, in order to generate the necessary customer flow, had to source products internationally to obtain quantity and variety of assortment (Pasdermadjian 1954; Ferry 1961; Gerlach 1988). Department stores provide many early examples of international flows of knowledge, for example the personal knowledge gained by Harry Selfridge on his visit to Europe in 1888 (Honeycombe 1984), the relocation of entrepreneurs taking knowledge internationally, for example in the early department stores in Hong Kong and Shanghai by Ma and Guo (Chan 1998; Hang and Godley 2009; Hang 2009), and the international transfers within the firm as it opened stores in new markets, as in the case of Whiteaway and Laidlaw in its expansion into Asian and African cities in the then British Empire. Hollander (1970) called this international flow of knowledge, 'international borrowing through visits, apprenticeships for managerial heirs and information exchanges' (p. 21) asserting that, 'Multicountry flows of ideas, merchandise, finance and entrepreneurship have helped shape the entire history of the department store' (p. 20). These activities were also important in generating awareness of international issues within the culture of the firm. International activity in terms of sourcing and knowledge accumulation, enhanced and increased the scale economies gained from the operations of large department stores. International activity was central to the development of department stores through the nineteenth and twentieth centuries.

The search for scale economies in store size, as exemplified by department stores, was paralleled by early attempts to gain scale economies through multistore operation. Again international activity was important in the early history of chain stores in creating scale economies. With the growth of larger firms, so purchasing relationships with manufacturers changed with increasing marginalization of wholesalers and a reduction in channel costs that were passed to consumers as lower prices. Larger scale provided cost economies in purchasing and reduced channel costs. To gain this larger scale of purchasing the retailers opened multiple stores which also then reduced overall firm-level risk of local market fluctuations. The increases in the store network in the domestic market steadily reduced the opportunity for domestic growth so expansion internationally became an attractive option. By extending the store chain to operate in countries adjacent to their home market the scale-related benefits were increased. Julius Meinl crossed boundaries in Central Europe in the early twentieth century with its coffee and provision stores, building a network across nine countries by 1939, whilst F. W. Woolworth in the USA opened stores in Canada, Mexico and Cuba as well as establishing subsidiary firms in UK, Germany and Spain. The lower cost and risk reduction advantages associated with being a large chainstore organization were enhanced by international operation.

These early international activities by retailers were characterized by specific entrepreneurial activity and can be seen as important, but isolated, examples which comprised a small part of total retailing. The activity was often opportunistic and was a response to local circumstances, with entrepreneurs responding to opportunities and specific aspects of the local socio–economic–political environment. The extent and variety of these activities have been considered by Hollander (1970) and, particularly those involving UK retailers, by Godley and Fletcher (2001) and Whysall (1997). These studies indicate a piecemeal approach to international activity with great variety of operational implementation, individual entrepreneurialism and activity characterized as responsive to events in the market. There was little systematic pattern to these activities. International retailing was of this type until around the early 1970s when the beginnings of a change of approach can be seen and from which the current extensive activity has grown.

Since the early 1970s, as part of wider changes in the sector there has been a substantive change in the form and intensity of the international activity in that there has there been a substantial increase not only in international sourcing (Dawson and Mukoyama 2006a) but also in operating stores outside the home market (Alexander and Doherty 2010; Swoboda *et al.* 2009). This expansion of international activity has been the result of more formal growth strategies rather than the entrepreneurial approach of previous decades. These formal strategies have continued the search for scale economies but have emerged with a stronger focus on scale-related benefits from organizational scale rather than establishment scale. This has encouraged the seeking of firm-level scale increases resulting not only from spatial expansion in market activity but also from greater diversification of international activity to address multiple markets. Internationalization has become a widespread strategy amongst large, mid-sized and even small retailers. In Western Europe, for example, it is estimated that by 2010 there were about 5,200 retail firms that were operating stores internationally through well over 100,000 stores.

International activity increased steadily, with the pace of development increasing in the 2000s. This has been evident across the world with more intra-continental moves within Europe, Asia and the Americas and additionally the emergence of a new dimension with major inter-continental moves. There has been a substantial increase in the scale and geographic scope of strategic actions such that by 2010, 80 of the 100 largest retailers in the world operated internationally and of the 20 that limited their operations to their home country ten were based in the USA.[1] Ten years previously 35 of the largest 100 limited themselves to domestic operations and in 1990, 52 were domestic market firms and of the 48 with international presence 14 were in only one additional country. For large retail firms internationalization has become an accepted and widely used growth strategy. Medium-sized firms are also following this approach with in 2010, according to Deloitte Touche Tohmatsu Limited (2012), 51 of the firms ranked 100–200 in their ranking of retailers on sales, operating internationally. For the large retailers pursuing this strategy, their growth in scale has enabled them not simply to respond to the market but also to be active in shaping their various markets through influencing consumer choice, supplier behaviour and attitudes of public policymakers (Dawson 2013). The shift from being reactive to the market environment to being active in shaping the environment, termed 'market driving' by Ghauri *et al.* (2008) and 'market making' by Petrovic and Hamilton (2011), is a consequence of the increased scale and international scope of retail firms and it has enabled retailers to gain more control over their developments in new markets and to reduce the risks inherent in international moves.

In moving from being an entrepreneurial activity responsive to local events to being an established growth strategy in which the retailers shape the market, the nature of international activity has changed. Internationalization is an evolving process within the firm. The changing international dimensions impinge on functions throughout the firm. The process evolves as the firm gains knowledge and as the international relationships become more important to the growth of the firm. This evolution of the internationalization process exists at the firm level and at the sectoral level. Within this evolution, earlier forms coexist alongside newer forms with innovation creating the new forms and strategies as retailers expand into new markets.

Phases of development of international retailing

The evolution from an entrepreneurial approach to a market-shaping approach to retail international growth strategy can be seen as involving several phases. This evolution is characterized by growing exploitation of a variety of benefits associated with increased scale of operation and, with this, a change in the relationship between structure and agency leading to evolution through a Giddens-type structuration process in the sector (Kilminster 1991; Sewell 1992). Alongside the structuration processes at firm and sector levels new dynamic capabilities (Teece 2009; Frasquet *et al.* 2013; Cao 2011) have emerged in firm-level processes. Several phases can be identified in the evolving process of retail internationalization. Discussion here is limited to the operation of sales methods but international sourcing and knowledge transfer have also became more complex as the overall process has evolved through several phases. These phases can be conceptualized either at the level of the individual firm or the sector in totality with the leading firms establishing new successive phases of development.

Entrepreneurial and opportunistic activity

The initial phase of international activity is the result of the entrepreneurial activity and commitment of an owner or key senior executive and results in established domestic firms establishing branch stores in foreign markets. Hollander (1970) provides many illustrations of this type of activity in the decades prior to the 1970s but it is still evident today amongst some small firms. Typically the retailer opens a small number of stores in one or two foreign markets. From these origins, in a few cases substantial and successful chains are developed in a strongly formalized way but the origins of such chains reside in an entrepreneurial response by a committed executive to a perceived commercial opportunity in a familiar market. The opportunity to become international may have arisen from some personal relationship or a cultural link to the foreign country or city: historically, for example, French and British firms opening stores in former colonies. More recently in Europe, 'border hopping' has been evident in these smaller stores. Within the totality of retailing the number of firms and the significance of the activity are small but for a few firms, for example C&A

Brenninkmeyer, Bata shoes (in its pre- and post-Second World War incorporations) and F. W. Woolworth, initial entrepreneurial activity resulted in substantial later development with the idea of international operation becoming entrenched in the firm's culture through the commitment of the entrepreneur.

Across the retail sector there is great variety of international involvement at this phase. Firms generally take their single operational format into the foreign market. The selected market is often, although not always, one with a lower demand per head in comparison with the domestic market. The opportunistic nature of many of the international actions results in exits from the foreign market being commonplace as the opportunity turns out to be less attractive than initially perceived by the entrepreneur. Direct and indirect costs of exit are small given the limited size of the investment. The tendency is to be market responsive and relatively passive in the interactions with the market environment (Knee 1966).

Experimental and learning orientated activity

A different type of internationalization started to became evident in leading firms from the early 1970s and through the 1980s. In this phase, retailers explore new markets in a more formal but still largely modest way. Managers gradually begin to develop knowledge and capabilities to facilitate international expansion. The survey by Corporate Intelligence Group (1991) recorded 338 European retailers involved in international activity. Retailers who had developed a strong presence in their home market sought out new countries into which to expand sometimes with trans-Atlantic moves. Kacker (1985) notes the surge in transatlantic acquisitions around this time but there were also moves by strongly branded firms exploring how the brand might 'travel' and by a small number of mass-merchandisers (Waldman 1978). For example Laura Ashley entered the USA with a store in downtown San Francisco in 1974 (Bunce 1989). More typical in terms of market spread is for expansion to take place into neighbouring countries with the firms remaining firmly rooted in their domestic operations and the internationalized format is a simple extension of the one used in the home market with little adaption. Typical in this respect is H&M with initial early moves from Sweden to Norway and Denmark and then through the 1970s to other culturally similar markets as shown in Table 1.1.

Table 1.1 H&M store network and sales shares at end FY 1979–1980

	Year of entry	*Number of stores*	*% of firm's sales*
Sweden		81	78.7
Norway	1964	15	11.9
Denmark	1967	14	5.1
UK	1976	6	1.9
Switzerland	1978	6	2.3
Germany	1980	2	0.1
Total		124	100

Other early examples of activity in this phase are the franchise activity of Body Shop, Carrefour's moves post-1969 into Belgium, Italy and Spain, Delhaize's entry into USA, Aldi's gradual expansion out of Germany into other European markets (Austria 1967, Netherlands 1973, Belgium and USA 1976, Denmark 1977) and the start of international expansion by Toys R Us and IKEA (Mårtenson 1981). A number of studies, for example (Laulajainen 1991a, 1991b, 1992) describe these moves but they must be seen as tentative attempts by the firms to gain knowledge about what was possible in terms of international expansion. The learning curve was steep and the new markets were often not profitable for several years; for example it took H&M five years post-entry before profit was made from stores in Germany and even longer for the UK stores to be profitable. For almost all of these firms historically the emphasis remained on building scale in their home market with international activity being a marginal activity. There were few specific capabilities associated with internationalization with domestic capabilities being simply transferred with minimal adaption for local market nuances. For many of the firms there was still an opportunistic aspect to the international activity at this phase, particularly at a local level within host countries, with the firm gaining knowledge of the managerial processes involved in moving international as well as collecting information on trading conditions and consumer behaviour in foreign markets.

Formalized market responsive activity

Changes in the market environment and the application of learning from previous experiences encouraged a new phase of activity to develop in leading firms in the late 1980s. Within Europe, activity increased fivefold in the 1990s compared with the 1980s (Retail Intelligence 2001). By the late 1980s, for most of the larger firms involved, the idea of internationalization had become a formalized, but non-core, strategy to be undertaken alongside their domestic market strategy (Burt 1991, 1993). Many of the international moves that took place were still small scale explorations of new markets, often in countries adjacent to existing operations (termed border hopping), rather than a mainstream strategy of full-scale internationalization but the evaluation of market entry was more formalized than the previous opportunistic approaches (Alexander 1990). There remained, however, a strongly opportunistic aspect to the implementation of many of the foreign moves, even when the idea of becoming international was a component of corporate strategy (Dawson 2001a). Flexibility linked to opportunism was present in development activity and resulted in considerable learning about the commercial environment in host countries. The knowledge gained was being used to create profitable operations outside the home market although the share of foreign operations to profits lagged behind the share of sales.

By the mid-1990s, for a few firms internationalization was becoming a mainstream strategy, in parallel to having a strong domestic market strategy (Burt 1991, 1993). Through the 1990s the number of these firms increased. In comparison with the manufacturing sector, retailing lagged in its international perspective in respect of both the extent and intensity of firm activity. But, from the late 1980s through the early 1990s a number of factors in the operational environment, particularly for European retailers, and in the internal management of firms encouraged the initiation and development of this new phase of internationalization. These changes facilitated greater interest in international expansion as a defined strategic option supplementing domestically orientated strategy.

Domestic market concentration. The growth of large retail firms in domestic markets through the 1980s, often through merger and acquisition and associated with the adoption of marketing by retailers, resulted in increasing levels of concentration in these domestic markets so increasing the difficulty of growth in the domestic market. The strategic options for these large firms, in order to achieve the sales growth that satisfied financial stakeholders, were increasingly limited to diversification or internationalization. Several firms selected internationalization. This is particularly noticeable in the smaller European markets so, for example, by 1990 H&M had more stores outside Sweden than within Sweden (Table 1.2) although the majority of profit was attributable to the Swedish stores.

Reduced barriers to cross-border movement. Within Europe the moves to the creation of a single European market between 1985 and 1992 made cross-border activity easier from an operational perspective and reduced perceived psychic differences between markets. Pellegrini (1992) forecast an increase in international activity as a result of the initiatives and the European Commission (1997a) in its review of the effects of the Single Market initiative confirmed this effect with a notable increase in intra-European retail merger and acquisition activity in the years prior to 1992, when the single market became operational, with a conclusion that 'After 1985, EU markets received significantly more attention from internationally expanding retailers than non-EU destinations' (p. 119). Van Geenhuizen *et al.* (1996) point to the reduced barriers encouraging activity particularly in border regions with the extension of networks across borders serviced from previously established infrastructure. The creation of

Table 1.2 Store network and sales shares of H&M at end FY 1989–1990

	Number of stores	*% of sales*
Sweden	102[1]	48.3
Norway	36	13.7
Denmark	26	15.0
Germany	28	10.4
UK	16	6.6
Switzerland	28	3.7
Netherlands	13	2.3
Total	249	100

Note
1 Includes small number of BK stores aimed at up-market shoppers and nine Galne Gunnar discount stores selling surplus and bankrupt stock, including non-clothing items.

NAFTA from 1 January 1994 had a similar, though less intense, effect in North America to the Single Market initiative in Europe with expansion into Canada and Mexico from the USA. The opening of borders increased the perception that minimal adaption of activity was needed with the transfer of current activities within a 'single market' and this was reinforced in Europe with ideas of the presence of 'euro-consumers'. This view was quickly dispelled as operations developed in the new markets and, in Europe, the idea of the standardized euro-consumer was realized to be a myth.

Privatization of Central Europe. The collapse of the centralized structures in the planned economies in Central Europe from 1989 opened new, large and under-provisioned markets with little local retail expertise (Rigoureau-Juin and Kerrad 1993). For example IKEA and BILLA entered Poland in 1990, GIB in 1991, and REMA in 1993. By 1996 the Institute of Home Market and Consumption (1997) estimated, that in Poland, there were 925 stores operated by foreign retailers and emphasized that their number belied their importance. By 1999, nine of the largest ten retailers in Poland were foreign owned (Pütz 1998; Dawson 2001a, 2001b; Dawson and Henley 1999). The Eurostat study of retailing in Central Europe (European Commission 1997b) points to an initial small group of pioneering firms that invested in central European countries early in the 1990s and 'A new wave of operations started in 1994 with more substantial acquisitions … and the opening of hypermarkets' (p. 18) all of which were foreign direct investments. Again, initially there was a widely held view that the new markets would be unquestioningly receptive to the simple transfer of existing retail practice and again this was dispelled as retailers gained knowledge of the particularities of local consumer demand and behaviour.

Adoption of new managerial practice. Longer term shifts in the evolution of the management of retail organizations resulted from the application of marketing in the 1980s and the integration of technology applications, particularly but not exclusively convergence of information and communication technology, by the mid-1990s. Integration of information and communication technology enabled the control of an international network of stores whilst advances in marketing enabled retailers to transfer marketing concepts to new markets but they often lacked knowledge in making the necessary adaptions to these local markets.

Demonstration effects of success. The demonstration effect of Wal-Mart deciding to develop internationally into Mexico in 1991 was important. The creation of an international division in 1993 legitimized internationalization as an acceptable retail strategy for investors and retailers in the USA. The successes of IKEA and H&M also demonstrated that international expansion could be successful in more specialist sectors. These high profile successes reinforced the view that a strong domestic format could be transferred with relatively little adaption.

By the early 1990s the conditions, internally within large firms and externally in market conditions particularly in Europe, were 'ripening' for the development of international retailing as a formal strategy. The view of strategy that was emerging was grounded in transferring existing operational knowledge from domestic to new market. Whilst knowledge was being gained in the new markets the knowledge was piecemeal and difficult to integrate into the existing knowledge base and operational practice. Awareness of the need for specific capabilities associated with internationalization was becoming apparent but the development of these capabilities was still at a very early stage.

European, and to a lesser extent North American, retailers developed international activity, but on a mainly intra-continental basis. Asian retailers began to explore expansion into other Asian markets (Pananond and Zeithaml 1998). The history of failure of several high-profile inter-continental transatlantic moves, for example Dixons in USA, Carrefour in USA, Marks and Spencer in Canada, K-Mart in the then Czechoslovakia, or the acute difficulties encountered in these investments, for example IKEA in Canada, encouraged strategists to focus on intra-continental moves with inter-continental moves often viewed as too high risk. The internationalization capabilities of retailers were seldom well enough established to make the transition to another continent. Analysts advising major financial institutions also questioned the ability of retailers to generate profits in international markets either distant or very different from the home market. Moving inter-continent was a step too far for internal control systems of many firms, other than when there was a very limited presence for example with Eddie Bauer and Gap entries into Japan, as well as raising questions about the capabilities of retailers to operate in fundamentally different consumer and management cultures.

The effect of these changes is seen in the internationalization of the 100 largest firms over the 1986–1996 period (Table 1.3). Between 1986 and 1996 the number of these 100 large firms operating in only one country fell from 53 to 40 whilst the number with stores in more than five countries increased from 16 to 35. More large firms became involved in internationalization and the scope of international activities widened. But the number of these 100 firms operating on more than one continent remained small.

By the mid-1990s the foundations for international activity had been laid and in the decade from the late 1990s there was a notable increase in activity that built on the foundations in marketing and technology convergence to create formalized internationalization strategies that were able to exploit cost economies of scale across several functions.

Table 1.3 Geographical spread of store operations of 100 largest firms, 1986–1996

Number of countries	1986	1996
1	53	40
2 to 4	31	25
5 to 9	11	17
10 to 19	4	13
20 and more	1	5
Average for top 100	2.8	5.5
Operating on more than one continent	7	13

Formalized market shaping and embedding

From the late 1990s we begin to see changes in the pattern of internationalization strategies constituting the start of a fourth phase of evolution. Whilst the number of firms in the top 100 that operated only in their domestic market declined steadily to only 20 in 2010 (Table 1.4), the very large, already international, retailers started to change strategy from further expansion of their market scope to focusing on a limited number of large markets in which they could build substantial market share and realistically aspire to be one of the top retailers, potentially in the top three of their market.

The perception of international markets changed with greater realization that foreign market activity could be undertaken on equal terms, and in some cases more substantive ways, to the domestic market. This required the identification of key foreign markets and then, not only, the development of a large-scale presence in the selected market, but also embedding the retailers into the economic, social and political environment (Wrigley *et al.* 2005; Hess 2004; Jones 2008). Scale economies for some functions began to be achieved in each of the several markets of operation in addition to those economies resulting from consolidation and sharing of activity across all the markets.

For the largest 50 firms the average number of countries in which they operate has changed little (Table 1.5). This meant withdrawing from some markets where they had a limited presence, but it also meant investment in large markets often on another continent. Retailers ranked 50–100 continued to expand internationally by entering new markets. These are mainly specialist retail firms, with many of them in the fashion sector, seeking to extend the spatial scope of their brand through expansion of a dominant format. The overall amount of international activity increased considerably in terms of market share accounted for by foreign markets (Table 1.6). Amongst the smaller and medium-sized firms there was a substantial increase in border hopping (in effect Phase 3-type activity for this group of firms), with the second tier of firms registering an increase in foreign sales percentage to match the increase in scope of operation. By 2010, around 25 per cent of the sales of the 100 largest retailers were from foreign markets, amounting, when converted to US$, to a sales total in excess of US$800 billion.

Table 1.4 Geographical spread of store operations of 100 largest firms, 1996–2010

Number of countries	1996	1999	2003	2006	2010
1	40	35	31	25	20
2 to 4	25	25	23	23	23
5 to 9	17	14	10	18	19
10 to 19	13	15	15	13	16
20 and more	5	11	21	21	22
Average for top 100	5.5	6.5	10.1	11.5	13.4
Operating on more than one continent	13	28	33	39	36

Table 1.5 Average number of countries in which retailers operated

Firms ranked by sales	1998	2000	2002	2004	2006	2008	2010
Largest 25	7.6	8.8	8.4	9.8	9.0	10.4	10.2
26–50	8.0	10.7	14.5	9.1	11.0	10.0	8.7
51–75	5.1	5.9	9.2	13.4	14.7	18.4	20.3
76–100	2.4	3.4	4.7	7.6	12.6	11.0	6.9
Largest 100	5.6	7.2	9.2	10.0	11.5	12.4	13.4

Table 1.6 Percentage of sales accounted for by foreign operations

	1998	2000	2002	2004	2006	2008	2010
Rank 1–25	23.0	20.3	18.5	22.5	21.2	24.9	26.3
Rank 26–50	14.8	19.3	22.0	18.0	20.9	22.8	22.9
Rank 51–75	8.9	8.6	9.3	13.8	23.2	27.9	26.8
Rank 76–100	9.2	9.8	9.9	16.1	20.2	21.5	23.1
All 100 firms	11.1	13.4	13.9	16.7	21.4	24.1	26.6

Inter-continental moves, notably by the larger retailers became more common. This activity was in part stimulated by the opportunities presented in South Korea and Thailand by the Asian financial crisis of the late 1990s and governmental policies to open markets to foreign direct investment. Rugman (2005; Rugman and Girod 2003) using data for the end of the 1990s showed that retail multinationals were, with one exception, strongly rooted in a single continent. Although they were starting to invest in operations in other continents it was argued that they remained in reality 'regional' not 'global'. The situation has changed since 2000 and whilst only a few retailers can be termed global there has been a steadily growing pattern of multi-continental activity (this is explored in Chapter 3). Within their international strategies, retailers became increasingly multi-format in their retail operations in the context of both single continent and multi-continent activity.

The increase in size and power of the international firms together with increasing control over their supply chains enabled them to become more directive in their operations such that they were able to create markets for their particular type of retailing (Hamilton *et al.* 2011). This became apparent particularly as major Western retailers moved into China, notably from the mid-2000s, but its beginnings were in central Europe from around 2000 as European retailers who had moved into these new markets realized that consumer culture was not well established and markets could be created as the spending power of consumers increased. Having gained knowledge in the emerging markets in Central Europe the opportunity then arose for a similar perspective to be adopted in developments in China. Thus, for example IKEA, H&M, Burberry, Inditex and Sephora, have been able to influence consumption styles and create markets for their products and more importantly for their total retail offer. Rather than being only responsive to the consumer they have also influenced the consumption culture of the host country.

The activity of H&M through the 2000s illustrates several of the features characterizing this fourth phase of international expansion. Scope and scale of international operations increased substantially. Directly owned stores were opened in 20 new country markets between 1999 and 2010 and over 2000 stores opened outside the domestic market. From its strong multinational European base developed through the 1990s, H&M moved inter-continentally in 2000 with stores in the USA which it identified as a key market and made substantial investment (Table 1.7) such that sales in the USA became larger than in the Swedish market within ten years. Opportunities opening up in Central Europe enabled further European development. In the second half of the decade further inter-continental expansion took place initially with China and Japan, which were again identified as key markets. The increased complexity of H&M operations is seen in a need to reorganize the firm on a regional basis and also in the use of franchising, after 2006, as an entry mode into markets with particularly complex political environments. The expansion into markets with a very different clothes fashion culture in East Asian, Eastern Mediterranean countries and Gulf States illustrates moves to create markets rather than being simply market responsive.

The fourth phase of international development exhibits an increase in scale, scope and complexity of the foreign-owned networks of stores. For example, the average number of stores operated by each of the largest 25 firms in 2000 was 4,824 and this had increased to 7,150 by 2009. Leading firms are operating on a multi-continental basis. From retailing being a response to culture, the retail firms, through their managers, now are active in shaping the market, culture and society in which they operate.

A further consequence of the increase in international activity has been a major increase in the extent of global concentration in retailing through the 2000s. Between 2000 and 2007 there has been a doubling of the share of global sales accountable to the foreign activities of the largest 100 retailers (Table 1.8). The growing power associated with international activities, and the associated scale-related benefits, is a consistent feature through the phases of internationalization

Structuration through the phases of evolution

The internationalization of retailing has passed through a number of phases since the 1970s. Through these phases various dimensions of the activity have evolved as scope, scale and organizational complexity of firms have all increased. Table 1.9 summarizes characteristics of the four phases. The evolution of international retailing clearly will continue. In Chapter 3 of this book we consider the emergence of a further phase that can be termed as a phase of the *Global Portfolio Strategy* in which the internationalization process becomes coordinated across multiple formats and with operations on several continents that are culturally distinct. In considering the patterns associated with the various phases, we can postulate their development as a process of structuration generated by the interaction between structure and agency with the interaction between structure and agency changing through the progression of the phases.

Theories that explore the integration of structure and agency have been important in providing insights into the nature of social change in a variety of

Table 1.7 H&M store network and sales shares by country

	Year of entry	Number of stores at year end		% of sales	
		1998–1999	*2010–2011*	*1998–1999*	*2010–2011*
Sweden		124[1]	173	16.1	6.5
Norway	1964	55	104	8.5	4.2
Denmark	1967	45	90	5.6	3.3
UK	1976	34	213	4.4	7.2
Switzerland	1978	41	80	7.5	4.7
Germany	1980	167	394	32.3	23.1
Netherlands	1989	32	118	6.7	5.4
Belgium	1992	33	66	4.4	2.5
Austria	1994	33	66	9.0	3.7
Luxembourg	1996	4	10	0.4	0.3
Finland	1997	12	47	2.6	1.8
France	1998	11	168	2.5	7.2
USA	2000	–	233	–	7.5
Spain	2000	–	132	–	4.5
Italy	2003	–	87	–	3.4
Poland	2003	–	89	–	2.1
Portugal	2003	–	23	–	0.7
Czech Republic	2003	–	24	–	0.6
Slovenia	2004	–	12	–	0.3
Canada	2004	–	58	–	2.1
Hungary	2005	–	20	–	0.3
Ireland	2005	–	15	–	0.4
China	2007	–	82	–	2.8
Greece	2007	–	22	–	0.6
Slovakia	2007	–	10	–	0.2
Japan	2008	–	15	–	1.2
Russia	2009	–	19	–	1.2
South Korea	2010	–	6	–	0.2
Turkey	2010	–	8	–	0.2
Romania	2011	–	11	–	0.2
Croatia	2011	–	6	–	0.2
Singapore	2011	–	1	–	0.1
Franchise[2]	2006	–	70	–	1.0
Total		613	2,742	100	100

Notes

1 Includes 13 Galne Gunnar discount stores. Four stores were closed during 1999 in anticipation of total closure in 2000.

2 Franchised operations in Gulf States, Lebanon, Israel, Jordan and Morocco.

Table 1.8 Estimates of retail sales as current prices converted to US$ and global market share of largest firms

	Retail sales $ '000 million		
	2000	2007	2010
Global sales	7,930	10,620	11,575
Sales of largest 100 retailers	1,732	2967	3,354
% global share largest 100	21.8	27.9	29.0
Sales of largest 25 retailers	987	1,773	1,998
% global share largest 25	12.4	16.7	17.3
% of global sales accounted for by foreign sales of 100 largest retailers	2.9	6.2	7.2

Sources: based on data from UN Statistical Office, Euromonitor, Planet Retail and large firm database.

situations (Bourdieu 1977; Giddens 1984; Archer 1982). The development of the phases of retail internationalization can be viewed as a form of social change with the phases as the outcomes of complex changes in the relationship between structure and agency. The integration of changes in structure and agency has been termed *structuration* by Giddens and the process has been theorized as a recursive one of mutual interdependence. Whilst the concepts on which the ideas of structuration are built have been used extensively as a way of interpreting social change within social theory (particularly useful in this context are Stones 2005; Parker 2000; Bryant and Jary 2001; and Cohen 1989) the idea of structuration can also be useful as a way of gaining insight into the nature and phases of international retail development from an empirical perspective.

Giddens argues that structuration is a process in which agency and structure are in continuous interaction and exhibit mutual influence. This corresponds well with the view of internationalization of retailing as a dynamic recursive process (Dawson and Mukoyama 2006b) in which agents, who are part of the commercial environment, take decisions with resulting changes in the structure of the firm and the environment in which it operates, with these changes in structure recursively influencing agent decisions. Structure and agency, however, should not be considered as simplistically synonymous with environment and management as management and environment contain aspects of both structure and agency. According to Giddens, structure changes as a result of agency whilst at the same time agency is constrained by structure. Agents – of many types, not simply managers in retail firms – attempt to appropriate aspects of retail structure in order to effect change in structure but these changes in retail structure introduce intended and unintended consequences that generate new catalysts and constraints to which agents then respond. An advantage of considering retail internationalization as a structuration process is that it moves consideration away from a view of a management – environment duopoly and the simple push–pull paradigm to describe retail expansion.

Table 1.9 Summary of characteristics of the phases of retailer internationalization

Dimension of activity	Phase 1	Phase 2	Phase 3	Phase 4
Style	Entrepreneurial, committed individual	Opportunistic	Strategic. Some opportunism still evident	Strategic Strong top level commitment
Market selection	Prior links to country	Border hopping Opportunistic	Intra-continent Widening scope	Exploratory multi-continent Focus on large markets
Key activity	Exploration and experimentation	Knowledge acquisition Identification of necessary capabilities	Market response Application of knowledge	Creating new markets Building market share in key markets
Format transferred	Existing format	Existing format	Existing format with adaptions	Existing format adapted New formats explored with existing format dominant Emerging multi-channel
Approach	Pioneering	Collecting countries Experimental	Increase number of markets Build scale in selected markets	Building scale in key markets Identification of new key markets
Entry and growth modes	Direct investment	Multiple: direct investment, franchising, acquisition	Formalized evaluation of entry and growth methods appropriate to country	Embed in economic, social, political environment
Role in firm	Marginal	Secondary to developing strong domestic presence	International requires support from strong domestic operation	International is core part of firm
Impact on firm	Ephemeral	Tactical	Medium term	Long term
Buying and sourcing	Existing sources of supply	Existing sources of supply	Identify new sourcing opportunities in host countries	Global supply chains to support global sales presence

In identifying how structuration can provide a better understanding of the processes of international retailing it is useful to consider how Giddens interprets the nature of structure and agency and to interpret these into the context of international retailing. Giddens defines: '*Structure*. Rules and resources, recursively implicated in the reproduction of social systems. Structure exists only as memory traces, the organic basis of human knowledgeability, and as instantiated in action' (Giddens 1984: 377). Structure can be construed in our current context as the non-domestic commercial environment in which the retailer operates and uses the accumulated knowledge within the retailer. Structure is considered as comprising *rules* and *resources*.

Rules or, as Sewell (1992) prefers to term them, 'schema' are 'generalizable procedures applied in the enactment/reproduction of social life' (Giddens 1984: 21). The rules can be seen as linked closely to the application of tacit knowledge within the commercial environment and within the retailer. Tacit knowledge of the rules facilitate people to take actions in the society hosting the international retailer and in the retailer. The generalizability of rules, Giddens argues, means that they can be used in a variety of contexts and a variety of levels but they are rules that also have context in that they can be applied to specific situations and events. This situational aspect is important in retailer internationalization with different structures of retailing evident as retailers move to different countries and at different times.

Building on Giddens' work it is usual to identify normative or external rules that are framed from outside the context of their use, and internal rules that are more closely linked to context and include rules about communication, legitimation and power determination within the retailer. In the case of international retailing, examples of normative rules are those associated with the established behaviour of consumers linked to their cultural values, and governmental rules on foreign retail investment. Examples of internal rules are communication rules associated with the information flows in the firm, legitimation rules about the measures that determine success in the firm, power-determined rules about controls over decisions in the firm. Whilst these can be conceptualized as having a 'virtual' existence they are capable of being applied in a variety of real situations involving actions by the firm in a commercial environment. As the retailer becomes international it is exposed to new external rules and agency adapts its internal rules to respond to the new situation and also tries to shape new external rules.

Resources, in Giddens' work, are interpreted as 'anything that can serve as a source of power in social interactions' (Sewell 1992: 9). Giddens differentiates two types: allocative resources being 'capabilities which generate command over objects or other material phenomena' and authorization resources as 'capabilities which generate command over persons' (Giddens 1979: 100). More specifically the resources are: first, allocative, essentially non-human resources being derived from material products, for example physical structures, communication infrastructures, and finance; second, authoritative, essentially human, resources, being derived from the coordination of human activity, for example: explicit knowledge that has been formalized, as in franchised agreements with retailers in another country; and the capabilities of individuals. The resources exist in the external commercial environment and also within the retail firm. Resources are important in establishing retail structure in that they are instrumental in creating the physical form of international retailing through format and formula (as explained in Chapter 2). The two types of resource can be used to enhance power and in effect shape decisions.

Rules and resources cannot really be seen as separate from each other but as integrated in the creation of structure. Structures as rules and resources do not 'do' anything themselves but have effect by being known and used by actors. Agency therefore is needed to make structure effective. Agency and structure cannot effectively exist without each other. 'Structures must not be conceptualized as simply placing constraints on human agency, but as enabling' (Giddens 1976: 161). 'Structures, then, are sets of mutually sustaining schemas and resources that empower and constrain social action and that tend to be reproduced by that social action' (Sewell 1992: 19). For the international retailer, structure can therefore be considered as spatially grounded (territorial embeddedness) in the commercial environment (network embeddedness) of a host society and organizationally grounded (social embeddedness) in the retailer.

Agency is purposeful action by agents. These agents may be people, firms or organizations and thus agency is both individual and collective (Meyer and Jepperson 2000) and exists at micro and macro scales. Agents have the deliberate intention to create changes in structure. They know what they want to do and know what they are doing. According to Giddens (1979) an agent, 'knows a great deal about the reproduction of the society' (p. 5) in which the agent is a member and the knowledge gives the agent power to change structure. Agents have knowledge of the current *rules* and have access to *resources*. Knowledge of the rules, although not necessarily the history of the rules, is essential in order to apply them in a new context. The actions change the structure, changing both rules and resources. Agents resist and manipulate the constraints and so structure becomes modified. Additionally, agents are enabled by structure in that they appropriate rules and resources and use them in an intentional way. Agents have the capacity to utilize resources through rules other than those that generated the resources. This capacity of agents to change rules is used to pursue directed actions. The consequences of actions are intended and can be unintended. In the context of international retailing, agents include not only managers of entrant and existing firms but also there are indirect agents including politicians, government officers, service providers and suppliers who all have knowledge of various aspects of structure and have agency power to change rules and create resources.

Within the context of retailing, opening stores in a new country, using the rules and resources available, is undertaken with specific intent but some consequences are uncertain and unintended. The intended and unintended consequences may then change some of the rules and resources that affect subsequent actions. For example, following the establishment of a presence in a market, agency may change allocative resource through increased investment for expansion; authoritative resource through improved knowledge on the development process generating changed managerial responsibilities; communication rules associated with information collection on market potential or communication with consumers; legitimation rules about store opening activity; and power determined rules about the relationship between country manager and store manager. These changes in structure then influence agents' subsequent actions, for example further expansion in one city to build market share rather than expansion to another city to extend market presence. The rules and resources available can be appropriated in different ways by different actors so, depending on the actors, the structures may change in different ways. Thus it is possible to have alternative, but equally valid, ways of progressing with the internationalization processes by different firms with their different forms of agency, as is indeed the case as firms use different entry and growth modes in foreign markets. The interplay between structure and agency is space- and time-dependent (grounded in situations) and, therefore in terms of the internationalization processes in retailing, the interaction is embedded in the firm but provides a catalyst for social change in the market being entered. The interplay between structure and agency contributes to societal embeddedness in the internationalizing firm and territorial and network embeddedness in the host country (Hess 2004; Coe and Hess 2005; Coe and Lee 2013).

The structuration process can be conceptualized as underpinning the various phases in internationalization and the activities of a particular firm. In the entrepreneurial stage the number of agents is small but individually they are powerful. The aspects of structure that are external to the firm are stronger than those within the firm which has little tacit knowledge of rules associated with internationalization and few relevant organizational resources. The rules and resources associated with the commercial environment of the host country are quite powerful but agents have limited power to influence these. In the experimental and learning phase the rules and resources in the firm become more clearly established and agents are interacting intensely with structure in order to gain knowledge of the internationalization process. Agents external to the retailer begin to be aware of some of the rules associated with international retailer activity. The structuration process is rapid to both gain rules related to knowledge and establish new structure. The likelihood of unintended consequences in the firm and in the commercial environment is high because of the relatively low level of knowledge about how rules and structure interact. Hence failures of the internationalization process may occur within the firm or within the commercial environment, for example with public policy organizations becoming involved in agency (Mutebi 2007) or retailers withdrawing from a country. In the third phase when international activity becomes more formalized as a strategy the internal rules and resources are strengthened by deliberate formalized managerial actions of agents. Thus, for example, firms develop rules and routines for the analysis of new market entry (Swoboda *et al.* 2007) and make investments in distribution centres as resources to support the growing store network. In these activities the knowledge of how to operate within the rules and resources of the commercial environment is also deliberately used by agency, within and external to the retailer, to change the structure of the commercial environment. Agency becomes more instrumental in the structuration process and creates change in structure. In the fourth phase agency is using the internal rules and resources to change the external rules and resources that exist in the commercial environment. The structuration process consists of agency appropriating new internal structure in order to change external structure. As the external structure is changed, i.e. markets are created and shaped, there is interaction with internal structure and the activities of internal and external agency again changes. In this fourth stage the power of agency, particularly agency of the firm compared to the agency of the entrepreneur, in the structuration process has increased compared to earlier stages. In this phase the external agents become more aware of the changes in structure and the changes in the rules within which the retail market operates.

A brief example of Tesco

Tesco plc is a UK food and general merchandise retailer that typifies many aspects of the change in the nature of retailer internationalization (Dawson *et al.* 2006) and can be used to illustrate the structuration process. There were tentative moves into Ireland and France in Phases 1 and 2 of the suggested sequence but neither of which provided a basis for substantive growth due the lack of knowledge and unintended consequences of the moves. Withdrawal in both cases was relatively easy with knowledge gained particularly about external agency. A strategic shift took place in Tesco in the mid-1990s (Phase 3) with decisions to re-enter Ireland, and to open stores in the newly opened markets in central Europe and in the high-potential markets of East Asia. Agency within Tesco acted with intent to extend the internationalization of the firm and create structure. Internal rules and resources were appropriated to establish stores and supporting infrastructure. In so doing the rules and resources were changed. Tesco, from being essentially a UK domestic retailer, made a substantial commitment to developing in specifically targeted foreign markets. Knowledge gained from the direct development in 1997 of hypermarkets in Poland and Hungary was fed back to influence the hypermarket development in UK (Palmer 2005). Agency resulted in a change in the rules and resources of the then-current structure. This change in structure in the UK then influenced agency development in South Korea after entry in 1999. The knowledge gained through entry by acquisition in Thailand in 1998 also fed into the management of the joint-venture established with Samsung in South Korea. The knowledge gained by agents generated changes in structure. A variety of entry and subsequent combinations of network expansion methods (direct development, acquisition, joint-venture, store exchange) are apparent across the markets in Central Europe, East Asia and, most recently, USA, with a complex sequence of investments over the decade from 2000 (Phase 4) that reflect a combination of strategic and opportunistic decisions with the aim of embedding Tesco into markets (commercial environments) so that these environments can be shaped. These investments have increased the number of stores in the format used for entry and also have launched new formats in the markets such that a multi-format strategy has been implemented within and across the multi-continental markets. A process of structuration has emerged in which there is dynamic interaction between agency and structure. The scale of expansion in the international markets has had impacts on competition, for example in the exit of Carrefour from Slovakia and with small retailers in Thailand, on suppliers, for example through supply chain quality and security agreements in Thailand and the close cooperation with suppliers in USA (Lowe and Wrigley 2010), and on consumer society, for example through the increased range of products and the new behavioural opportunities for consumers in Poland and Malaysia. By the fourth phase Tesco has become instrumental in changing aspects of consumer society in these countries and at the same time responding to local consumer cultures, using the term 'glocalization' to describe their approach. Table 1.10 summarizes the change in the international footprint of Tesco in the decade from 2000. The scope and scale of activity has increased substantially such that 33 per cent of sales and 67 per cent of floorspace were accounted for by non-UK operations in the financial year 2011–2012.

The ideas of the process of structuration are applicable to aid understanding of the macro-scale phase changes for Tesco but also allow insights into development at country level. The expansion of Tesco in South Korea can be used to exemplify this.[2] South Korea, in 2010, was Tesco's largest non-UK retail investment (Table 1.10) (Choi 2003; Yahagi 2003; Coe and Lee 2006, 2013). Coe and Lee (2013) provide deep insights into the development of Tesco in Korea and the aim here is not to replicate their analysis but to use the development of Tesco in South Korea as an example of how ideas of structuration can be used in an empirical context. The potential applicability of an approach through structuration can be considered through a series of questions that explore structuration as a theoretical framework to address international retailing.

Can the approach be used at different activity 'levels' in respect of internationalization? Giddens does not explore structuration at different organizational levels but the approach can be seen to operate at multiple scales although clearly the components of, and interaction between, structure and agency would be different at the various levels. At the level of corporate strategy the approach can be applied to the initial entry in 1999 by Tesco through a joint venture with Samsung as a result of changed rules of structure consequent from the financial crisis and IMF intervention in 1998 (Kim 2005). Rules, including the encouragement given by the South Korean government for the opening of the market for inward investment, were created by these conditions that were appropriated by the agency of Tesco executives in order to gain entry to the market. The agency both of Tesco and Samsung and the external agency of politicians resulted in changes in structure within the retail market in the creation of the joint venture with new resources and rules being created in the process. The structure was also changed by Carrefour and Wal-Mart entering the commercial environment.

Table 1.10 The expansion of the international presence of Tesco stores 2000–2010

Country	Year of entry	FY year end February 2001[1]				FY year end February 2011[1]			
		Stores		Floorspace '000 sq. ft.	Sales £m[1]	Stores		Floorspace '000 sq. ft.	Sales £m
		Total	Of which: hypermarkets			Total	Of which: hypermarkets		
Ireland	1997 (re-entry)	76	–	1,652	859	130	110	3,241	2,332
France	1992	1	–	16	N/A	1	–	16	N/A
Czech Republic	1996	12	6	1,191	236	158	73	5,238	1,355
Hungary	1994	45	15	1,646	296	205	115	7,185	1,649
Poland	1995	40	10	1,432	223	371	68	8,146	2,156
Slovakia	1996	10	5	833	142	97	54	3,383	996
Turkey	2003	–	–	–	–	121	46	3,016	700
China	2004	–	–	–	–	105	93	8,135	1,141
Japan	2003	–	–	–	–	140	–	505	476
Malaysia	2001	–	–	–	–	38	37	3,325	794
Taiwan	2000	1	1	107	3	–	–	–	–
Thailand	1998	24	24	2,847	532	782	124	11.342	2,844
South Korea	1999	7	7	689	326	354	121	11,676	4,984
USA	2007	–	–	–	–	164	–	1,702	495
Total		216	68	10,413	–	2,665	841	66,894	–

Source: company reports and presentations.

Note

1 Sales converted to £ sterling at average exchange rate for the year.

Important in the structuration process were authoritative resources in key executives, notably Seung-Han Lee as chief executive of the joint-venture with his background in Samsung Retail and David Reid, as board member of Tesco responsible for international expansion with his background in finance. At an operational level we can see structuration in the development of the Tesco store and distribution centre network as allocative resources. By the start of 2001, seven stores were operating. During 2001, seven more hypermarkets were opened and a further eight in 2002 followed by six in 2003. This rapid growth triggered the need for the new distribution centre at Mokdong, opened in 2003 serving all South Korea and intended to serve an expanding store network. By the autumn of 2005, 35 hypermarkets were in operation. This rapid expansion early in the internationalization processes built market share quickly and provided access to Samsung-Tesco for an increasing number of consumers with consequent change in their buying behaviour, a change in agency relationships with suppliers and the start of Samsung-Tesco initiating social change. In this rapid early expansion, agency is represented by the firm and local governments with both groups, as agents, seeking to appropriate aspects of structure, including the authoritative and allocative resources in place. The expansion also involved and reflected the way non-store allocative resources became available for example, in the new distribution centre at Mokdong in 2003 and another opened in late 2010 in Ansung. These centres reflect the steady resource increase in investment in new stores. As more stores were built, with 114 hypermarkets in operation in February 2010. Structure changed and generated changes in agency. Structuration, as recursive changes in structure and agency, can be seen therefore at both strategic and operational levels of international retailing.

Can the approach be matched with empirical study of multi-format development? Structure is both the medium and the outcome of agency. Structure can be seen as analogous to the 'format model' that the retailer is attempting to transfer (this is explored more generally in Chapter 2). The format model, derived through and constrained by rules and resources is the medium and the outcome of the agency activity involved in undertaking the international transfer. In the case of Tesco in South Korea the development of a multi-format model illustrates the structuration process. The initial purchase of Samsung Homeplus stores represents a first phase of format development with the second generation being hypermarkets that were influenced by Tesco's knowledge of hypermarkets obtained in Central Europe and more importantly in Thailand, with its Asian consumer culture. A third generation of hypermarkets was initiated in 2007 with the store in Jamsil. This generation has a stronger reflection of Korean society than earlier phases, and contains social, educational and leisure services alongside the more traditional commercial aspects (Coe and Lee 2013). This evolution of the hypermarket format through the Homeplus formula can be seen as a dynamic interaction between the format (structure), managers using knowledge of the market (agency) and consumers (agency). Over the eight years to 2007 the interaction of structure and agency had resulted in a series of changes to the hypermarket format to respond to Korean society and at the same time the evolution of the Homeplus formula changed society by introducing new product choices and a new way of shopping. Subsequent market penetration has been substantial with hypermarket numbers increasing from 75 in 2007 to 114 in 2010. The evolution of the Homeplus formula reflects the explicit social role and direct involvement in social change apparent in Samsung-Tesco's retail philosophy in South Korea. A second format developed in 2004 in South Korea was a convenience store formula, Homeplus Super Express (structure) with its particular rules and resources. This structure is modelled on Tesco Express stores in other markets but is larger and has a wider product range, reflecting agency's (consumer driven) adaption of the formula to the Korean market (Suh and Howard 2009). A third format of internet shopping has been introduced and the coverage has been gradually increased as more hypermarkets have acted as supply points for the home shopping delivery service. The development of a multi-format approach can be seen as the interaction between structure and agency that generated structuration in store development activity.

Can we distinguish between communication, legitimation and power determination as modes of rule related to the situation? Samsung-Tesco has pursued communication rules to create strong environmentally friendly credentials that accord with the emergent social rules on green issues. The firm was awarded the title of Most Ethical Firm in 2003. An international retailer needs to communicate its values to the society into which it has entered and this requires a variety of rules within the structure. The medium, message and execution reflect the interplay between the values (rules) of the firm, i.e. the green credentials of Samsung-Tesco, and the existing norm (rules) of communication within the commercial environment of South Korea. This norm is the widespread use of flyers, in-store messaging, print advertising etc. In respect of power-determined rules, the relationships of retailers and suppliers in an international context operate within generic rules The use of non-Korean suppliers has been necessary for some of its private brand products because the rules in South Korea require the manufacturer's name to be provided on the product packaging meaning that major Korean suppliers (agency) with their own strong brands (resources) are unwilling (rules) to provide private brand items (Cho 2009; Cho *et al.* 2013). Samsung-Tesco buyers (agency) have appropriated these rules to enable them to seek competitive non-Korean suppliers and in so doing develop a retail brand (resources) appropriate to the market. Consumer acceptance of a private brand has strengthened the power-determined rules of buyers with the share of sales accounted for by private brand products rising to 21 per cent by 2008.

Can we distinguish allocative and authoritative resources in international retailing? The presence of external resources, for example external finance, and the internal resources associated with knowledge are widely recognized in international retailing studies. The identification of the two forms of resources is useful. For example it is useful to consider the authoritative resource of knowledge brought to Samsung-Tesco from the transfer to South Korea of senior managers into key positions and the knowledge provided by Korean managers either originally in Samsung Retail on its acquisition by Tesco or subsequently appointed to the firm. Drawing on knowledge gained from international activity elsewhere, Tesco transferred only a small number of senior executives to Samsung-Tesco. The number of Tesco executives was quickly reduced even further to four as the joint venture became established. These included a key executive involved in the development of Tesco Express in the UK. The four provided a direct conduit to Tesco knowledge resources in the UK and to the 'Tesco in a box' transferable suite of IT systems. The nature of the authoritative resource base changed, as the joint venture became successful, becoming more Korean. These authoritative resources can be contrasted with the allocative finance resource provided by investors to enable the initial joint venture with Samsung and the subsequent process of purchasing a steadily larger share of the firm. The initial joint venture comprised 51 per cent for Tesco at a cost of $250 million. Phased investment increased Tesco's share to 89 per cent by 2005 and agreement was reached in 2006 for Samsung to sell the remaining 11 per cent to Tesco by 2011. Agency appropriation of this allocative resource facilitated the further expansion of the store network and resulted in change in structure. The growth of the store network (Table 1.11) also provided allocative resource which enabled agency to implement further changes in structure with the changed structure having recursive effects on agency.

Is there evidence of unintended consequences in the internationalization processes? According to Giddens, the interaction of structure and agency is theorized as generating intended and unintended consequences in the structuration process. Within international retailing the outcomes of decisions are a mix of intended and unintended consequences of the appropriation of structure by agents. Agents deal with situation contingency. Thus, in international retailing some developments are opportunistic (Dawson 2001b) in which agents appropriate resources to seek advancement of a strategy and opportunism tends to increase the potential for unintended consequences. In South Korea the announcement in March 2006 of the planned exit of Carrefour from South Korea provided Tesco with a potential opportunity to expand their store network (Joe and Kim 2007). Samsung-Tesco became one of four shortlisted bidders but E-Land, a Korean firm, was the successful bidder at $1.77 billion for the 32 Carrefour stores. But in May 2008 Tesco was able to acquire for $1.9 billion 36 Homever stores which included those obtained from Carrefour, when E-Land, the operators of Homever, decided to sell its hypermarket assets. The network of Homeplus Tesco hypermarkets thus was extended substantially by this acquisition in 2008 which occurred because of the failed bid two years previously. Over the intervening two years Samsung-Tesco had increased its hypermarket network by direct development of 24 stores and had moved to be the second largest hypermarket operator in South Korea. The additional stores acquired in 2008 provided a scale increase to enable Samsung-Tesco to challenge E-Mart for the position of largest retailer in the sector. The larger size enabled scale economies to be obtained which changed the structure of Tesco in South Korea and the South Korean commercial environment.

Table 1.11 Samsung-Tesco in South Korea

FY ending	Store number		Sales space m²		Estimated sales volume '000 mill won			Market share
	Homeplus	Homeplus Express	Homeplus	Homeplus Express	Homeplus	Homeplus Express	e-Homeplus	
2000	2	—	18,600	—	278,994	—	—	0.6
2001	7	—	68,900	—	592,220	—	—	0.9
2002	14	—	137,800	—	1,368,988	—	—	1.6
2003	21	—	212,500	—	2,282,377	—	1,875	2.2
2004	28	—	285,152	—	3,076,636	—	1,951	2.7
2005	31	7	310,234	3,716	3,612,653	10,539	2,108	3.2
2006	42	20	366,220	17,372	3,983,036	164,403	2,259	3.4
2007	52	39	449,000	24,340	4,694,799	248,034	2,572	3.9
2008	66	71	549,524	30,843	5,222,033	316,203	2,967	3.8
2009	111	131	889,260	46,898	6,306,543	627,404	4,655	4.1
2010	114	191	954,385	60,758	7,914,060	982,292	5,187	4.3
2011	121	233	1,011,245	74,768	8,292,140	1,129,004	7,340	4.4
2012	127	331	1,072,844	93,181	8,192,448	1,226,266	N/A	4.4

Sources: company reports and presentations, press releases, Planet Retail.

Is the framework able to be used to explore the adaptive capacity of a retailer as it adapts to and also changes the market into which it has entered? Reflexivity of agents means they can adapt and change the use of the knowledge they use to change the structure. Such adaptions are a central theme in international retailing as operations are changed to meet consumer needs and so gain a stronger competitive position. The re-launch of the private brand packaging in 2009 by Samsung-Tesco, using knowledge gained from private brand development elsewhere but adapted to Korean products and to sensory perceptions of Korean consumers, has enabled Tesco to increase its private brand share and profitability. Private brand items have become more widely accepted by South Korean consumers generating agency changes across the commercial environment. Other examples of this adaption are seen in the changes made to the hypermarket format to be more reflective of the social values of Korean society (Kim 2009). In adapting in this way, the new hypermarkets have also resulted in changes in Korean society in terms of consumption and behaviour. Social change has resulted from the adaption process. The appropriation of the term 'glocal' to describe Samsung-Tesco's approach to the market (Suh and Howard 2009) indicates an approach to adaption with global values and systems acting as the agency to change society and local markets constituting the structure that constrains and enables the operation of agency.

These questions are only some of those that can be used to illustrate, in a specific context, the applicability of structuration to international retail processes. Coe and Lee (2013) state that, 'the localization of Tesco (in South Korea) should be seen as a dynamic process that unfolds within, and is shaped by, the context of a developing host retail market' (p. 3 doi version). The ideas of structuration provide a basis for adopting this perspective and enable us to move beyond the management versus environment dichotomy to take a more nuanced view. This view of retail internationalization is of a complex process of interaction between, on the one hand, internal and external rules and resources and, on the other, agency in the form of managers, consumers and other agents in relationships with the retail firm. This view of retailer internationalization can be viewed as structuration. Archer (1982) emphasizes that ' "Structuration" itself is ever a process and never a product' (p. 457) which clearly has close parallels with the accepted view of retail internationalization as a continuing process. Existing theory in international retailing is limited in its consideration of these issues which reflect the increased social components of international retailing in its fourth phase of development. Within retailer internationalization there are increasingly issues of social change alongside issues of corporate change and these require a more inclusive theoretical framework than has been the case to date.

Conclusion

Whilst there is a long history of retailers exploring markets in countries beyond their domestic sphere much of this activity was small-scale entrepreneurial operations. Since around 1970 the exploration of foreign markets began to be more seriously considered and several phases of development are to be seen. The latest, from around 2000 is a period of substantive increase in scale and scope of activity. Driving the increase in foreign investment in all the phases of development is a search to exploit economies of scale in the retail business model. This is evident particularly in scale benefits from sourcing products, in scale benefits of replication of selling points and scale benefits in the operation of information systems and communication networks. Whilst there has been a reduction in the barriers and constraints to international operation it is the search for increased sales and scale economies which underpin the strategies of international expansion. The extended international scope of operations is a consequence of the search for scale economies.

Several phases of development illustrate the pattern of international retailing at a sectoral level and also for the individual firm. Thus whilst a few retailers are developing their activity in what is described as a fourth phase, and have several decades of accumulated knowledge about the internationalization process, other retailers are still at a much earlier phase exhibiting entrepreneurial characteristics and are at an early stage in their learning. Across the sector as a whole however the amount of international activity is increasing with the retail firms that are operating internationally gradually gaining market share from the purely domestic firms.

The progression through the phases exhibits an increasingly complex approach to the use of scale economies within the strategy of the retailers. Initial phases enable the retailer to increase the scale-related benefits domestically by incorporating the added scale gained for international expansion, for example in buying arrangements. A strong domestic position can be further enhanced providing the platform for foreign investment. In later phases as non-domestic operations become more substantial so some scale-related benefits begin to appear in countries where operations have built a market share to a level giving negotiating power over local suppliers. Moves to focus development on a limited number of markets provide the opportunity to gain scale economies within these markets for some functions but to consolidate scale across all markets to gain scale benefits in other functions. The growth of multi-format operations adds a further level of complexity as the different formats generate their own cost economies of scale, which may involve both establishment- and organizational-scale economies.

The process of internationalization of retailing, we argue, can be conceptualized as one of structuration with the dynamic integration of structure and agency at multiple levels. The rules, resources and agents that generate the structuration process differ by phase both at macro sector level and micro firm level. At each level the integration of structure and agency is affected by key events in the commercial environment and in the management of the firm. These key events have expected, intended and unintended consequences but interrupt the structuration process in some way or change the direction of the process. The progression of the structuration process provides a dynamic for the internationalization activities.

Each later phase involves a greater willingness of the retailer to exploit scale economies by expanding geographical scope so that moving to multi-continental activity, with consequent increased cultural gap between home and host operations, becomes inevitable in the progression of the internationalization process. The need to adapt increases. Adaption is a process in which agents empowered by control of real resources and knowledge of the virtual rules, or schema, aim to change the structure of activity in the new host market. Purposive action by agency when there is a move to a new continent involves different rules and resources than are applied in earlier border-hopping phases of internationalization.

As internationalization moves through the phases so agency becomes more directive by its use of rules and resources such that management in the international retailer is more influential on consumption and in creating a market for its retail formula in the host country. Changing the market in line with purposeful agency generates new rules and resources and so changes structure that can be appropriated by agency to further drive the market. The agency and structure associated with the continuous development of the retail formula in the host market is central to a market-driving approach to international expansion. The development of the retail formula is the focus of the next chapter.

Notes

1 The chapter draws on a database of the activities of the 100 largest retail firms in terms of sales and estimates of global retail sales. This database has been developed from reports of the firms involved, collations of material from Retail Forward, Management Horizons, Deloitte, Planet Retail and Euromonitor, and UN and Eurostat statistical series. It is limited to the 100 largest firms each year and so the population of the database changes slightly each year. By limiting it to the largest 100 firms some firms with a very wide geographical scope, for example Amway, Arcadia, and Body Shop, are not included as they are not amongst the 100 largest firms. It is therefore not a database on the international scope of firms but of the largest retail firms in overall sales size.
2 This section is based on interviews in November 2003, April 2004 and June 2009 with senior executives in Samsung-Tesco, South Korea, and store visits.

References

Alexander N. (1990) Retailers and international markets: motives for expansion. *International Marketing Review*, 7(4), 75–85.

Alexander, N. and Doherty, A. M. (2010) International retail research: focus, methodology and conceptual development. *International Journal of Retail and Distribution Management*, 38(11/12), 928–942.

Archer, M. (1982) Morphogenesis versus structuration: on combining structure and action. *British Journal of Sociology*, 33(4), 455–483.

Bourdieu, P. (1977) *Outline of a theory of practice*. London: Cambridge University Press.

Bryant, C. G. A. and Jary, D. (eds) (2001) *Contemporary Giddens: social theory in a globalising age*. Basingstoke: Palgrave Macmillan.

Bunce, M. L. (1989) The international approach of Laura Ashley. In: *Adding value to retail offerings*. Amsterdam: ESOMAR Proceedings, pp. 101–116.

Burt, S. (1991) Trends in the internationalisation of grocery retailing: the European experience. *International Review of Retail, Distribution and Consumer Research*, 1(4), 487–515.

Burt, S. (1993) Temporal trends in the internationalisation of British retailing. *International Review of Retail, Distribution and Consumer Research*, 3(4), 391–410.

Chan, W. K. K. (1998) Personal styles, cultural values and management. In: K. L. MacPherson (ed.) *Asian department stores*. London: Curzon, pp. 66–89.

Cao, L. (2011) Dynamic capabilities in a turbulent market environment: empirical evidence from international retailers in China. *Journal of Strategic Management*, 19(5), 455–469.

Cho, Y.-S. (2009) Retailer brand development and handling processes: a comparative study of Tesco Korea and local Korean retailers. PhD thesis, University of Stirling.

Cho, Y.-S, Burt, S. and Dawson, J. (2013) Why do local South Korean market leaders supply retailer grocery brands? *Journal of Asia Pacific Business*, 14(4), in press.

Choi, S. C. (2003) Moves into the Korean market by global retailers and the responses of local retailers: lessons for the Japanese retail rector? In: J. Dawson, M. Mukoyama, S. C. Choi and R. Larke (eds) *The internationalisation of retailing in Asia*. London: RoutledgeCurzon, pp. 49–66.

Coe, N. M. and Hess, M. (2005) The internationalization of retailing: implications for supply network restructuring in East Asia and Eastern Europe. *Journal of Economic Geography*, 5(4), 449–473.

Coe, N. M. and Lee, Y.-S. (2006) The strategic localization of transnational retailers: The case of Samsung-Tesco in South Korea. *Economic Geography*, 82(1), 61–88.

Coe, N. M. and Lee, Y.-S. (2013) 'We've learnt how to be local': The deepening territorial embeddedness of Samsung-Tesco in South Korea. *Journal of Economic Geography* (advanced access) doi:10.1093/jeg.lbs057, now published in 13(2), 327–356.

Cohen, I. J. (1989). *Structuration theory: Anthony Giddens and the constitution of social life*. London: Macmillan.

Corporate Intelligence Group (1991) *Cross-border retailing in Europe*. London: Corporate Intelligence Group.

Dawson, J. A. (2001a) Strategy and opportunism in European retail internationalization. *British Journal of Management*, 12(4), 253–266.

Dawson, J. A. (2001b) Retail investment in central Europe and its implications. *Thexis*, 18(3), 23–28.

Dawson, J. A. (2013) Retailer activity in shaping food choice. *Food Quality and Preference*, 28(1), 339–347.

Dawson, J. A. and Henley, J. S. (1999) Internationalisation of hypermarket retailing in Poland: West European investment and its implications. *Journal of East-West Business*, 5(4), 37–52.

Dawson, J. A. and Mukoyama, M. (2006a) The increase in international activity by retailers. In: J. Dawson, R. Larke and M. Mukoyama (eds) *Strategic issues in international retailing*. Abingdon: Routledge, pp. 1–30.

Dawson, J. A. and Mukoyama, M. (2006b) Retailer internationalisation as a process. In: J. Dawson, R. Larke and M. Mukoyama (eds) *Strategic issues in international retailing*. Abingdon: Routledge, pp. 31–50.

Dawson, J. A., Larke, R. and Choi, S. C. (2006) Tesco: Transferring marketing success internationally. In: J. Dawson, R. Larke and M. Mukoyama (eds) *Strategic issues in international retailing*. Abingdon: Routledge, pp. 170–195.

Deloitte Touche Tohmatsu Limited (2012) *Switching channels: global powers of retailing 2012*. London: Deloitte Touche Tohmatsu Limited.

European Commission (1997a) *The single market review: Subseries II: Impact on services, Vol. 4. Distribution*, Luxembourg: Office of Official Publications of European Community and London: Kogan Page.

European Commission (1997b) *Retailing in the central European countries 1996*. Luxembourg: Office for Official Publications of the European Communities.

Ferry, J. W. (1961) *A history of the department store*. New York: Macmillan.

Frasquet, M., Dawson, J. and Molla, A. (2013) Post-entry internationalisation activity of retailers: an assessment of dynamic capabilities. *Management Decision*, 51, in press.

Ghauri, P. N., Tarnovaskaya, V. and Elg, U. (2008) Market driving multinationals and their global sourcing network. *International Marketing Review*, 25(5), 504–519.

Gerlach, S. (1988) *Das warenhaus in Deutschland*. Stuttgart: F. Steiner.

Giddens, A. (1976) *New rules of sociological method.* London: Hutchinson.

Giddens, A. (1979) *Central problems in social theory*. London: Macmillan.

Giddens, A. (1984) *The constitution of society*. Cambridge: Polity Press.

Godley, A. and Fletcher, S. R. (2001) International retailing in Britain 1850–1994. *Services Industries Journal*, 21(2), 31–46.

Hamilton, G. G., Petrovic M. and Senauer, B. (eds) (2011) *The market makers: how retailers are reshaping the global economy*. Oxford: Oxford University Press.

Hang, H. (2009) *The emergence of international retailing in China: pre-conditions and contexts*. Saarbrücken: VDM.

Hang, H. and Godley, A. (2009) Revisiting the psychic distance paradox: international retailing in China in the long run (1840–2005). *Business History*, 51(3), 383–400.

Hess M. (2004) 'Spatial' relationships? Towards a reconceptualization of embeddedness. *Progress in Human Geography*, 28(2), 165–186.

Hollander, S. (1970) *Multinational retailing*. East Lansing: Michigan State University.

Honeycombe, G. (1984) *Selfridges: 75 years. The story of the store, 1909–1984*. London: Park Lane Press.

Institute of Home Market and Consumption (1997) *Poland's domestic trade in 1996*. Warsaw: Ministry of Economy.

Joe, K.-C. and Kim, S.-H. (2007) Factors causing the withdrawal of foreign retailers from Korean retail market. *Journal of Rural Development*, 30(5), 61–81.

Jones, A. (2008) Beyond embeddedness: economic practices and the invisible dimensions of transnational business activity, *Progress in Human Geography*, 32(1), 71–88.

Kacker, M. (1985) *Transatlantic trends in retailing*. Westport: Quorum.

Kilminster, R. (1991) Structuration theory as a world view. In: C. G. A. Bryant and D. Jary (eds) *Giddens' theory of structuration*. London: Routledge, pp. 74–115.

Kim, J. (2005) Entry strategies of Tesco into the Korean market. *Research in Business Administration*, 8, 81–104.

Kim, J.-H. (2009) Tesco Homeplus: Adding creativity to the discount retail business. *SERI Quarterly*, 2(2), available at: www.seriquarterly.com/05/ qt_contents_page. html?p_pubseq=20130119.

Knee, D. (1966) Trends towards international operations among large-scale retailing enterprises. *Rivista Italiana di Amministrazione*, 2, 107–111.

Laulajainen, R. (1991a) Two retailers go global: the geographical dimension. *International Review of Retail, Distribution and Consumer Research*, 1(5), 607–626.

Laulajainen, R. (1991b) International expansion of an apparel retailer: Hennes and Mauritz of Sweden. *Zeitschrift fur Wirtschaftsgeographie*, 35(1), 1–15.

Laulajainen, R. (1992) Louis Vuitton Malletier: A truly global retailer. *Annals of the Japan Association of Economic Geography*, 38(2), 55–77.

Lowe, M. and Wrigley, N. (2010) The 'Continuously Morphing' retail TNC during market entry: interpreting Tesco's expansion into the United States. *Economic Geography*, 86(4), 381–408.

Mårtenson, R. (1981) *Innovations in multinational retailing: IKEA on the Swedish, Swiss, German and Austrian furniture markets*. Goteborg: University of Goteborg.

Meyer, J. W. and Jepperson, R. L. (2000) The 'actors' of modern society: the cultural construction of social agency. *Sociological Theory*, 18(1), 100–120.

Mutebi, A. M. (2007) Regulatory responses to large-format transnational retail in southeast Asian cities. *Urban Studies*, 44(2), 357–379.

Palmer, M. (2005) Retail multinational learning: a case study of Tesco. *International Journal of Retail and Distribution Management*, 33(1), 23–48.

Pananond, P. and Zeithaml, C. (1998) The international expansion process of MNEs from developing countries: a case study of Thailand's CP group. *Asia Pacific Journal of Management*. 15(2), 163–184.

Parker, J. (2000) *Structuration*. Buckingham: Open University Press.

Pasdermadjian, H. (1954) *The department store: its origins, evolution and economics*. London: Newman.

Pellegrini, L. (1992) The internationalisation of retailing and 1992 Europe. *Journal of Marketing Channels*, 1(2) 3–27.

Petrovic, M. and Hamilton, G. G. (2011) Retailers as market makers. In: G. G. Hamilton, M. Petrovic and B. Senauer (eds) *The market makers: how retailers are reshaping the global economy*. Oxford: Oxford University Press, pp. 31–49.

Pütz, R. (1998) *Einkelhandel im transformationsprozess*. Passau: L.I.S.

Retail Intelligence (2001) *European retail briefing* 18 July 2001, London: Mintel.

Rigoureau-Juin, A. and Kerrad, K. (1993) *L'Europe du commerce: encore à faire, déjà dépassée*. Paris: Economica.

Rugman, A. (2005) *The regional multinationals*. Cambridge: Cambridge University Press.

Rugman, A. and Girod, S. (2003) Retail multinationals and globalization: the evidence is regional. *European Management Journal*, 21(1), 24–37.

Sewell, Jr, W. H. (1992) The theory of structure: duality, agency and transformation. *American Journal of Sociology*, 98(1) 1–29.

Stones, R. (2005) *Structuration*. London: Palgrave Macmillan.

Suh, Y.-G. and Howard, E. (2009) Restructuring retailing in Korea: the case of Samsung-Tesco. *Asia Pacific Business Review*, 15(1) 29–40.

Swoboda, B., Zentes, J. and Elsner, S. (2009) Internationalisation of retail firms: state of the art after 20 years of research. *Marketing – Journal of Research and Management*, 2, 105–126.

Swoboda, B., Schwarz, S. and Hälsig, F. (2007) Towards a conceptual model of country market selection: selection processes of retailers and C&C wholesalers. *International Review of Retail, Distribution and Consumer Research*, 17(3), 253–282.

Teece, D. J. (2009) *Dynamic capabilities and strategic management*. Oxford: Oxford University Press.

Van Geenhuizen, M., Van Der Knaap, B. and Nijkamp, P. (1996) Transborder European networking: shifts in corporate strategy? *European Planning Studies*, 4(6), 671–682.

Waldman, C. (1978) *Strategies of international mass retailers*, New York: Praeger.

Whysall, P. (1997) Interwar retail internationalization: Boots under American ownership. *International Review of Retail, Distribution and Consumer Research*, 7(2), 157–169.

Wrigley, N., Coe, N. M. and Currah, A. (2005) Globalizing retail: conceptualizing the distribution-based transnational corporation (TNC). *Progress in Human Geography*, 29(4), 437–457.

Yahagi, T. (2003) The internationalisation process of Tesco in Asia. *Hosei Journal of Business*, 39(4), 45–67.

2 Building international strategy with formats and formulae

John Dawson and Masao Mukoyama

If we came up to Canada and didn't offer ketchup-flavored potato chips, then we would have looked like we didn't know what we are doing.

Tony Fisher, President Target Canada (Lee 2013)

Seeking economies of scale by spatial market growth has been a significant motive for retailers to expand internationally. Alongside this expansion into new geographic markets retailers have also increased organizational scale, domestically and internationally, by developing a multi-format and multi-formula approach through stores to target additional market segments. It has also become apparent that retailers have to adapt these formulae to local markets, not only in merchandise but also across a range of operational activities. Before exploring the implications of this multi-format approach for internationalization it is useful to consider the concepts of format and formula as a means by which retailers and consumers interact so enabling retailers to achieve their primary objective in international retailing, namely growth of sales.

The place of transaction

The transaction is a central element in the overall complex interaction between the retailer and the consumer. The transaction is important as it represents the formalization of the exchange of value. The transaction occurs at a place. The idea of a place of transaction is a core concept in strategy and operations in retailing. Whilst often thought of simplistically in terms of geographic location, as in much of the retail marketing literature that draws on ideas of the marketing mix, the place of transaction needs to also be considered as an a-spatial concept. There are very many possibilities for the place of transaction. Most typically it is some variety of shop – a specialist boutique, department store, supermarket, flagship store, superstore, in-store concession, etc. – which is established by the retailer and where geographic space is important. But alongside the varieties of shop there are many other places, again created by the retailer, where a transaction can occur, for example, over the phone, with a mail order catalogue, on a website. Geographic space provides no constraints in these cases and the transaction place is an a-spatial concept.

From the perspectives of the retailer and consumer, their respective activities and behaviours during the transaction relate directly to the nature and characteristics of the place in which the transaction takes place. The consumer has different behaviour when undertaking a transaction at different places; sometimes the transaction is impersonal, sometimes it involves price negotiation, sometimes an extended period of evaluation takes place before a transaction, and so on. Not only is the behaviour of the consumer affected by the place of transaction but also the place of transaction is chosen in terms of the consumer's expectation of value from that place.

The retailer also behaves differently in the different transaction places; sometimes a large variety of goods are offered, sometimes technology is introduced to facilitate the transaction, sometimes heavy promotional activity is used, sometimes technology replaces the sales person, and so on. The place of transaction is a creation of the retailer, being in a sense the 'product' of the retailer. The behaviour of the retailer and the design of the place are partly a response to consumer expectations but they are primarily a consequence of the business objectives of the retailer. The place is where the consumer makes a purchase of values and the retailer presents an offer of alternative values. An individual retailer may decide to operate through several types of place in order to implement their business model. The consumer may use several types of place to satisfy their needs. Place in this context is not simply a geographical place but is a locus for the transactional exchange of values that contain market and non-market elements.

The transaction place is an output of a retail business model. At the transaction place value is generated for consumer and retailer. Within retailing there are a number of business models that relate input to output. Some models focus on the exploitation of scale economies, at establishment and organizational levels, while others use economies of scope at these different levels to define their cost structures and competitive position. The different forms of scale and scope economies, and their interactions, generate alternative business models. Success is possible through different models, even within a single retail sector (Hilditch 2010; Sorescu *et al.* 2011). The different business models also provide a range of experiential outputs that reflect values, such as convenience, entertainment, personalization, surprise, etc. sought by consumers (Messinger and Narasimhan 1997). These values for the retailer and consumer are the outputs of the business model delivered through the place of transaction. There is great variety in the values the retailer and consumer seek and so there is great variety of transaction places (Shields 1992).

Format and formula as the place of transaction

For the retailer the output of the business model at a place of transaction is the retail format. There has been extensive debate over the idea of retail format and the classic models of the evolution of the retail sector, for example retail lifecycle models, have been based on the concept of format. There is a substantial literature on consumer behavioural issues associated with different formats (for example Uusitalo 2001; Messinger and Narasimhan 1997; Rousey and Morga-nosky 1996; Carpenter and Moore 2006) but relatively little discussion on what constitutes a format and its close relative, the formula (Reynolds *et al.* 2007; Ishii and Mukoyama 2009). In essence, the format has been conceptualized as a generalized set of relationships that create a particular cost structure for the place of transaction. The cost of physical space associated with the accumulation, pre-sentation, sale and rotation of an assortment of products are one set of costs. Labour costs are another part of this cost structure. Betancourt (2004) views these several costs as associated with types of distribution service provided for potential consumers with the format as the delivery vehicle for a bundle of serv-ices. The ideas of distribution services and of business format model have been viewed as closely related. Thus, a department store, as a format, represents the output of a business model that uses scale economies of store operation with scope economies of assortment and brand ranges. The model uses these cost eco-nomies to establish relationships amongst revenues, costs, margins, inventory rotation, etc. across a particular mix of assets (physical property, employees, products for resale, technology for recording transactions, etc.) used to manage the transaction with consumers and provide consumers with a particular mix of values or, in Betancourt's analysis, distribution services. A fashion brand flag-ship format is defined by a different set of relationships amongst the cost and revenue elements and so has a different business model from the department store and generates a different set of values for the consumer (Kozinets *et al.* 2008). A hypermarket has yet another business model, the transactional website has another model, and so on. Each format business model generates a different set of values to consumers and retailers. The way that the bundle of distribution services is constructed creates the format that generates value at the transaction place.

Whilst the core model of these different formats can be clearly differentiated the boundaries are more difficult to determine because the composition of the bundle of services is flexible and dynamic. The extent to which a business model can be flexed is often unclear. In the food and general merchandise sector, for example, the sequence of formats of supermarket, superstore, hypermarket illus-trate this issue. Whilst the core business model for each is well defined, the model is flexed for example in terms of the balance between food and non-food items and the implications for this for overall margins, inventory rotation, working capital, labour costs, etc. so that boundaries between the formats become blurred. The capacity of the format to be flexed in this way illustrates the dynamic nature of the format concept. This flexing of the format allows the format to evolve in response to market changes and technological and manage-rial developments. The supermarket format, and its associated business model, of 1970 was different from that of 1990 or 2010 but despite the changes some aspects remain consistent to the design of the core business model. Flexing and evolution of the model may reach a point at which the relationships in the model change to the extent that a new format is created. Thus in the late 1960s in the UK, for example, the supermarket model was flexed in terms of increased product categories and expanded assortments thus requiring an increase in shelf space, floorspace and car park space, a changed structure to the labour force and changes in financing. As a result the food superstore emerged as a distinctive format (Dawson 2003).

A format, and the business model that underpins it, is the result of the prevailing society and the economic and political institutions that exist. The department store as a format emerged in the nineteenth century as a response to the then prevailing social conditions. The trader in a periodic market, as a format, emerged much earlier as a basic format in societies moving from a subsistence society to a commercial society. There are many studies of the origins and histories of different formats (for example Appel 1972; Lancaster 1995; Marseille 1997; Lhermie 2003; Coopey *et al.* 2005; DeMarco 2006; Markin 1968; Freathy and O'Connell 1998) and these studies generally point to the socio-environmental influences as critical issues in their early development. The studies of the transfer of supermarkets to societies where more traditional formats dominate emphasize the importance of the socio-environmental conditions for the success of the transfer (Goldman 1981, 2001; Kaynak 1985; Reardon *et al.* 2003, 2007) but also illustrate the dynamic nature of the retail format.

The retail format therefore is a result of the operation of a generalized business model in which a transaction place is created that is directed at a group of consumers with broadly similar expectations for deriving value from the transaction.

The format is interpreted in different ways by each retailer, according to their culture, historical development, managerial style, innovativeness and capabilities to generate and use resources. The way that a retailer individually interprets the format creates the formula which the specific retailer presents to the consumer. The formula is a bundle of distribution services that the retailer designs within the confines of the format business model. Stremersch and Tellis (2002) review the extensive literature on bundling as a marketing concept, provide definitions and relate the concept to strategy. Their discussion is limited to traditional product-based views of marketing, rather than the wider view of marketing required in a retail context, but by extension their work is relevant to the concept of formula. The formula is the bundle of distribution services that is bought by the consumer and it comprises not only product items but the operational routines and design of the transaction point to which it applies. Stremersch and Tellis make the important point that when the firm provides a bundle that is tightly bound, what they term 'pure bundling', in which the firm provides no opportunity to deconstruct it, performance is optimized. This in effect is the position with the design of a formula with the formula in total being what is offered to the consumer and the means by which the retailer penetrates a market. They conclude that 'developing expertise in designing bundling strategies may be of prime importance in achieving long-term success' (2002: 70) and this is likely to be the case with formula development.

In the case of the department store format, for example, each firm that operates this format has slightly different interpretations of the model and so creates their own formula as their version, often branded, of the format. In the UK, the department store formula branded as Harvey Nichols is different from that branded as John Lewis or that branded as House of Fraser. In Japan, similarly, Takashimaya is different from Isetan, and Hankyu is different again, whilst all operate a generic department store model. They all use the same general business model that underpins the operational format but each has subtle and individual ways of interpreting the format to reflect the particularities of the firm. For any format, individual firms create their own formula using managerial capabilities applied to the resources in the firm and its environment.

The formula is the place in which the retailer–consumer transaction takes place. The supermarket, doorstep seller, specialist boutique, vending machine and market-place trader are each the format resulting from a particular business model and each of the formats have different formulae dependent on the firm that operates the model. Design of the formula, within the confines of the format, is central to inter-firm competition. The formula is the place at which the consumer chooses to seek value and at which product and service choices are made.

As with the format, so also there is evolution of the formula. Whilst the format evolves in terms of social, technological, market, etc. changes – essentially macro-level forces – the formula evolves through micro-level managerial interpretations of the macro-level forces. For example, whilst technological developments have resulted in self-service checkouts becoming part of the hypermarket format, the self-service checkout is used in different ways by the various firms operating hypermarkets. In addition, as a firm gains more knowledge about the use of self-service checkouts so this specific aspect of the firm's formula evolves. A firm develops their formula and it undergoes a constant process of renewal and development. The capability to adjust and adapt their formula is an important aspect of competitiveness for the retail firm. Capabilities of sensing, seizing and transforming resources have been identified as important dynamic capabilities (Teece 2007, 2009; Luo 2002) and these are required capabilities of retailers as they develop their formula. The dynamic capabilities of the firm are instrumental in creating and evolving the formula. The formula is the creation of the retailer and acts as their constantly evolving 'selling machine'.

Brand as integral to formula and format development

The concept of brand is central to the creation of the retail formula. Branding constitutes one mechanism, alongside others such as technology application, corporate culture, etc. for the retailer to differentiate its formula(e) from those of competitors. As with branding generally, the branding of a formula serves as a way of communicating to the consumer the offer of values created by the retailer. The retailer uses branding to change the format to a formula and this can be undertaken in the home context or as part of the internationalization process. In the current context of considerations of internationalization we can point to multiple ways that this creation of a branded formula is achieved in an international context.

At the simplest level the retailer operates through a single format and has a single brand applied to a single formula. Evolutionary developments of the formula, at different times or in different markets, continue to have the same brand name. This was once the most common type of format–formula model but has become less common as retailers have embraced marketing activity and the resulting more complex format–formula strategies. Woolworths, in their early expansion in USA and internationally, used this approach. Laura Ashley, Body Shop and Lush began in this way but as they developed, domestically and internationally, they expanded with new format models (for example in-store concessions, franchised operation and transactional websites) but retained the same brand for their various formulae.

The single brand applied to multiple formats is now a more widely used approach with many of the apparel retailers using this approach with no distinction between domestic and international operation. Ted Baker, Mango, Desiguel and Paul Smith for example, all operate with a single brand but through a combination of flagship store format, in-store concession format, airport shop format, standard store format, outlet store format and transactional website format with each format having a distinctive, but common branded, formula. An important aspect of the formula in this approach is the close correspondence and integration of brand of the products with the brand of the formula. The integration of the product brand and the formula brand are an essential part of the internationalization process for firms using this strategy of linking format and formula.

Some firms prefer to operate multiple brand formulae across several formats. At a simple level, L'Occitane en Provence, which started internationalizing its stores in 1996 and was in 70 countries by 2007, operated a single brand through multiple operational formulae and then added a second brand formula, Melvita, which has been taken international to several countries in Europe, Asia and also to the USA, in parallel with the main formula brand. The branded formula is not a static concept with evolution in store design and systems, for example, in the case of L'Occitane en Provence, with the trial of a new POS and replenishment IT system in Australia in 2008 and subsequent roll-out of the system across the international store network in 2011 and 2012 and the implementation of SAP in Hong Kong in 2012 as a pilot for gradual integration through the chain.

H&M have followed a similar strategy with the main H&M brand formula operating through several operational formats. The COS brand formula was then developed with a different branding position and marketing approach, initially limited to Europe but then taken more widely international. This was followed in 2008 by the purchase of 60 per cent of Swedish fashion company FaBric Scandinavien AB, which included the brands Monki, Weekday and Cheap Monday. In 2010 the acquisition was completed with 100 per cent H&M ownership. The Monki, Weekday and Cheap Monday brands have been developed internationally into branded formulae but through a limited number of format routes. A sixth branded formula, & Other Stories, was launched within European markets in 2013. Inditex is the leading exponent of this approach and has developed individual brands that for many functions operate independently but for some activities use shared corporate services. The retailing functions of Inditex operate through eight branded formulae – Zara, Pull & Bear, Massimo Dutti, Bershka, Stradivarius, Oysho, Zara Home and Uterqüe. A variety of operational formats are involved with major flagship stores, in-store concessions, standard store units, transactional websites, etc. The branded formulae also are the subject of evolutionary development with refurbishments, new store designs and development of store systems. The formula evolution within a format is a continuous process. An example is within the flagship format with the Zara store in central London (Inditex's 6,000th outlet) being refurbished in 2012 on the model of the new formula design for the Zara flagship format that had been established in New York earlier in the year. The new Zara brand formula for flagship stores involves more clearly identified areas for individual collections, an emphasized simplicity of layout, more integration of hard and soft fixtures and fittings and a greater emphasis in eco-efficiency and environment sustainability. Maintaining a level of independence for the various branded formulae is an important aspect of Inditex's capacity to adapt to changing conditions in the various geographic markets, allowing the brands to shift direction without being slowed by corporate policy in operational issues.

The multi-brand formulae delivered through several formats enables targeting of a wide range of consumer groups with transaction places being tailored to the particular needs, tastes and behaviours of different consumer groups. In addition the variety of brand formulae diversifies risk and helping to protect firms from some of the volatility inherent in the market. Whilst the brand formulae, for example in Inditex, often have considerable autonomy there is a sharing of services, for example in the location of brand formulae in shopping centres where central negotiation of rents is of benefit allowing several of the brand formulae a presence in a centre and there can also be the sharing of airfreight logistics across brand formulae particularly in markets where the firm's presence is still relatively small. Inditex and Mothercare, for example, both use these approaches to the sharing of services internationally across their formulae and so gain economies of scope across their mix of brand formulae. For all the firms using this approach of multiple branded formulae delivered through multiple formats, the branded formula is used throughout their international operation.

An alternative to the H&M and Inditex type format–formula model is one where the brand formulae are limited to specific countries. Again there is a multi-format framework but individual markets have a specific brand formula. The advantage of this model is the building of market-specific brand attributes relevant to the local market. This approach is illustrated by the Jerónimo Martins Group which has stores in its home country, Portugal, and in Poland and Columbia. In Poland it uses the formula brand Biedronka for over 2,000 discount stores, HeBe for its small chain of 60 drugstores, and Na Zdrowkie for its pharmacies. These formula brands are limited to the Polish market. Ahold follows a similar approach to its internationalization of format and formula with North American operations using their brand formulae limited to those markets. A somewhat similar approach is used by Wal-Mart which in 2012 had 55 combinations of format and brand formulae across its 15 markets. For example, in its various discount supermarket operations it uses Smart Choice, changomas expresss, ekono, Super Ahorras, Bodega Aurrera, DESPENSA FAMILIAR, TodaDia, and PALi in the various markets. These generally have been the result of retaining the brand following acquisition although many of the operational systems of the formula will have changed subsequent to acquisition. A similar pattern is seen in the other formats operated by Wal-Mart although in some cases the same brand formula is used in more than one country, for example with the hypermarket Wal-Mart brand formula which is used in Canada and Mexico in addition to USA (Brunn 2006).

This more complex use of format and formula with both market-specific and market-shared brand formulae is used by large firms operating through a variety of formats and generally growing through acquisitions. It is used, for example, by Tesco and A. S. Watson. Acquired firms retain their previous brand, for example Superdrug in UK acquired by A. S. Watson, or may have the acquirers brand added, for example Tesco Lotus in Thailand and Tesco Homeplus in South Korea. At the same time, however, in some markets a common brand formula is used across several markets for example with the use of Tesco Extra brand formula for the hypermarket format across central Europe and the Marionnaud brand formula for A. S. Watson's perfumery format across Europe. Building a new brand formula in a new market is extremely difficult as Tesco found in USA with its Fresh & Easy brand formula for its supermarket format (Lowe and Wrigley 2009). Retaining a formula brand after acquisition or transferring an existing brand formula enables the firm to develop a relationship with consumers more quickly than establishing a totally new formula.

There are several combined ways that formats and brand formulas are used strategically in internationalization processes. There is no single preferred model for this strategy. There are examples of success and failure with all the combinations discussed above. The criterion for success is not the form of the strategy but the dynamic capabilities exhibited by management in interpreting the format to create a brand formula and then to manage its adaption and evolution. The capabilities have to be dynamic because the brand formula is in constant evolution. The evolution results from the retailer responding to changes emanating from consumers, attempting to shape consumer behaviour to better achieve retailer objectives and changing operations systems to seek cost reductions. The capabilities required are ones of sensing and seizing opportunities in respect of interfacing with consumers. There are also necessary capabilities in respect of understanding and gaining knowledge about operational systems so that they can be changed to generate improved performance. In addition, because retail activities are relatively open, there are also capabilities required in respect of monitoring the operational and strategic activity of competitors. As retailers have become multi-format and multi-formula through their networks of transaction places so the importance of these dynamic capabilities has increased. The development of multi-format and multi-formula networks is a key aspect of the way retailer internationalization strategy has been implemented.

Multi-format and multi-formula competition

The distinction between format and formula is central to ideas of retail competition and retail strategy in domestic and international markets. The format decisions are an answer to 'with what consumer markets does the retailer wish to engage?' The formula decisions are an answer to 'how does the retailer engage with consumers?' Decisions in both cases depend on the extent to which the retailer, in order to meet overriding strategic objectives, seeks to respond to and influence the consumer in creating the transaction place.

Historical accounts of retailers and retail entrepreneurs frequently explore the ways that entrepreneurs saw the activities (formulae) of others and adapted them to the particularities of their own firm. A format often becomes diffused through the retail system by the development of formulae with entrepreneurs learning from others. The diffusion of modern formats in Asian markets has been strongly influenced by the entry into those markets of several foreign retailers each with their own formula (Goldman 1981, 2001; Goldman *et al.* 2002; Coca-Cola Retailing Research Council 2007).

Inter-format and intra-format competition have long been recognized as being different types of competition within retailing and reflect competition at macro and micro levels (Bucklin 1972; Betancourt 2004; González-Benito *et al.* 2005; Bhatnagar and Ratchford 2004). The inter-format competition takes place as the formats are flexed, as discussed above, and cost structures in the business model change. The intra-format competition takes place between the formulae of different firms in their interpretations of the format business model. Competition between firms therefore takes place not on *either* an inter- *or* intra-format basis but on an inter- *and* intra-format basis. From the consumer perspective the competitive value obtained from a transaction place is generated by a combination of the format and the formula.

In this competitive process, over time the variety of formats and formulae has increased, but for different reasons. The increase in the variety of formats comes about as consumers become more affluent and more differentiated. Retailers, implicitly for several decades from the nineteenth century and explicitly from around the 1960s, have embraced ideas in marketing, initially viewing the market as comprising segments and more recently addressing market fragments rather than segments (McGoldrick 2002). The early department stores and catalogue retailers (Emmet and Jeuk 1950; Katz 1987), for example, had target markets in mind although they predate the formalization of marketing ideas within retailing. With a more formal acceptance of marketing and continued growing affluence of consumers and related expansion of consumer demand for experiential variety, so more sophisticated segmentation concepts were related to consumer behaviour as well as socio-demographics. Consumer mobility increased, for example, facilitating new possible shopping behaviours. The roles of leisure in society changed also, creating new experiential possibilities for consumers with associated new shopping behaviours (Eastbury 1986). Retailers responded to these social and market changes by creating new formats, for example, with supermarkets, hypermarkets, in-store concessions, discount drug stores, convenience stores, flagship stores, direct selling, museum shops, transactional websites and many others. The variety of formats present in a society is the result of retailers' interpretations of the variety of shopping behaviours that can be identified as being undertaken by consumers.

In contrast to formats, the increase in the variety of formulae results from changes within the retail sector and the dynamic capabilities of the large firms that have come to dominate retail sectors. The development of new managerial capabilities has resulted in the faster evolution of formulae. Retailers have embraced new technologies, for example in physical display, information use, sensory stimulation, packaging, material handling and other areas, that have enabled them to fast prototype and test changes in formulae not only to speed the evolutionary and adaptive aspect but also to create new formulae to operate alongside existing ones. The change in retailing that has enhanced the importance of organizational scale economies has meant that the coordination and sharing of some services, for example in sourcing and logistics, has resulted in retailers addressing multiple consumer fragments with, in consequence, multiple formulae. Inter-firm competition has become increasingly focused on intra-format competition with the formula used as the mechanism for competitive action. Therefore within a format, formula design to elicit customer responses, the use of new technologies to reduce costs, product ranging, pricing and promotion to stimulate consumer purchasing, and routines to improve customer service have become key dimensions of competition. How well the formula operates, essentially the effectiveness of the firm's dynamic capabilities, establishes the success or otherwise of the retailer.

Formula adaption, evolution and embeddedness

The formula of the retailer is the basis for competition in the internationalization process. There has been considerable debate over the need for the retailer to standardize or adapt their operations when moving to a new market. Much of the discussion has been at a very general level without consideration of the way the formula operates and of the process by which a formula is created or transferred to a new market. The simple dichotomy of standardization or adaption is too crude a concept to explain the process of formula transfer (Burt *et al.* 2011). In reality, adaption and standardization are both necessary. In moving to a new a market a retailer keeps some things the same as in the home market and also makes changes to the transferred formula. There is often a transfer of standardized IT and financial systems and adaption of marketing and merchandizing activities that interface directly with consumers, but the detail is more complex than this simple functional division. Often competitive success, or otherwise, rests in the detail.

The degree of adaption has been related to the extent of cultural difference between home and host markets, particularly where the home market is in Western Europe or North America (Evans and Bridson 2005). The idea of psychic distance affecting the degree of adaption is widely discussed in international business although Hang and Godley (2009) point out in a study of international retailer moves to China, 'psychic distance remains one of the most vaguely measured constructs in the domain of international business' (p. 387). Whilst this relationship involving adaption is likely in consumer-facing activity when there are substantial differences in consumer culture, but there is likely to be more standardization of IT and accounting systems when there is a big difference in managerial cultures. Although the degree of adaption of consumer-facing activity may be greater when cultural difference are large, even for small cultural difference adaption is necessary. Understanding the nuances of consumer culture, and adapting to them is essential (Simmons and Schindler 2002) otherwise consumers complain about the absence of key products from ranges (Park 2005) or the incorrect sizes and colours available. Knowledge gained at a local level supports adaption processes and also enables rapid expansion in unfamiliar markets (Bhardwaj *et al.* 2011). Gaining knowledge of the detail of local consumer needs allows the retailer to understand the consumer culture so that as well as responding to it the retailer can also consider ways to shape the consumer culture to respond positively to their particular brand formula and so generate demand (Desvaux and Ramsay 2006).

Adapting the formula to meet and shape local consumer needs is a major, but not the only, part of formula adaption. Glocalization has emerged as a concept to address the extent to which firms operating globally adapt their operating practices to the local commercial and cultural environments. As a concept it tends to focus on the responsiveness of firms to the local conditions rather than the changing of the local situation by the firm involved (Friedman 2005). Glocalization extends beyond responding only to consumers but also includes adaptions of employee relationships and working conditions and, in addition, adaption to relationships with public policy agencies and administrative practices. These are all relevant to the adaption of the formula. Matusitz and Leanza (2009) consider how Wal-Mart has adapted to China, including examples of changes to store design. Matusitz and Forrester (2009) apply a similar approach to Wal-Mart in Japan. Many of the glocalization studies tend towards over-generalization in considering adaption to be at country level whereas national markets often have considerable internal variety that results in adaption at a finer spatial level than the country. The highly segmented, even fragmented, nature of the commercial market and consumers in China means that local adaption and local embeddedness become particularly important.

The capabilities of the retailer to manage these different functional and spatial levels of adaption is an important factor for the success or otherwise of the retailer in a foreign market (Evans *et al.* 2008). These capabilities involve accumulating knowledge about the dynamics of consumer culture and behaviour at a local level, monitoring competitor activity, and importantly having a deep implicit and explicit knowledge of the processes that constitute the retail formula (Cao and Dupuis 2009). With these capabilities it is possible to make evolutionary changes to the adaptions that have been introduced to fit the initial position in the market. It is necessary not only to adapt the formula to be appropriate for the market but also the formula has to evolve as the consumer and competitive market evolves and as new managerial requirements are placed on the formula. Local management may play a major part as the agency for the local evolutionary changes. The extent to which local management can initiate these changes varies by firm but can be present in centralized firms and in franchise networks (Streed and Cliquet 2010; Perrigot 2010). Much depends on the use of the capabilities of the firm rather than its form of organization. Over a period, therefore, the formula in a host market changes to become embedded in the commercial culture and retail structure of the host market.

Ideas of embeddedness, as a feature of international retailing, have been developed by Hess (2004) and enlarged upon by Wrigley *et al.* (2005), Wrigley and Currah (2006) and Coe and Lee (2013). Hess argued that embeddedness takes three forms: societal embeddedness reflects the historico-cultural factors that have created the firm in its home market; network embeddedness reflects the relationships the firm has with other market participants; and territorial embeddedness relates to the cultural, political and economic specificities of the spatial market in which the firm operates. The international retailer has different intensities of involvement with the three types of embeddedness dependent on decisions made on the nature of the formula. The importance of the concept of embeddedness to the discussion on multi-format and multi-formula strategies is that embeddedness stresses the dynamic nature of the systems, procedures and capabilities in retailer operations in diverse markets. Embeddedness must be seen as a process and not as a state. Initial activities of the internationalizing retailer draw on societal embeddedness factors. As the formula becomes established in the market so the factors of network and territorial embeddedness become more important. Coe and Lee (2013) in their discussion of Tesco in Korea stress the territorial embeddedness in stating, 'the localization of Tesco should be seen as a dynamic process that unfolds within, and is shaped by, the context of a developing host retail market' (p. 3 of doi version). It should not be ignored, however, that the firm, in this case Tesco, also plays an active role in shaping the retail market in which it operates through the interaction of structure and agency. Innovations developed in product branding that have been incorporated into several Tesco formulae in South Korea have changed consumer perceptions of retailer branding and also influenced the commercial activity of competitors and food suppliers. The processes of embeddedness are influenced by the environment but also generate responses from that environment.

Network embeddedness can also be important in the way a formula is developed in a host country. The network of suppliers and particularly the introduction of local suppliers into the network can result in adaptions to otherwise normally standardized systems in logistics and product handling. Some retailers seek to keep the systems highly standardized, transferring established routines and systems; for example Wal-Mart in China (Lichtenstein 2009) follows this route, whilst others allow some flexibility in local supplier relationships, as is the situation with Carrefour in China. These different approaches to network embeddedness affect the nature of the adaption of the formula to the local market.

Embedding the formula involves the firm having the capability to integrate aspects of the three types of embeddedness proposed by Hess. Several capabilities are involved. These include: the capability to integrate knowledge about the market and consumer values from different sources; the capability to seize technological and institutional opportunities; the capability to form and manage alliances; and the capabilities to sense and respond rapidly to changes in the competitive environment. Cao (2011) in a study of international retailers in China, concludes that the formula is, 'potentially an autonomous centre of innovation, embedded in (and shaped by) a unique local context' (p. 468). As such adaption and evolution drive embeddedness.

An important issue in the adaption, evolution and embedding of a formula in a market is the extent to which the branded formula can be changed without the brand losing its essential brand values and its integrity. Parry (2013) quotes the Development Director of Ted Baker commenting on their entry into China, 'We've had to re-imagine our business for the Chinese market. We're Ted Baker, but optimized to efficiency "China Style"' (p. 33). All formula brands have to be adapted to local markets to some extent but establishing the balance between retaining core brand values and allowing change is difficult and is not the same for all markets. The management control systems, as Gennari (2010) points out, are critical in achieving and monitoring this balance. Managing the balance is particularly relevant when internationalization is taking place through franchised formulae (Cliquet 2000; Cliquet and Nguyen 2003). In this case the opportunities for the franchisee to make local adaptions are considerable but control systems of the franchisor are required to identify those changes that are compatible with the balance and can be adapted by the franchisee and those which are fundamental to the brand formula and are only changeable by the franchisor. Whilst the systems to achieve this balance are internal in retailers with a corporate network, for franchise operations they become more externally explicit. This has an effect on the nature of embeddedness for franchise systems such that the embeddedness is a more top-down process with the likelihood of fewer informal feedbacks from the host country market in which embedding is taking place.

Managing the adaption, evolution and embedding processes of the formula occurs in all international retailers irrespective of home and host country, sector of operation and format model being used. A range of dynamic capabilities are required to collect and apply knowledge to generate the necessary routines for the processes. Different firms have different approaches to this issue and so require a different mix of capabilities. There is no single optimal approach. Firms have different ways of managing the process of formula transfer and development with the process often at a different stage of sophistication in different host markets where the firm is present. It is important therefore to see adaption and embeddedness as processes that can have a variety of outcomes for a retailer depending on the dynamic capabilities available to the firm.

Conclusions

Format and formula are central concepts for the study of retailer internationalization. Whilst the format is a generalized concept related to the output of the business model employed by the retailer, the formula is the transaction place where interaction occurs between retailer and consumer. Formats and formulae may be grounded in locations, as is often the case with shop-based formats, but they may also depend on technologies that do not require a physical spatial presence.

Whilst the multi-format and multi-format strategy has been well established, since at least the 1980s, by larger retailers in their domestic markets, the development of the strategy, particularly since the late 1990s as suggested in Chapter 1, has come to characterize activity in international markets. In order to expand internationally retailers have a range of format and formula options. In many cases a strategy based on multi-format and multi–formula operation is implemented. Pederzoli (2006) has pointed out that such a strategy enables multiple consumer segments to be addressed and reduces risks in international expansion. It also enables sharing of various support services and so generates economies of scope alongside the scale-related benefits associated with development in new markets. In addition the linking of brand formula in such a strategy can increase consumer awareness of the retailer and increase the level of communication with the market.

The increased use of a multi-format multi-formula approach across diverse markets has placed greater emphasis on the need to adapt, evolve and embed the formula in the host market. The evolution process has become faster as knowledge has been gained and used to adapt the formula and to shape the consumer market. Embedding the formula has become more complex as a wider perspective of the role of the formula in the commercial environment has been realized. The networks of the formulae used by a retailer become more extensive as market penetration and growth in the host market is achieved.

In order to operationalize a multi-format and multi-formula approach retailers have had to harness a range of dynamic capabilities that are both generic to international activity and also are specific to the retail activity of the individual firm. Cao (2011) identifies sensing, shaping and transforming capabilities in a study of capabilities relevant to the total internationalization process. Within this are changes to local competitiveness that relate to format and formula development. Frasquet *et al.* (2011, 2013) also point to generic and specific capabilities suggesting that, whilst being generic, the capabilities of knowledge acquisition and learning, ability to adapt and entrepreneurial vision, have a specific retail interpretation and all are relevant to formula creation and development in the host market. They also suggest the presence of four specific retail capabilities of brand building, formula design, multi-format channel management and customer relationship management. These are all relevant to the operation and evolution of multi-format and multi-formula networks in host markets with the aim to embed the retailer, as a passive and active agent, in the commercial environment.

We can see therefore, the importance of dynamic capabilities in the development of a multi-format multi-formula strategy and the copious literature on capabilities of sensing, seizing and transforming resources in the firm is highly relevant to our understanding of retailer internationalization.

Three clear conclusions emerge from this consideration of format and formula in international retail development. First, the international operations of retailers are very diverse, even within a product sector, and attempts to overgeneralize, by academics and managers alike, through generic strategies are likely to fail. There is no single automatically successful model. The dynamic capabilities of each firm combine to create different results and firms are at different stages in the adaption, evolution and embedding processes of their formula networks. Second, the development of a multi-format and multi-formula approach generates economies of scope for retailers that complement the search for scale economies that are central to the internationalization process. Third, the international strategy of retailers now has to include a multi-format and multi-formula approach to operations if the retailer is serious about operating outside their domestic market.

References

Appel, D. (1972) The supermarket: early development of an institutional innovation. *Journal of Retailing*, 48(1), 39–53.

Betancourt, R. (2004) *The economics of retailing and distribution*. Cheltenham: Edward Elgar.

Bhardwaj, V., Eickman, M. and Runyan, R. (2011) A case study on the internationalization process of a 'born-global' fashion retailer. *International Review of Retail, Distribution and Consumer Research*, 21(3), 293–307.

Bhatnagar, A. and Ratchford, B. T. (2004) A model of retail format competition for non-durable goods. *International Journal of Research in Marketing*, 21(1), 39–59.

Brunn, S. D. (ed.) (2006) *Wal-Mart world*. Abingdon: Routledge.

Bucklin, L. P. (1972) *Competition and evolution in the distributive trades*. Englewood Cliffs: Prentice Hall.

Burt, S., Johansson, U. and Thelander, Å. (2011) Standardized marketing strategies in retailing? IKEA's marketing strategies in Sweden, the UK and China. *Journal of Retailing and Consumer Services*, 18(3), 183–193.

Cao, L. (2011) Dynamic capabilities in a turbulent market environment: empirical evidence from international retailers in China. *Journal of Strategic Marketing*, 19(5), 455–469.

Cao, L. and Dupuis, M. (2009) Core competence, strategy and performance: the case of international retailers in China. *International Review of Retail, Distribution and Consumer Research*, 19(4), 349–369.

Carpenter, J. M. and Moore, M. (2006) Consumer demographics, store attributes, and retail format choice in the US grocery market. *International Journal of Retail and Distribution Management*, 34(6), 434–452.

Cliquet, G. (2000) Plural forms in store networks: a model for store network management. *International Review of Retail, Distribution and Consumer Research*, 10(4), 369–387.

Cliquet, G. and Nguyen, M.-N. (2003) Innovation management within the plural form network. Paper presented at the *EMNet*-Conference on *Economics and Management of Franchising Networks*, Vienna, Austria, 26–28 June.

Coca-Cola Retailing Research Council (2007) *Food retail formats in Asia: Understanding format success*. Report by Coca-Cola Retailing Research Council Asia.

Coe, N. M. and Lee, Y.-S. (2013) 'We've learnt how to be local': The deepening territorial embeddedness of Samsung-Tesco in South Korea. *Journal of Economic Geography* (advanced access) doi:10.1093/jeg.lbs057, now published in 13(2), 327–356.

Coopey, R., O'Connell, S. and Porter, D. (2005) *Mail order retailing in Britain*. Oxford: Oxford University Press.

Dawson, J. (2003) Retail change in Britain during 30 years: the strategic use of economies of scale and scope. In: *Distribution and Society in Modern Japan*: *Essays in Honour of Yoshiaki Shiraishi*. Kobe: Minerva Press, pp. 56–68.

Desvaux, G. and Ramsay, A. J. (2006) Shaping China's home improvement market: an interview with B&Q's CEO for Asia. *McKinsey Quarterly*, July, 82–91.

DeMarco, E. S. (2006) *Reading and riding: Hachette's railroad bookstore network in nineteenth-century France*. Bethlehem: Lehigh University Press.

Eastbury, L. (1986) Concept retailing. *Management Horizons Retail Focus*, Autumn.

Emmet, B. and Jeuk, J. J. (1950) *Catalogues and counters*. Chicago: University of Chicago Press.

Evans, J. and Bridson, K. (2005) Explaining retail offer adaptation through psychic distance. *International Journal of Retail and Distribution Management*, 33(1), 69–78.

Evans, J., Mavondo, F. T. and Bridson, K. (2008) Psychic distance: antecedents, retail strategy implications and performance outcomes. *Journal of International Marketing*, 16(2), 32–63.

Frasquet, M., Mollá, A. and Dawson, J. (2011) Dynamic capabilities in retailing: a perspective for the study of international fashion retailing. Paper to *EAERCD* conference, University of Parma, 29 June–1 July.

Frasquet, M., Dawson, J. and Mollá, A. (2013) Post-entry internationalisation activity of retailers: an assessment of dynamic capabilities. *Management Decision*, 51(7), in press.

Freathy, P. and O'Connell, F. (1998) *European airport retailing*. Basingstoke: Macmillan.

Friedman, T. L. (2005) *The world is flat*. New York: Farrar, Straus and Giroux.

Gennari, F. (2010) Management control in global mass market retailers. *SYMPHONYA Emerging Issues in Management*, 1, 57–65.

Goldman, A. (1981) Transfer of retailing technology into lesser developed countries: the supermarket case. *Journal of Retailing*, 57(2), 5–29.

Goldman, A. (2001) The transfer of retail formats into developing economies: the example of China. *Journal of Retailing*, 77(2), 221–242.

Goldman, A., Ramaswami, S. and Krider R. E. (2002) Barriers to the advancement of modern food retail formats: theory and measurement, *Journal of Retailing*, 78(4), 281–295.

González-Benito, Ó., Muñoz-Gallego, P. A. and Kopalle, P. K. (2005) Asymmetric competition in retail store formats: evaluating inter- and intra-format spatial effects. *Journal of Retailing*, 81(1), 59–73.

Hang, H. and Godley, A. (2009) Revisiting the psychic distance paradox: International retailing in China in the long run (1840–2005). *Business History*, 51(3), 383–400.

Hess, M. (2004) 'Spatial' relationships? Towards a reconceptualization of embeddedness. *Progress in Human Geography*, 28(2), 165–186.

Hilditch, G. (2010) *European apparel: international, internet and inflation.* London: J. P. Morgan Cazenove.

Ishii, J. and Mukoyama, M. (eds) (2009) *Innovation of retail formats. Tokyo:* Chuokeizai (in Japanese).

Katz, D. R. (1987) *The big store: Inside the crisis and revolution at Sears.* New York: Penguin Books.

Kaynak, E. (1985) Global spread of supermarkets: some experiences from Turkey. In: E. Kaynak (ed.) *Global Perspectives in Marketing.* New York: Praeger, pp. 77–93.

Kozinets, R. V., Sherry, J. F., DeBerry-Spence, B., Duhachek, A., Nuttavuthisit, K. and Storm, D. (2008) Themed flagship brand stores in the new millennium: theory, practice and prospects. *Journal of Retailing,* 78(1), 17–29.

Lancaster, B. (1995) *The department store: a social history.* London: Leicester University Press.

Lee, T. (2013) Canada in Target's bull's eye. *Minneapolis Star Tribune,* 15 February. Available at: www.startribune.com/business/191491891.html.

Lichtenstein, N. (2009) *The retail revolution: how Wal-Mart created a brave new world of business.* New York: Picador.

Lhermie, C. (2003) *Carrefour ou l'invention de l'hypermarché.* Paris: Vuibert.

Lowe, M. and Wrigley, N. (2009) Innovation in retail internationalization: Tesco in the USA. *International Review of Retail, Distribution and Consumer Research,* 19(4), 331–347.

Luo, Y. (2002) Capability exploitation and building in a foreign market: implications for multinational enterprises. *Organization Science,* 13(1), 48–63.

Markin, R. (1968) *The supermarket: an analysis of growth development and change.* Pullman: Washington State University Press.

Marseille, J. (1997) *La revolution commerciale en France: Du Bon Marche a L'hypermarche.* Paris: le Monde.

Matusitz, J. and Forrester, M. (2009) Successful glocalization practices: the case of Seiyu Japan. *Journal of Transnational Management,* 14(2), 155–176.

Matusitz, J. and Leanza, K. (2009) Wal-Mart: an analysis of the glocalization of the cathedral of consumption in China. *Globalizations,* 6(2), 187–205.

McGoldrick, P. J. (2002) *Retail marketing.* Maidenhead: McGraw-Hill.

Messinger, P. R. and Narasimhan, C. (1997) A model of retail formats based on consumers' economizing on shopping time. *Marketing Science,* 16(1), 1–23.

Park, C. (2005) Complaints of Asian shoppers toward global retailer: a content analysis of e-complaining to Carrefour Korea. *Asia Pacific Journal of Marketing and Logistics,* 17(3), 25–39.

Parry, C. (2013) Solving retail's Chinese puzzle. *Retail Week,* 18 January, 32–34.

Pederzoli, D. (2006) Conception and test of a comprehensive model of international strategy for retail companies. *International Review of Retail, Distribution and Consumer Research,* 16(4), 415–431.

Perrigot, R. (2010) Plural form and the internationalization of franchising networks: exploring the potential relationship. In: G. Hendrikse, M. Tuunanen, J. Windsperger and G. Cliquet (eds) *Strategy and governance of networks, cooperatives, franchising and strategic alliances.* Heidelberg: Physica-Verlag, pp. 147–164.

Reardon, T., Henson, S. and Berdegué J. (2007) Proactive fast-tracking diffusion of supermarkets in developing countries: implications for market institutions and trade. *Journal of Economic Geography,* 7(4), 399–431.

Reardon, T., Timmer, C. P., Barrett, C. B. and Berdegue, J. (2003) The rise of supermarkets in Africa, Asia, and Latin America. *American Journal of Agricultural Economics*, 85(5), 1140–1146.

Reynolds, J., Howard, E., Cuthbertson, C. and Hristov, L. (2007) Perspectives on retail format innovation: relating theory and practice. *International Journal of Retail and Distribution Management*, 35(8), 647–660.

Rousey S. P. and Morganosky, M. A. (1996) Retail format change in US markets. *International Journal of Retail and Distribution Management*, 24(3), 8–16.

Shields, R. (1992) *Lifestyle shopping: the subject of consumption*. London: Routledge.

Simmons, L. C. and Schindler, R. M. (2002) Cultural superstitions and the price endings used in Chinese advertising. *Journal of International Marketing* (special issue on marketing in transitional economies), 11(2), 101–111.

Sorescu, A., Frambach, R. T., Singh, J., Rangaswamy, A. and Bridges, C. (2011) Innovations in retail business models. *Journal of Retailing*, 87S(1), S3–S16.

Streed, O. and Cliquet, G. (2010) Concept uniformity: control versus freedom in business format franchising. In: G. Hendrikse, M. Tuunanen, J. Windsperger and G. Cliquet (eds) *Strategy and governance of networks, cooperatives, franchising and strategic alliances*. Heidelberg: Physica-Verlag, pp. 127–146.

Stremersch, S. and Tellis, G. J. (2002) Strategic bundling of products and prices: a new synthesis for marketing. *Journal of Marketing*, 66(1), 55–72.

Teece, D. J. (2007) Explicating dynamic capabilities: the nature and microfoundations of (sustainable) enterprise performance. *Strategic Management Journal*, 28(13), 1319–1350.

Teece, D. J. (2009) *Dynamic capabilities and strategic management*. Oxford: Oxford University Press.

Uusitalo, O. (2001) Consumer perceptions of grocery retail formats and brands. *International Journal of Retail and Distribution Management*, 29(5), 214–225.

Wrigley, N. and Currah, A. (2006) Globalizing retail and the 'new e-economy': the organizational challenge of e-commerce for retail TNCs. *Geoforum*, 37(3), 340–351.

Wrigley, N., Coe, N. M. and Currah, A. (2005) Globalizing retail: conceptualizing the distribution-based transnational corporation (TNC). *Progress in Human Geography*, 29(4), 437–457.

3 Global portfolio strategy as a new strategic paradigm

Masao Mukoyama and John Dawson

> *The difference between Chinese culture and European culture is something exceptional.*
>
> Jean-Luc Chéreau, President Carrefour China 1999–2006
> (Child 2006)

Since the late 1990s the major firms in the retail sector have been the subject of substantial increases in scale, an expanding geographical scope, and diversification into multiple formats and formulae. In Chapter 1 the gradual emergence of multi-continent. multi-format retailer activity was described and in Chapter 2 the detail of the multi-format. multi-formula approach was explored. In this chapter the focus is first on the advantages and difficulties of operating on a multi-continental basis and second, the exploration of the concept of a global portfolio strategy that can be used to link the multi-continent and multi-format approaches.

The approach to multi-format, multi-continent operation is evident for large firms irrespective of their home continent. This is well illustrated by the fmcg sector retailers with Wal-Mart present on five continents with eight formats and in excess of 55 branded formulae. Seven&I operates on four continents through ten formats and Carrefour on four continents through five formats and with 12 branded formulae. Only slightly less spatial and format scope is evident in Tesco, Ahold and Delhaize. In all these firms the spatial and format scope has increased in recent years. This pattern is repeated for major retailers in many other sectors as they have sought ways to increase sales volumes. For example in 2012, in clothing Inditex operates across six continents through eight branded format ranges and H&M has five brand formula chains operating within multiple formats across five continents with plans to add Australia as a sixth continent in 2013. Gap and Fast Retailing both operate on three continents with five and four brand formulae and multiple formats, respectively. All these large clothing retailers operate multiple operational formats (flagship store, online e-commerce, in-store concession, pop-up store, standard format store, etc.) alongside their brand formula stores. In the luxury sector most major firms are similarly now multi-continental, multi-format and multi-formula. Major specialist retailers have developed a similar strategy. For example, Toys-R-Us operates on six continents with five brand formulae and multiple operational formats; Staples operates on five continents with several operational retail formats but within a single brand formula. This complex market facing operating strategy, which we term a *global portfolio strategy*, has emerged as the latest of the phases of internationalization proposed in Chapter 1.

Expanding the continental scope of activity

As retail internationalization became more accepted as a strategy many retailers had a preference to remain within their general region of operations. Rugman (2005) using data from the late 1990s termed them 'regional multinationals'. Since around 2000, as was discussed in Chapter 1, there has been increasing activity to move beyond this regional pattern and to attempt to move out of home continents into often geographically and culturally distant markets. This move by some retailers follows the general trend of the globalization of markets. Rugman points out that at the time of his study only 10 per cent of Wal-Mart stores were outside North America. By 2012, however, the majority of stores were outside the USA. Whilst much of the academic globalization literature has ignored the activities of retailers who have been somewhat late movers compared to manufacturers, there have been some studies using the term 'retail globalization' (Bell *et al.* 2004; Wrigley *et al.* 2005; Coe 2004) but generally much of the discussion has followed Rugman and has been on regional internationalization. The increasingly widespread use of the term 'trans-national' (for example Coe and Wrigley 2007; Mutebi 2007; Tacconelli and Wrigley 2009) in studies of retail internationalization seldom makes the distinction between regional and global scopes of activity. The differences between regional multinational and global multi-continental retailers requires exploration. It is relevant therefore to consider first, the reasons behind the increased willingness to become more global and second, how inter-continental activity is different from the regional internationalization.

Why has multi-continental activity increased?

There are a number of reasons for the steady increase in multi-continental expansion of retailers since the early 2000s. Most of this trend is accounted for by retailers based in the already competitive markets of North America, Europe and Japan moving away from their respective home region. With a few notable exceptions, for example Billabong, and A. S. Watson, the international retailers based in other continents and in Asia outside Japan, at the current stage of internationalization, have tended to remain regional in their activity. The retailers in developed economies have moved strongly into the emergent developing economies (Planer 2009) and also to a lesser degree into other already highly competitive regions. Golub (2009) calculates that in respect of foreign direct investment (FDI) stocks in wholesaling and retailing between 1990 and 2005, the ratio of stocks in developing: developed countries has decreased from 1 : 7.8 to 1 : 4.4 with the total of FDI stocks in developing countries having increased to US$200 billion in 2005. Since 2005 the increased presence of foreign investment in the developing countries, through direct investment and acquisition, for example Wal-Mart's acquisition of Massmart in South Africa, and through acting as integrators of global supply chains (Reardon 2005) has further increased the stock of retail-based FDI investment in developing countries. Much, although certainly not all, of this new foreign investment has been directed at China (Zhen 2007; Siebers 2011; Pennemann 2013; Wang and Du 2007; Yahagi *et al.* 2009; Huang and Liu 2011).

The slowdown in retail sales in Europe, North America and Japan which was evident for several years before the crisis of 2007/2008 is an important factor in retailers from these markets moving into markets where sales are growing more quickly. Reisman (2010) shows that from 2004–2008 the annual growth of real GDP averaged 7 per cent in developing countries compared to 2 per cent in developed countries. Figure 3.1 shows comparisons of average percentage real growth in GDP for key countries on different continents. After 2009 this disparity increased considerably with real GDP going into decline in several developed countries. Retail sales generally track real GDP per head but in developing countries retail sales grow faster than growth in real GDP per head because the high GDP growth results in substantial increases in discretionary incomes of consumers. The fundamental business model of retailers, and particularly large retailers, is anchored in continuous growth of sales volumes so expansion into new markets is essential (Dawson 2013). The high growth in South America and East Asia became very attractive to retailers with extensive exposure in low-growth Europe and North America The combined share of global retail sales of the four 'BRIC' countries (Brazil, Russia, India and China) grew from 13 per cent in 2003 to 18 per cent in 2008 (Reisman 2010). Whilst the increasing income of consumers in emerging economies generates an increase in discretionary spending there is also increase in retail sales in the food and grocery sector. Table 3.1 shows the historic and forecast difference in growth in the food sector retail sales as between North America and Western Europe compared with Asia and Latin America. Moving to a high-growth market in a new continent is potentially attractive for retailers, in all sectors, faced with low growth at home.

A second contributing factor to the increase in multi-continent retailing is associated with the increase in sourcing on a global basis and, for some retailers, global sourcing (Branch 2009; Burch and Lawrence 2007; Bair 2009). Sourcing on a global basis has increased awareness of retail expansion opportunities in the countries from which product is sourced and so has encouraged retailers to consider expansion in these markets. Knowledge has been gained by retailers not only of the production capabilities in these countries (Reardon *et al.* 2012) but also of their potentialities for retail expansion. Baron (2007), with particular reference to the food sector, points out that the foreign retailers rely on local

Table 3.1 Grocery sector estimated retail sales, excluding tax, converted to US$

	Index at current prices year on year exchange rates		Increase sales US$ million	Forecast growth US$ million
	2001	2011	2001–2011	2011–2016
North America	100	149.6	350,424	120,368
of which USA	100	144.1	284,854	98,571
Western Europe	100	183.5	687,814	131,643
Eastern Europe	100	348.9	302,357	217,866
of which Russia	100	608.9	190,114	167,797
Asia Pacific	100	200.8	744,213	536,609
of which China	100	282.4	325,756	269,844
Latin America	100	190.6	221,225	136,747
of which Brazil	100	370.7	82,500	34,754
Middle East and Africa	100	217.3	160,763	86,722

Source: based on Dawson (2013).

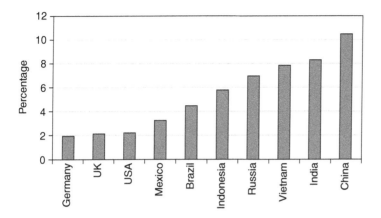

Figure 3.1 Average annual percentage real growth in GDP 2004–2008 (source: IMF data).

procurement and invest in local production but that these production sources can also be used to service home as well as local operations as has been evident in some food supply chains in Thailand and Vietnam (Raynolds 2004; UNCTAD Secretariat 2005).

Changing social structures and consumer demand in the fast-growth emergent economies in South America and Asia have generated new demands for modern forms of retailing, for example supermarkets (Reardon and Hopkins 2006; Maruyama and Trung 2007; Reardon *et al.* 2007), and iconic brands from Europe and North America. The retailers with efficient operational formats and strong brand formulae have benefited from the more general globalization of brand awareness. This has been particularly, but not only, the case in the fashion sector with multi-continental activity by luxury brands, for example within LVMH and Paul Smith; street fashion, for example TopShop and Forever 21; fast fashion, for example H&M, Fast Retailing and Inditex brands; young casual fashion, for example Bestseller brands; and affordable luxury, for example Ted Baker. In all these examples the retailers have moved beyond their regional scope to become multi-continental. The globalization of brand concepts, for example Apple and IKEA, has widened the horizons of consumers and generated global demand for key brands resulting in the retailers initially following demand into new markets but more importantly creating sustained demand and changing consumption patterns post entry into the market. Lee *et al.* (2012), for example, report changes in food consumption patterns in Korea that took place alongside the growth of modern retailing and the increasing influence of foreign firms in the food retail sector (see also Pingali 2007). The ability of retailers to create demand for brands and to shape consumer behaviour and values has enabled them to build on their initial multi-continental activity. The opportunities for shaping consumption cultures and making markets is greater when the retailer moves to a new continent (Desvaux and Ramsay 2006).

A further encouragement for retailers to consider inter-continental moves has been the gradual reduction of the great variety of restrictions on international investment and operations in the retail sector (Arkell 2010). Whilst many restrictions still exist in terms of direct investment, for example in India and Malaysia (Mukherjee and Patel 2005; Mukherjee 2011), and in other operational areas of retailing, for example in relationships between retailers and suppliers and the licensing of specific formats (Reardon and Hopkins 2006; Kalirajan 2000; Nielson and Taglioni 2004; Mutebi 2007) there has been a steady reduction in these constraints. The presence of these more open markets has encouraged multi-continental foreign investment (Roy 2008). The financial crisis in East Asia in 1997/1998 forced the hand of several governments to open the market to retail FDI and a substantial stock of foreign-owned investments built up through the decade from 2000. Since 2000 there has been pressure from WTO, World Bank and OECD for a reduction in the barriers to international investment in retailing. But, as Roy (2008) points out, 'many WTO members remain without international trade commitments in this key sector [i.e. retailing], and a number of barriers continue to affect providers and raise costs for consumers' (p. 224). Nonetheless, the reduction in regulations and opening of markets has been an important factor in allowing entry, into emergent Asian and South American markets, of modern retail formats mainly developed by retailers from Europe and North America as well as increasing the opportunities for inter-continental supply chain integration (Nordås 2008). Whilst the relaxation of these restrictions has often generated negative responses from traditional retailers it has encouraged more inter-continental flows of investment.

Advances in information and communication technologies have been a further factor in reducing the constraints on multi-continental expansion. Retailers have developed sophisticated models of their operations so that they can transfer the key operating systems as a package when they enter a new country. For example, the Tesco Hindustan Service Centre has created a transferable package that models 'a well defined common set of business processes and IT systems that can meet the diverse needs of various countries where Tesco sets up shop'.[1] This package has been used in the entry stage of Tesco into Turkey, Japan, China and the USA in order to reduce the time needed to establish basic systems for store operation, accounting and trading with suppliers. Whilst implemented in alternative ways by different firms (Burt *et al.* 2006) this transfer of explicit knowledge, in some cases held on a corporate Cloud (Dawson 2009) and in other cases using outsourced expertise (Lanz *et al.* 2011), has made it easier and faster for retailers to move standard practice systems into foreign operations thus enabling more effort to be given to local adaptions of customer-facing practices and systems, such as people management (Gamble 2006, 2011) and merchandizing. With operational systems becoming standardized there is more time spent on embedding the retailer into the local consumer culture. For example, by having standard business systems that are transferable to culturally different markets, IKEA has been able to spend more resource on adapting stores to local consumer needs often using advanced computer-aided design software. IKEA transferred its core operational systems to Japan so that control was established using common systems. Therefore, this has allowed adaption of in-store merchandizing to local conditions. For example IKEA introduced in late 2012 a third generation of room sets based on Japanese apartment layouts in districts around the specific store with the new room sets developed having outer walls cut away so that the entire layout is positioned to provide better lines of sight into the rooms as customers walk around the store (Larke 2013). Jonsson and Foss (2011) term this standardize core and market adaption in IKEA as 'flexible replication'. The easier knowledge transfer systems that reduce the constraints of distance for inter-continental expansion are linked to technological advances in network architectures so that secure information flows have become more reliable.

Linked to technological changes has been the growing use of e-commerce to effect market entry for retailers and for retailers to evaluate markets outside their current operational region. E-commerce has provided a low-cost and low-risk method of prospecting a market for more substantial entry. Monitoring the origin of orders on a transactional website provides an indication of whether or not a move into a market on another continent is worth serious exploration. This is of particular relevance for clothing brand retailers. For example Ted Baker monitored web-based demand from Japan before deciding to open a store in 2012. Mothercare had a similar approach before deciding on franchising in Asian markets.

Critical events can, but not always, create opportunities for inter-continental expansion. A change in government policy in China, for example, whilst certainly not removing barriers to entry, provided an opportunity for American and European retailers to create joint ventures with Chinese businesses. In contrast, however, the opening of markets in Central Europe after 1989 resulted in little inter-continental retailer investment with, other than the K-Mart purchase of 13 department stores in the then Czechoslovakia, most of the investment coming from regional sources. Only much later has Central Europe started to attract the attention of American and Asian retailers. These recent moves (for example TK Maxx to Poland in 2009 and Gap and Footlocker to Poland in 2011) have been more the result of the new availability of shopping centre locations than the collapse of central economic planning. Thus a different type of critical event, the development of shopping centres, can provide the catalyst for multi-continental expansion.

There are a number of sector-wide factors that have encouraged and acted as a catalyst for moves to explore multi-continental operation. Individual firms have responded to these factors in different ways and at different times in their overall internationalization strategy depending on perceptions of the benefits and risks of moving to a new continent. In considering the importance of these triggers for strategic action it is useful to explore why, in terms of risks and rewards, becoming multi-continental for retailers is different from staying within their own region.

How is inter-continental expansion different?

Moving into new continents requires different managerial capabilities from internationalization within a continent. Enderwick (2007), in considering doing business in emerging markets, explores some of these by implication through a focus on China and India and contrasting the risks and constraints with conditions in Europe or North America. It is useful to consider what issues, for a retailer, make moving to another continent different from internationalization within a region. It is not only the differences in the external commercial environment that have to be considered but also the differences in operating essentially the same format in very different cultural environments and the operation of different format mixes. The magnitude of differences between major cultural regions can require different capabilities for a firm to succeed in a multi-continental framework.

Ways of conducting business and concepts of contractual relations can differ greatly between continents whilst essentially being the same across countries on a continent despite differences in legal frameworks. Thus the ways contracts are executed can be very different with non-legal factors having different strength in, for example, Asia compared to Europe. In the early development of Carrefour in Taiwan formal legal contracts for five new stores were signed by a departing country manager but the new country manager failed to get the stores developed being told that 'Just because (the Taiwanese developer) signed a 20 year contract two years ago with your former boss – a person who is not you – does not mean (the Taiwanese developer) will respect the contract' (Child 2006: 72). The contract had to be re-negotiated with the new country manager before development could begin. This more flexible interpretation of contracts evident in Asia is very different from the situation across countries within Europe or in North America.

The cultural differences from continent to continent are substantial and affect the norms of consumption and consumer behaviour. Although there are consumer differences between countries within the main continents the differences tend to be rooted in some common cultural and consumption values. Inter-continental differences can be based on different root values. Gao (2012) in a detailed review of differences between East Asian Chinese and Western European cultural values points to the grounding of Chinese values in a more generic Asian cultural value structure. Five key value constructs were identified that defined Chinese values drawn from the Asian culture realm. The five were identified as 'Moderation and Harmony'; 'Guanxi and Reciprocation'; 'Conformity and Authority'; 'Practical Rationalism'; and 'Face and Status' had implications for product symbolic meaning, for consumer behaviour and provide fundamental differences with the European or North American cultural value influences on consumers (de Mooji 2010). These contrasts between Chinese-based and European-based values are substantial (Sun *et al.* 2004; Xiao and Kim 2009) and create a considerable barrier for retailers who wish to operate in both continents. Whilst studies have tended to focus on comparisons involving China the broad culture realms represented by the continents each have distinctive features that underpin behavioural norms and accommodating these distinctions of consumption and consumer behaviour are a factor making inter-continental retailer activity different from border-hopping activity within a continent. European and American retailers moving into each other's home continents have often discovered that consumer values are much more different than expected even for broadly similar goods. Dixons for example found the price-driven attitudes of consumers in the USA very different from Europe and failed in the USA whilst Best Buy's failure to meet UK consumer expectations led to their withdrawal from Europe. In both cases the cultural differences in consumers on the two continents played a role. The social mechanisms of consumption reflect the cultural patterns of consumers. As a result, often on a different continent, products have different social meanings, customs and practices of shopping are different, values attached to activities and relationships are different, and the semiotics of the sales outlet are different. The capabilities and routines required by management, particularly the capabilities to sense the dynamics of consumer culture, are different for intra-continent and inter-continent expansion with attention to the foundations of consumer culture needing to be sensed more explicitly in the inter-continental situation.

Whilst consumer cultures are often very different on different continents, it is also well established that managerial cultures and styles differ in significant ways (Whitley 1992; Easterby-Smith *et al.* 1995; Horwitz *et al.* 2002). This is particularly relevant in retailing and other service sector firms where a network structure to operations involves a large cadre of middle managers who have a direct influence on consumer interactions and so have a strong impact on the commercial success or failure of the network of outlets. For the foreign retailer it is essential to have managers drawn from the local managerial culture. In an inter-continental move this usually involves having an interface between a limited number of senior executives drawn from the home and the larger number of local managers so the need to understand local managerial cultures is essential for the internationalizing retailer. This does not mean that the internationalizing firm cannot bring in new practices, as Gamble (2003, 2006) has pointed out in respect of a UK retailer moving to China, but it does mean that the introduction of these practices has to take into account the very different managerial values and styles. Whilst Gamble has focused on transfers between UK and China for a predominantly food retailer similar issues are raised for other retailers, for example Wal-Mart (Chuang *et al.* 2012), and other sectors involved in inter-continental moves. Whilst all international moves by retailers pose issues about convergence of managerial styles, particularly when expansion by acquisition is involved, nonetheless the complexity of the issues is greater when inter-continental activity is involved.

When a retailer moves into a new market there is usually a transfer of the formats and formulae. Adaptions have to be made to the firm's formulae and the capability to make transformations of formats for new markets is a fundamental dynamic capability for retailers. An aspect of this capability is knowledge about the process of formula evolution within the context of the commercial culture of the market. This is the capability to transform routines to adapt the way the retailer communicates to consumers through its formula. The greater the difference in the commercial culture from the one where the formula was developed then the greater the complexity in making the necessary transformations and the more knowledge required by the retailer. In moving to a market on a new continent therefore more knowledge is required about the relationships in the business model associated with a formula and more knowledge is required about the variables involved in the evolution of the formula. Lowe *et al.* (2012), in an analysis of the development of Tesco in the USA, suggest that there is evidence of three important capabilities used by Tesco in moving from the UK. They term as 'splicing' the capability to transform routines relevant to creating the new formula used by Tesco in the US market. The differences in the commercial environment in USA caused Tesco to develop transforming capabilities in order to adapt its format mix and create a formula specific to their US operation. Intercontinental moves involve the need for new dynamic capabilities to create the adaptions to the established formulae of the retailer.

Moving to a new continent may require the development of a different supplier network with new relationships having to be made with a group of new suppliers. This is particularly the case in the food and grocery sector. For regional internationalization, existing supply networks often can be extended to accommodate border hopping. In such cases adjustments to logistics networks are often sufficient. When inter-continental moves take place, however, a new supplier network and associated logistic network have to be developed *ab initio*. For food retailers this may involve the creation of an integrated supply chain through to primary production to ensure that product security and traceability are maintained (Swinnen and Maertens 2007). This type of radical creation of a new supply chain increases the complexity and the risk of moving into a new continent.

More generally the risk is higher for an inter-continental move compared with one within the home operating continent. Risks of mistaken perceptions of environmental factors and competition, of mistakes in the operational systems in the different consumer and managerial culture, and of misunderstanding the dynamics of the market, including political risks, are all higher when the retailer expands to another continent. Making assumptions about a market carries high risks when the new market is on a different continent. The chairman of Marks and Spencer, Sir Stuart Rose, in an interview with *Financial Times*,

> admitted that the company had misunderstood the local market, assuming that M&S expertise in Hong Kong, where the group has 10 stores and has been trading for 20 years, would translate easily to the mainland. Shanghai clothing sizes were based on Hong Kong sizing but the smaller sizes rapidly sold out.

Adding 'We need to get the A to Z of sizing right and we need better market research' (Waldmeir 2009). Not only is the level of risk higher but also the analysis of the risk may have to take different factors into account making the capabilities to evaluate the risks somewhat different from when expansion into a home continent is involved. Typical in this respect is the experience of Staples in moving from USA to Europe. In an interview in 2009 the chairman and CEO admitted,

> We probably made nearly every mistake one could make in Europe over the ten years. As a US company, we thought Europe would be a single market like in the States, which of course it isn't. We tried to operate the business with US managers and initially sited our European corporate headquarters in the UK rather than on the Continent. Also our store sizes were too large, and some of the product decisions we made were wrong.
>
> (Sargent 2009)

One approach to reducing these types of risk is through the use of regional franchise agreements in which established local firms become agents, franchisees and region-wide sub-franchisors for an internationalizing retailer based outside the region. International retailers entering the Gulf States region often have taken this approach. Large locally based firms, for example Majid Al Futtaim, Alshaya and Fawaz Alhokair Groups, have used their knowledge of cultural values and consumption processes to become successful strategic partners actively taking foreign retailers internationally through several countries in the region. The risks linked with inadequate levels of local knowledge and associated absence of key capabilities has been reduced through the use of local partners. The frequency of failures in inter-continental expansions reflect the higher levels of risk and the need for different capabilities for evaluating risk (Evans and Mavondo 2002; Burt *et al.* 2003) and for establishing partnering relationships.

The costs of moving to a new continent are often high compared to border-hopping activity. Planer (2009), in a consideration of Western food retailers moves into emergent markets, asserts that,

> Western market participants usually need deep pockets (ideally filled by highly profitable home market operations) to cross-finance start-up losses for several years. The numbers of Western retailers operating profitably in Russia or in India, for example, are very low indeed.
>
> (Planer 2009 p. 15)

Pederzoli (2006) similarly points to the need for substantial investment which may be necessary for several years before profits are made. Whilst small-scale incremental investment is feasible in border-hopping expansion, going to a new continent requires the retailer to rapidly generate a scale of operation that quickly covers the high start-up costs. With a commitment to major investment, however, the returns can be substantial. For example Tesco have made substantial commitment to investment in South Korea (over £2 billion) and

Thailand (over £1 billion), outside their European home base, with a return on investment of around 17 per cent in 2007–2008 and 2008–2009. In Japan, by contrast the investment was small and insufficient to begin to gain scale economies and cover start-up costs with the result that a decision was made, in 2011, to withdraw from the market. Attaining scale economies and a better return on investment in a large market, such as USA or China, is likely to require a substantial increase in the level of investment compared to border hopping in the home region. In a market with a very different commercial culture and an environment different from the comfort zone of home, the evaluation of investment opportunities can be particularly difficult. The evaluation of acquisition targets also can be problematic as Wal-Mart found with its ill-fated move into Germany (Korr and Arndt 2003; Christopherson 2007). Tackett (2006) in a review of Wal-Mart's failure points out that, 'Wal-Mart's haste to set up shop in Germany, however, proved costly. The 21 Wertkauf and 74 Interspar hypermarkets Wal-Mart purchased in 1998 and 1999, respectively, were overpriced and many needed remodelling or were in less-desirable locations' (p. 1). This view is reinforced by Dawson (2009) pointing out that the $715 million for Wertkauf was 'far in excess of anything that local German retailers were prepared to pay at the time' and the error was compounded by the purchase of '74 Interspar hypermarkets from Germany's crumbling Spar organization for around $690m'. When the largest retailer in the world with access to potentially the best acquisition tools available makes these types of mistakes, then clearly acquisitions in a new continent with different commercial environment are difficult to assess.

There are many reasons why moving retail operations away from the home continent to markets in a very different consumer commercial culture poses different issues and requires different dynamic capabilities to those required for internationalization within a continent. The issues have different degrees of importance depending on the sector so that for the food sector the differences in consumer food culture take on particular importance but for brand-driven fashion the contrasts in importance of brand advocacy may be more important. In general, however, the limits on retailers that affect their ability to operate on a multi-continental basis have been steadily eroded. Limits associated with managing large multi-format networks, limits on the availability of capital to support early stage development, limits associated with the cost of extended supply chain, and limits linked to governmental constraints on foreign firms, have all been reduced in the 2000s. With the change in limits the inter-continental activity has increased and different managerial issues arise. Formerly there were issues about dealing with east–west difference in time as between East Asia and Europe or North America and north–south differences in seasonality, particularly for clothing retailers. Now however, issues concerned with knowledge management and the processes of embeddedness are more evident and new capabilities are required to address these new and more complex issues associated with multi-format, multi-continent retailing.

The GPS concept and GPS map

The character of retail internationalization activity changed greatly with the simultaneous expansion of geographic scope and increase in number of formats. In effect we begin to see a true globalization of retailers as they construct two types of network: a network that links countries and a network that involves formats. A successful strategy involves growth of both networks simultaneously but with different processes of entry, growth and exit exhibited by the two networks. The networks can be conceptualized as a portfolio of markets and formats and we term the strategy to develop and manage this as a *retail global portfolio strategy* (GPS). Becker and Freeman (2006) in a survey of company performance across a range of industries show how successful firms, 'shift the business mix of their portfolios in response to the competitive dynamics of their industries' and the 'companies that tweak portfolios to align them with favourable competitive factors are quite likely to grow faster and offer higher returns to shareholders than companies that don't' (p. 21). We can therefore view the retailers changing their corporate portfolio within their market and format networks. The previous chapter explored the diversification of formats and earlier in this chapter the expansion of the country-level network to several continents has been explored. Bringing the two networks together we can conceptualize, as an example, a schematic network of a GPS of three formats across four continents as illustrated in Figure 3.2.

In Figure 3.2 a small square represents a format (A, B, C). The ovals enclosed represent continents (a, b, c, d) within each of which the retailer has multiple formats across several national markets. For example, the format C has a network linking markets in continents b, c and d. The format D network involves markets in continents a, b and d. On the other hand, a format network

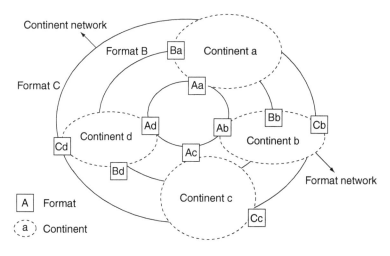

Figure 3.2 A stylized GPS network of continents and formats.

that consists of format A and B is constructed in continent a, and format network that consists of three formats A, B, and C is constructed in continent b. Decisions about strategic growth link the format and the continent networks and are not simply dependent of the characteristics of a particular country market. Expansion and contraction decisions have to be taken in the light of the situations across the networks. Whether or not a retailer will enter into a country or withdraw from another is decided after evaluating which format is adopted and whether it is possible to operate the business model necessary to develop the format from a viewpoint of format network construction across (multi-continent) markets.

However, Figure 3.2 shows a static situation of a retailer at a point in time. It is necessary to clarify the process of evolution. If the GPS concept is used, it becomes possible to develop the idea of networks that evolve simultaneously as the retailer expands its operations.[2] If we consider a GPS network map as shown in Figure 3.3 we can place retailers at initial positions on this, then it is possible to consider their transition into other quadrants.

The first dimension is the geographic scope in continental terms with the possibilities of international operation within the home continent (region) and of moving to other continents and building international networks there. As discussed above, moving to being international in one or more continents outside its home region requires of the retailer different capabilities to those of border hopping in the home region. Factors in the commercial environment of the target are influential in the extent of this spatial scope with Bell *et al.* (2004) even going so far as to state that 'decisions about mode, scale and timing of entry are dictated by the state of economic development in the foreign market' (p. 304). This is an extreme deterministic view that underplays the role of the second dimension, that of format complexity. A retailer with a single dominant format may use this as the vehicle for multi-continental expansion but more commonly retailers have become multi-format and use this to reduce the risks associated

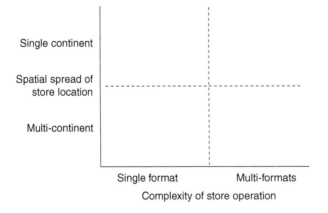

Figure 3.3 GPS network map.

with multi-continental expansion by developing different format mixes in different continents. As explained in Chapter 2 the different formats require different knowledge capabilities and so exporting a format requires exporting and adapting knowledge specific to the format.

A hypothetical sequence of the internationalization activity begins with a retailer developing a single format in its home national market. The choice then is to diversify by format in the home market or to become international in markets in the same region thus remaining in a single continent. As the retailer becomes international in its home continent it may remain with a single format (SC–SF in Figure 3.4) or may take multiple formats to other markets in the home continent (SC–MF). SN and MN in the figure refer to single nation and multi-nations. As the geographic scope is expanded to operations beyond the home continent again there is the scope to either focus on the singe dominant format or to develop format mixes in the new continental regions. The final stage of globalization can be hypothesized as having different format mixes on the different continents with each continent having multinational operations (MC–MF in Figure 3.4)

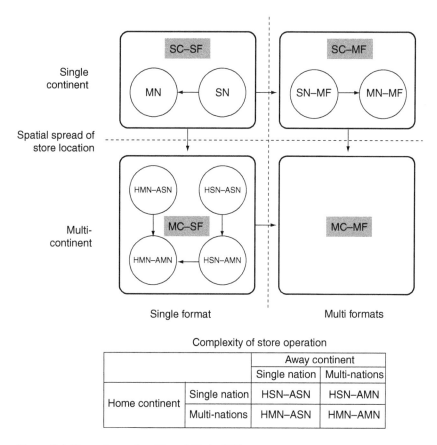

Figure 3.4 The pattern of position shifts in GPS.

When a new continent is entered with a specific format (SC–SF to MC–SF) there is first a move to enter a particular country. The retailer may either be only in its home nation (HSN) or be international (HMN) within its home continent. On entering the new continent the retailer may remain in only one nation (ASN) or become multi-national (AMN) in the new continent. Likely developmental links are indicated in Figure 3.4.

The GPS Network Model in Figure 3.5 summarizes the above-mentioned pattern of movement. The solid line arrow indicates the generation of the continent network and the broken line indicates the move to creating format networks.

To illustrate this approach we can consider the case of Carrefour as shown in Figure 3.6. It is summarized in Figure 3.7. The following features become apparent in this GPS mapping:

*   The starting point for Carrefour is the establishment of a hypermarket in 1963 in its home country France.
*   Carrefour became a European multinational after six years with entry to Belgium in 1969.
*   Within Europe it entered 14 countries in 40 years although it did not remain in all of these.
*   Carrefour became multi-continental in 1975 when it opened stores in Brazil.[3] This was six years after it became multinational in Europe.
*   Within South America, Carrefour became multi-national on entering Argentina, seven years after entering Brazil.
*   Carrefour opened its first store in Asia in Taiwan in 1989. This was 20 years after its first international move in Europe compared with six years for its move to South America.

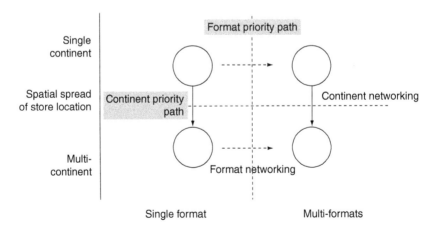

Figure 3.5 The GPS Network Model.

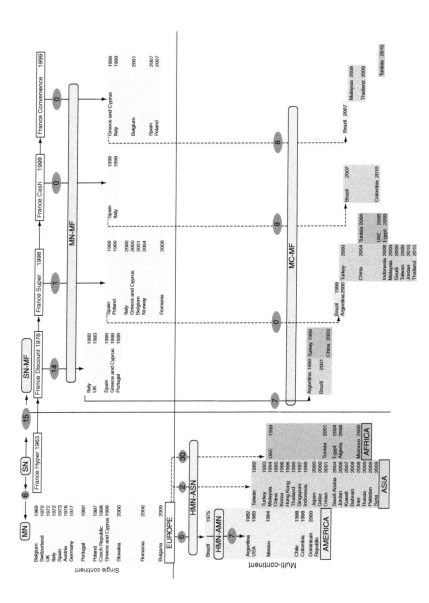

Figure 3.6 GPS map of Carrefour.

- Development in the Middle East began in UAE in 1999, ten years after Asia, and in Africa in 2001 in Tunisia.
- Carrefour began format diversification with a discount store in 1978 in France.
- Another 20 years were required to establish a supermarket with cash and carry and convenience store being developed almost at the same time.
- Multi-national activity within Europe after format diversification required 14 years when it entered Italy with the discount store in 1992. Other formats very quickly became multi-national in Europe after initial development in France.
- In Argentina in 1999 the discount store was developed in a continent other than Europe.
- Carrefour required six years to develop its core hypermarket format in the European continent, and also required a further six years to enter a new continent. In contrast, 15 years were required for Carrefour to establish a new format in its home country, another 14 years were required to develop stores overseas within the same continent as the home country, and a further seven years required for Carrefour to become multi-content and multi-format.

It has taken 36 years from creating a hypermarket in France, for Carrefour to become multi-continent and multi-format.

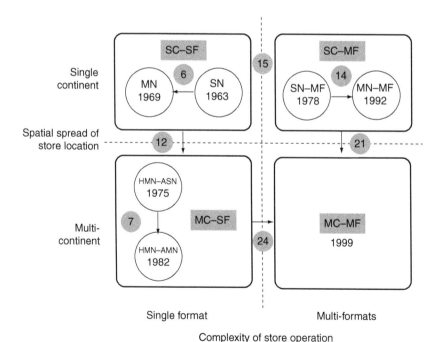

Figure 3.7 Summary of GPS position shift of Carrefour.

Factors encouraging the position shift on the GPS map

In viewing retailer internationalization as continent and format transitions a key issue is why, at a particular time, a retailer makes a decision to diversify its format or move to another continent. We can conceptualize this as a turning point in the gradual development of the firm. A turning point is when the development of the firm makes a radical shift to take the firm onto a different growth trajectory. 'Shifts occur when forces creating pressure for change overcome forces that create resistance to change' (Ginsberg 1988 p. 562). These forces are often seen solely in terms of environmental and competitive pressures. Tushman and O'Reilly (1996) point out that, 'Almost all successful organizations evolve through relatively long periods of incremental change punctuated by environmental shifts and revolutionary change. These discontinuities may be driven by technology, competitors, regulatory events, or significant changes in economic and political conditions' (p. 11). In our consideration of international retailing we need to consider not only environmental issues but also innovations and capabilities internal to the firm as well as 'random' events as triggers for shifts in strategic direction (Dawson 2001). Crucial events within the firm and the wider environment act as triggers to set in motion structural changes associated with the development of the format and market networks of the retailer as illustrated in Figure 3.8. Examples of these events are provided in Table 3.2.

In our example of Carrefour, the acquisition of Groupe Promodès S. A. in 1999 changed the format and market network of Carrefour as seen in Figure 3.6. Originally announced as a merger it became in effect an acquisition. The move was widely seen as a response to Wal-Mart's moves into Germany and the UK at this time (Sordet and Wantz 2004; Brosselin and Sordet 2011; Cliquet 2001). Promodès, formed in 1957 and coming from a wholesaling background, operated five formats, hypermarkets, supermarkets, discount supermarkets, convenience stores and institutional food services, when it was acquired by Carrefour. Within the formats there was a combination of directly owned and franchise

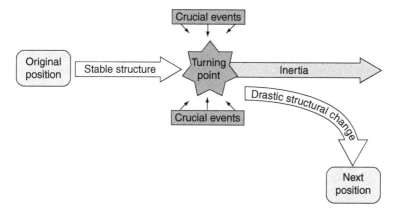

Figure 3.8 Turning points and crucial events.

Table 3.2 Examples of crucial events acting as triggers for major shifts in GPS

Events within the firm	*Environmental events*
• Culture change introduced into the firm that changes the perception of the international ambitions. For example, Fast Retailing in Japan changed its culture, from being strongly Japanese to being more international, to emphasize its need to become multi-continental in scope in order to compete with other major apparel retailers.	• Changes in public policy related to market access or firm development. For example, the removal of restrictions on access to South Korean market following the financial crisis in 1997 allowed Tesco to gain entry through joint venture with Samsung.
• Change of senior executives or new specialists and consultants result in review of strategic direction. For example, Fat Face Ltd, the UK apparel retailer, following the appointment of a new chief executive in 2010 and subsequent strategy review, engaged consultants in autumn 2012 to help them develop a strategy to expand the international activity of the firm outside Europe.	• A competitive shift in the market – either the existing or a target market. For example, the emergence of the internet as a sales channel resulted in Inditex developing interactive websites for Zara specific to countries in their sales network.
• Changes in product procurement network or in logistics that reduces barriers to international expansion. For example, upgrades in logistics were important in enabling Mango to move out of established markets in Europe and enter Asian markets	• Changed economic conditions. For example, the financial crisis in Greece in 2011–2012 resulted in Aldi withdrawing from the market and provided an opportunity for Lidl to expand its operations.
• Merger or acquisition of retailer operating in a different region or operating different formats. For example, the acquisition of Promodès by Carrefour in 1999 brought new geographic and format networks into Carrefour (see text)	• Shifts in consumer behaviour. For example, the emergence of a relatively affluent middle class of consumers in China has moved China to be a target market for many Western retailers.
• Changes in organizational structure or the acceptance of new operational modes. For example, the acceptance by Mothercare of franchising as mode of growth enabled them to expand their geographic network to new continents	• Changes of socio-cultural values. For example, the acceptance of self-service as a way of buying food, instead of through markets, in Vietnam has opened up the opportunity for investment by Western supermarket and hypermarket firms.
• Emergence of new managerial capabilities to create new formats or to control a more extensive geographic network. For example, Tesco developed new capabilities to develop hypermarkets when it moved into Poland in 1995 giving them the capability to take the format back to UK and then to other countries.	• Advice from a supplier. For example, B&Q entered Taiwan in 1996. The CEO for Asia in an interview in 2006 said that, 'a supplier from Taiwan had this crazy idea of opening a home-improvement store there. So we thought, why not Asia? That's how the first store opened in Taiwan, in 1996' (Desvaux and Ramsay 2006, p. 82).

operations. Promodès had a growth pattern of acquisition or partnership into a region where it could realistically become a dominant retailer. This enabled cross-format operational and sourcing synergies to control entry costs. French governmental restrictions in the 1990s encouraged the firm to seek markets outside France but initially in Europe, notably in Spain, Italy, Greece, Portugal and Turkey. The firm entered partnerships outside Europe in Morocco, Dubai, Taiwan and Argentina. Salto, the deputy chief operating officer, speaking at a conference in 1998, emphasized the entrepreneurial aspect of early international-ization, 'At Promodès our first moves into international markets came about by chance, and it was only later that they became a necessity. The chance was a matter of unforeseen events and meetings, and unexpected opportunities' (Salto 1999 p. 5). Continent (Continente in some markets) became the hypermarket format. Champion was the supermarket format of which there were three opera-tional formulae based on size. Most were franchised. A third format was the Dia discount supermarket chain. Shoppi and 8 à Huit were convenience store formu-lae. The fifth format was Promocash which operated as a cash and carry format. Promodès had entered the USA market in 1979 and built up substantial opera-tions in the east of the USA before selling to Ahold in 1994 so that these were not included in the Carrefour acquisition. By the late 1990s, however, Promodès had stores outside Europe in Dubai, Morocco, Taiwan, Indonesia and Argentina. The acquisition of Promodès by Carrefour was a critical event in the develop-ment of a global strategy, creating a merged firm of 9000 stores in 26 countries across three continents (Figure 3.6) and introduced into Carrefour cash and carry and convenience store formats, took supermarkets outside France and outside Europe, and made the discount store network multi-continental. The format network, the market network, and the GPS map were fundamentally changed by the acquisition.

Conclusion

As international retailers widen their geographic scope there is a growing rea-lization of significant differences between the internationalization process in the home region and operating on a multi-continental basis. The requirement placed on retailers to move to markets in which they can use their formulae knowledge and capabilities to grow overall sales has resulted in more moves outside their home region and into very different consumer and commercial environments. The high levels of economic growth, and thus access to growing levels of con-sumer spending, coupled with indigenous retail structures of relatively low pro-ductivity, present in emergent economies have powerful attraction to retailers. But, 'As retailers have moved into unfamiliar and unpredictable territory, many have been unprepared for the unique challenges posed by a different economic, political, and cultural environment' (Deloitte 2012 p. 1). Whilst there has been a general reduction in politically inspired barriers to entry in these emergent eco-nomies there remain many substantive differences between home and host conti-nents across many culturally related consumer and managerial variables.

In these multi-continental networks adaption by the retailer is needed to accommodate the consumer and commercial environment of several host countries. The consumers and the commercial structures in the host country respond to the presence of the foreign retailer. Minahan *et al.* (2012) illustrate this duality of response in their study of Costco's entry to Australia and the complex process of recursive mutual adaption by the firm and consumers to the new structures in the market. Despite the higher risks and more complex dynamic capabilities required by management to operate a multi-continental network the number of retailers moving in this direction, to become in effect global, is increasing.

Moves by retailers to develop a multi-format, multi-continent approach can be considered as a portfolio issue with strategy having to simultaneously develop spatial networks of markets and operational networks of formats. The Global Portfolio Strategy map is presented as an analytical framework to model the pattern of multi-format, multi-continent retail internationalization. The GPS map can be considered in a dynamic way by exploring the key events that result in directional changes of market and format expansion and contraction.

The approach through the idea of GPS and GPS map provides possibilities of linking a number of conceptual approaches to the study of retailer internationalization. By a focus on the process of structuration as evolution and adaption, process tracing (Tamura 2006), within the networks then links become evident with institutional theory, embeddedness and dynamic capability approaches. These links open up the possibility of new conceptual approaches to the study of retailer activity across multiple markets through synthesis of established concepts. The established approaches, whilst having been useful in gaining insights into the earlier stages of retailer internationalization, are inadequate for analysis of the complexities associated with emergent multi-format, multi-continent retailer networks.

Notes

1 Story 5: 'Development, implementation and support of Operating Model' at www.tescohsc.com/knowledge_centre/success_stories.html.
2 Conceptually it is possible also to add the network of suppliers to this model and this would link to both the geographic and the format networks. For simplicity the discussion in this chapter is limited to the geographic and format networks.
3 This excludes development of stores in French *départements* outside metropolitan France.

References

Arkell, J. (2010) Market structure, liberalization and trade: the case of distribution services. In: M. Engman, S. Sáez and O. Cattaneo (eds) *International trade in services: what's in it for developing countries?* Washington: World Bank, pp. 141–176.
Bair, J. (2009) *Frontiers of commodity chain research*. Palo Alto: Stanford University Press.
Baron, M.-L. (2007) European retailing multinationals: investment in Asia and return effects. In: J.-K. Kim and P.-B. Ruffini (eds) *Corporate strategies in the age of regional integration*. Cheltenham: Edward Elgar, pp. 131–152.

Becker, W. M. and Freeman, V. M. (2006) Going from global trends to corporate strategy: will your business catch them before they catch it? *McKinsey Quarterly*, August, pp. 17–27.

Bell, D. E., Lal, R. and. Salmon, W. J. (2004) Globalization of retailing. In: J. A. Quelch and R. Deshpande (eds) *The global market: developing a strategy to manage across borders*. San Francisco: Jossey-Bass, pp. 288–312.

Branch, A. E. (2009) *Global supply chain management an international logistics*. Abingdon: Routledge.

Brosselin, C. and Sordet, C. (2011) *La grande histoire des regroupements dans la distribution*. Paris: Editions Harmattan.

Burch, D and Lawrence, G. (eds) (2007) *Supermarkets and agri-food supply chains*. Cheltenham: Edward Elgar.

Burt, S., Dawson, J. and Larke, R. (2006) Royal Ahold: multinational, multi-channel and multi-format food provider. In J. Dawson, R. Larke and M. Mukoyama (eds) *Strategic issues in international retailing*. Abingdon: Routledge, pp. 140–169.

Burt, S., Dawson, J. and Sparks, L. (2003) Failure in international markets: research propositions. *International Review of Retail Distribution and Consumer Research*, 13(4), 355–373.

Child, P. N. (2006) Lessons from a global retailer: an interview with the president of Carrefour China. *McKinsey Quarterly*, June, 70–81.

Chuang, M.-L., Donegan, J. J. and Ganon, M. W. (2012) Culture implications for the operations strategy: Walmart experience in China. Paper to 15th Conference on *Interdisciplinary and Multifunctional Business Management*, Soochow University. Available at: www.scu.edu.tw/ba/2012conference/papers/PDF/ 5211.pdf (accessed 18 December 2012).

Christopherson, S. (2007) Barriers to 'US style' lean retailing: the case of Wal-Mart's failure in Germany. *Journal of Economic Geography*, 7(4), 451–469.

Cliquet, G. (2001) The megamerger: Carrefour-Promodès. *European Retail Digest*, 30, 32.

Coe, N. M. (2004) The internationalisation/globalisation of retailing: towards an economic geographical research agenda. *Environment and Planning A*, 36(9), 1571–1594.

Coe, N. M. and Wrigley, N. (2007) Host economy impacts of transnational retail: the research agenda. *Journal of Economic Geography*, 7(4), 341–371.

Dawson J. (2001) Strategy and opportunism in European retail internationalization. *British Journal of Management*, 12(4), 253–266.

Dawson, J. (2009) European retailer challenges from ICT including cloud-based services. Paper at *Does Cloud Computing Contribute to Solve Social Problems*, Research Institute for Socio-network Strategies. Osaka: Kansai University.

Dawson, J. (2013) Retailer activity in shaping food choice. *Food Quality and Preference*, 28(1), 339–347.

Dawson, M. (2009) Wal-Mart Germany revisited. *German Retail Blog* 20 August. Available at: www.german-retail-blog.com/2009/08/20/wal-mart-germany-revisited.

de Mooij, M. (2010) *Consumer behavior and culture: consequences for global marketing and advertising*. Thousand Oaks: Sage Publications.

Deloitte (2012) *Retail globalization: navigating the maze*. London: Deloitte Global Services.

Desvaux, G. and Ramsay, A. J. (2006) Shaping China's home improvement market: an interview with B&Q's CEO for Asia. *McKinsey Quarterly*, July, 82–91.

Easterby-Smith, M., Malina, D. and Yuan, L. (1995) How culture-sensitive is HRM? A comparative analysis of practice in Chinese and UK companies. *The International Journal of Human Resource Management*, 6(1), 31–59.

Enderwick, P. (2007) *Understanding emerging markets: China and India*. Abingdon: Routledge.

Evans, J. and Mavondo, F. T. (2002) Psychic distance and organisational performance: an empirical examination of international retailing operations. *Journal of International Business Studies*, 33(3), 515–532.

Gamble, J. (2003) Transferring human resource practices from the United Kingdom to China: the limits and potential for convergence. *International Journal of Human Resource Management*, 14(3), 369–387.

Gamble, J. (2006) Introducing Western-style HRM practices to China: Shopfloor perceptions in a British multinational. *Journal of World Business*, 41(4), 328–343.

Gamble, J. (2011) *Multinational retailers and consumers in China: transferring organizational practices from the United Kingdom and Japan*. Basingstoke: Palgrave.

Gao, L. (2012) Chinese cultural values and purchase behavior of technology products: An empirical research on smartphone users in Shanghai. PhD thesis, University of Rennes 1.

Ginsberg, A. (1988) Measuring and modelling changes in strategy: theoretical foundations and empirical directions. *Strategic Management Journal*, 9(6), 559–575.

Golub, S. C. (2009) Openness to foreign direct investment in services: an international analysis. *The World Economy*, 32(8), 1245–1268.

Horwitz, F. M., Kamoche, K. and Chew, I. K. H. (2002) Looking east: diffusing high performance work practices in the southern Afro–Asian context. *International Journal of Human Resource Management*, 13(7), 1019–1041.

Huang, L. and Liu, A. (2011) *China grocery retailers*. Hong Kong: Macquarie Research.

Jonsson, A. and Foss, N. J. (2011) International expansion through flexible replication: learning from the experience of IKEA. *Journal of International Business Studies*, 42(9), 1079–1102.

Kalirajan, K. (2000) Restrictions on trade in distribution services. *Productivity Commission Staff Research Paper*. Canberra: AusInfo.

Korr, A. and Arndt, A. (2003) Why did Wal-Mart fail in Germany? University of Bremen: Institute for World Economics and International Management. Available from: www. iwim.uni-bremen.de/publikationen/pdf/w024.pdf (accessed 12 January 2013).

Lanz, R., Miroudot, S. and Nordås, H. K. (2011) Trade in tasks. *OECD Trade Policy Papers*, 117, Paris: OECD.

Larke, R. (2013) IKEA Japan: playing the long game. *Japan Consuming*, 14(1), 1.

Lee, H.-S., Duffey, K. J. and Popkin, B. M. (2012) South Korea's entry to the global food economy: shifts in consumption of food between1998 and 2009. *Asia Pacific Journal of Clinical Nutrition*, 21(4), 618–629.

Lowe, M., George, G. and Alexy, O. (2012) Organizational identity and capability development in internationalization: transference, splicing and enhanced imitation in Tesco's US market entry. *Journal of Economic Geography*, 12(5), 1021–1054.

Maruyama, M. and Trung, L. V. (2007) Supermarkets in Vietnam: opportunities and obstacles. *Asian Economic Journal*, 21(1) 19–46.

Minahan, S. M., Huddleston, P. and Bianchi, C. (2012) Costco and the Aussie shopper: a case study of the market entry of an international retailer. *International Review of Retail, Distribution and Consumer Research*, 22(5), 507–527.

Mukherjee, A. and Patel, N. (2005) *FDI in Retail Sector: India*. New Delhi: Academic Foundation, ICRIER and Ministry of Consumer Affairs, Food and Public Distribution, Government of India.

Mukherjee, S. (2011) Policies of retail sector of India and other selected countries. *UTMS Journal of Economics*, 2(2), 171–180.

Mutebi, A. M. (2007) Regulatory responses to large-format transnational retail in southeast Asian cities. *Urban Studies*, 44(2), 357–379.

Nielsen, J. and Taglioni, D. (2004) Services trade liberalisation: identifying opportunities and gains. *OECD Trade Policy Papers 1*. Paris: OECD.

Nordås, H. K. (2008) The impact of services trade liberalization on trade in non-agricultural products. *OECD Trade Policy Working Paper 81.* Paris: OECD.

Pederzoli, D. (2006) Conception and test of a comprehensive model of international strategy for retail companies. *International Review of Retail, Distribution and Consumer Research*, 16(4), 415–431.

Pennemann, K. (2013) *Retail internationalization in emerging countries: the positioning of global retail brands in China*. Wiesbaden: Springer.

Pingali, P. (2007) Westernization of Asian diets and transformation of food systems: Implications for research and policy. *Food Policy*, 32(3), 281–298.

Planer, B. (2009) *Emerging markets: playground for the rich and fearless*. London: Planet Retail.

Raynolds, L. T. (2004) The globalization of organic agro-food networks. *World Development*, 32(5), 725–43.

Reardon, T. (2005) *Retail companies as integrators of value-chains in developing countries*. Report commissioned by Federal Ministry for Economic Cooperation and Development, Germany, published in Trade Matters series by GTZ Trade Programme, Eschborn.

Reardon, T. and Hopkins, R. (2006) The supermarket revolution in developing countries: policies to address emerging tensions among supermarkets, suppliers and traditional retailers. *European Journal of Development Research*, 18(4), 522–545.

Reardon, T., Henson, S., Berdegué, J. (2007) 'Proactive fast-tracking' diffusion of supermarkets in developing countries: implications for market institutions and trade. *Journal of Economic Geography*, 7(4), 399–431.

Reardon, T., Timmer, C. P. and Minten, B. (2012) Supermarket revolution in Asia and emerging development strategies to include small farmers. *Proceedings of the National Academy of Science*, 109(31), 12332–12337.

Reisman, M. (2010) Recent trends in U.S. service trades. Paper to OECD Experts Meeting on Distribution Services: Towards a service trades restrictiveness index (STRI) 17 November. Available at: www.oecd.org/tad/servicestrade/ 46278882.pdf.

Roy, M. (2008) Out of stock or just in time? Doha and the liberalization of distribution services. In: J. A. Marchetti and M. Roy (eds) *Opening markets for trade in services: countries and sectors in bilateral and WTO negotiations*. New York: Cambridge University Press, pp. 224–263.

Rugman, A. M. (2005) *The regional multinationals*. Cambridge: Cambridge University Press.

Salto, L. (1999) Towards global retailing: the Promodès case. In: M. Dupuis and J. Dawson (eds) *European cases in retailing*. Oxford, Blackwell, pp. 5–14.

Sargent, R. L. (2009) Ronald L. Sargent, Chairman & CEO of Staples, Inc. interviewed by M. Dawson, 16 January. Available at: www.german-retail-blog.com/ 2009/01/16/talk-with-staples (accessed 28 January 2013).

Siebers, L. Q. (2011) *Retail internationalization in China*. Basingstoke: Palgrave.

Sordet, C. and Wantz, J.-F. (2004) *Paul-Louis Halley: De Promodès à Carrefour*. Paris: Editions d'Organisation.

Sun, T., Horn, M. and Merritt, D. (2004) Values and lifestyles of individualists and collectivists: a study on Chinese, Japanese, British and US consumers. *Journal of Consumer Marketing*, 21(5), 318–331.

Swinnen, J. F. M. and Maertens, M. (2007) Globalization, privatization, and vertical coordination in food value chains in developing and transition countries. *Agricultural Economics*, 37(S1), 89–102.

Tacconelli, W. and Wrigley, N. (2009) Organizational challenges and strategic responses of retail TNCs in post-WTO-entry China. *Economic Geography*, 85(1), 49–73.

Tackett, K, (2006) *Auf wiedersehen, Wal-Mart. Retail Perspectives*. Columbus: Retail Forward.

Tamura, M. (2006) *Research design*. Tokyo: Hakuto Shobo (in Japanese).

Tushman, M. L. and O'Reilly, C. C. III (1996) Ambidextrous organisations: managing evolutionary and revolutionary change. *California Management Review*, 38(4), 8–30.

UNCTAD Secretariat (2005) *Distribution services*. Geneva: UNCTAD Commission on International Trade in Goods and Services, and Commodities. Ref: TD/B/COM.1/EM.29/2.

Waldmeir, P. (2009) M&S admits Shanghai errors. *Financial Times*, 9 February. Available at: www.ft.com/cms/s/0/2bac61ae-f6e2-11dd-8a1f-0000779fd2ac.html# axzz2JC6eGmeZ (accessed 28 January 2013).

Wang, S. and Du, B. (2007) *Foreign retailers in China: stories of success and setbacks.* Toronto: Center for the Study of Commercial Activity, Ryerson University.

Whitley, R. (1992) *Business systems in East Asia: firms, markets, and societies*. Newbury Park: Sage.

Wrigley, N., Coe, N. M. and Currah, A. (2005) Globalizing retail: conceptualizing the distribution-based transnational corporation (TNC). *Progress in Human Geography*, 29(4), 437–57.

Xiao, G. and Kim, J.-O. (2009) The investigation of Chinese consumer values, consumption values, life satisfaction, and consumption behaviors. *Psychology and Marketing*, 26(7), 610–624.

Yahagi, T., Sekine, T., Chung, S. and Taotao, Bi-M. (2009) *Distribution in China.* Tokyo: Hakto-Shobo (in Japanese).

Zhen. Y. (2007) *Globalization and the Chinese retailing revolution: competing in the world's largest emerging market*. Oxford: Chandos.

4 Nitori

From local furniture store to largest home furnishing chain in Japan

Jung-Yim Baek

Nitori is a Japan-based retailer that manufactures and retails furniture and interior goods in Japan and Taiwan. The company is the largest furniture retailer in Japan and provides a full range of furniture products, soft furnishings, domestic housewares, interior accessories and gardening items. Despite adverse recessionary conditions in recent years Nitori has continued to grow. Two key reasons for the success of Nitori have been, first, its policy of moving sourcing and production offshore to foreign countries with lower labour and operating costs and second, changing its company structure to better operate under recessionary conditions (Baek 2009).

In this chapter it is argued that the creation of global sourcing networks are particularly important in exploiting opportunities in the home furnishing market in Japan. In order to develop these networks it is necessary for the retailer to acquire knowledge about manufacturing processes to enable private label development. The development of off-shore sourcing and manufacture linked to the development of private label products has enabled Nitori to develop from a local Hokkaido-based furniture speciality store to be the largest home furnishing chain in Japan with a nationwide network of stores and with an emergent internationalization strategy.

This case study will use the framework outlined in Chapter 3 that seeks to highlight the importance of key events to the international development of the retailer. The focus, however is the sourcing network which enables Nitori to have aspirations to be a substantive international retailer whist continuing as the leading furniture retailer in Japan.

Historical background

Initial conditions

Asahikawa city in Hokkaido, the home city of Nitori, has a long tradition as a centre of furniture manufacture. Nitori was a part of this furniture cluster beginning as a traditional home furniture retailer initially sourcing its products from local furniture manufacturers. The business concept employed by Nitori was different from other retailers in Hokkaido in that it attempted to source products directly from manufacturers rather than through wholesalers. Although attempting to be different, it was difficult to differentiate itself from competing stores when it came to the price of goods because procurement costs and traditional product designs were similar to those of other retailers.

In the furniture production map of Hokkaido there are five major manufacturing and wholesale centres: Asahikawa, Sapporo-Otaru, Obihiro, Kitami, and Hakodate. Nitori first opened in the Sapporo-Otaru district in 1967 where there were many furniture manufacturers who were still making furniture by hand and to order. At that time, other than for a small number of firms, a change to a mass production system was viewed very negatively. In the first half of 1970s, manufacturers and wholesalers in Hokkaido wanted their traditional Japanese high-quality furniture from Hokkaido to be sold on mainland Japan. Typical of this view were the manufacturers in Asahikawa and Sapporo-Otaru markets, where the traditional Japanese-style furniture, like the Paulownia chest of drawers were made using wood native to Hokkaido. These firms had expanded after the war and took the lead in making and selling the high-quality home furniture until the bubble economy era.

However, competition developed among the major sources for home furniture as mass production became accepted and new designs which imitated Western-style legged furniture became demanded by consumers. Japanese consumers nationwide had considered Asahikawa as a major source of home furniture in the past, but Asahikawa did not respond to changes in consumer sentiment. A new design development was needed to meet the diversified needs of the consumers, and simultaneously adapt to the growing demand of furniture that was functional and integrated within an overall design of a room.

Development of stores limited to a local market

In the late 1960s the retail furniture market in Sapporo centred on the offerings of a few department stores. Their only significant competitor was Hasegawa, which initially was a table manufacturer but established a store in conjunction with other wholesale and retail outlets at a location on the highway connecting Sapporo to Chitose. Hasegawa established a shop and showroom at this site. In general the wholesale trading companies exercised leadership in furnishing distribution and marketing. Wholesalers increased their channel leadership over manufacturers in Hokkaido and retail stores. Rationalization of physical distribution was considered as particularly important to them, because 30 per cent of the entire production in Hokkaido was supplied to other parts of Japan at that time.

The home furnishing market in Hokkaido was driven by wholesalers. Consumers in Sapporo were changing their expectations of home furnishing retailers in demanding new styles of furnishings. The retailers were mostly small furniture stores of long standing in the centre of Sapporo city, but a few medium- and large-sized stores started to be established, typically four to six kilometres from the centre of Sapporo city. There was a favourable consumer environment for a different type of retailing not being fully met by the combination of the few department stores, many small traditional stores and a few out-of-town stores. Nitori began to establish stores within Sapporo city with a chain of seven established through the 1970s. Nitori's stores were located in the centre of the city, were medium and large size, and had assortments of not only Japanese traditional high quality furniture like chests for Kimono but also Western style furniture with legs, for example dining tables, priced lower than the traditionally designed products. Nitori did not limit sourcing to within Hokkaido in order to provide the variety of furniture and tried to buy its products directly from national furniture manufacturers.

Nitori's new type of large stores was successful in competition with traditional furniture stores of long standing within Sapporo city. Consequently, Nitori expanded its operation by opening another store in Tomakomai in June 1981. The expansion of the chain of Nitori stores was limited to Hokkaido until 1992. The company established its first store on the mainland in 1993. This led to the establishment of a store development office for the east of Japan, in Matsudoshi, Chiaba-ken in 1988. During the following ten years, Nitori opened about 100 stores to become a nationwide chain.

Current conditions

Nitori, in 2012, operated 258 stores across Japan and had ten stores in Taiwan. Having built a strong base on Hokkaido it was possible to launch its business nationally and then into the south of Taiwan in 2007. The pattern of store growth is shown in Figure 4.1. Table 4.1 shows the sales of the major retailers operating in the home furnishing market in Japan. Nitori has been the largest since 2003 when it overtook Otsukakagu.

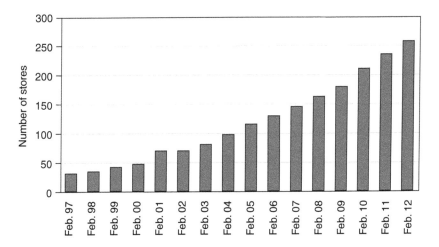

Figure 4.1 Number of Nitori stores in the Japanese market (source: Nitori annual reports).

Table 4.1 Sales of major home furnishing store groups in the Japanese market (JPY Mil)
(FY 2011)

1 Nitori	331,016
2 Nafuko	220,347
3 Shimachu	158,982
4 IKEA	67,500
5 Otsuka Kagu	54,367

Source: website (https://kmonos.jp/industry/91, accessed 30 September 20120; each company homepage.

While sales in the home furniture sector in Japan have decreased, Nitori continues to increase its sales and profit (see Figures 4.2 and 4.3). The annual sales for the Japanese furniture retailers peaked in 1991 and have fallen steadily since then.

Nitori was established as a specialized furniture retailer, and in the mid-1990s expanded its product ranges of furnishings, which consumers purchased more frequently. To achieve the extensions to the ranges Nitori integrated all processes in-house from acquisition of raw materials to manufacturing, distribution and sales. This enabled a focus on retailing and merchandizing to be established in order to respond to consumer demands and the changing behaviour of consumers.

With this change of range balance and the focus on merchandizing Nitori changed its store name to Home Furnishing Nitori in 1985 and built a specialized distribution centre limited to furnishings and household fittings. The sales proportion of furnishing goods to furniture increased from 3 : 7 in 1987 to 6 : 4 in 2007. This change in balance of the sales is shown in Figure 4.4.

In addition to their home furnishing stores, many of which are located on main roads in suburban areas, Nitori has a home fashion store formula. Home fashion stores are located in shopping centres and shopping districts. These

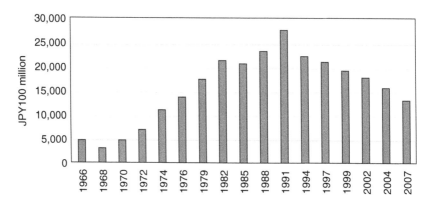

Figure 4.2 Annual sales of Japanese furniture retailers (source: Ministry of Economy, Trade and Industry, commercial statistics).

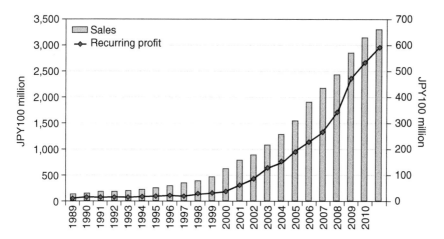

Figure 4.3 Nitori's sales and recurring profit (source: Nitori annual reports).

stores do not sell large furniture but specialize in an array of product categories purchased with high frequency such as seasonal merchandise. Nitori also developed a further store formula in the February 2011, called Decohome. These stores do not sell furniture but are more a home variety store selling clothing, pet accessories, travel goods, stationery, and health and beauty items. Nitori currently operates four of these stores in eastern Japan.

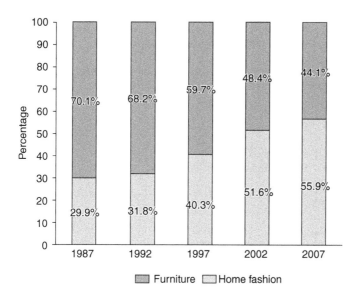

Figure 4.4 Sales proportion of home furnishing to furniture (source: company internal materials).

In October 2011 Nitori opened a focused shopping mall in Higashi Osaka. The shopping centre has 16 tenants specializing in clothing and household products, anchored by a Nitori store. The developments in recent years have increased the store network in Honshu whilst numbers of stores in Hokkaido has remained almost constant (Figure 4.5). From this Japanese base Nitori opened its first foreign store in Kaohsiung, Taiwan in 2007 and as at 2012 had ten stores in Taiwan.

Figure 4.6 shows the GPS map of Nitori. It is clearly positioned in the single format single continent sector although it is now also operating also in a country relatively close to Japan. Within Japan it is operating several formulae having flexed its original store concept. The essential business model that generates the format has not changed despite major changes to its back office systems and the impetus of its sourcing offshore.

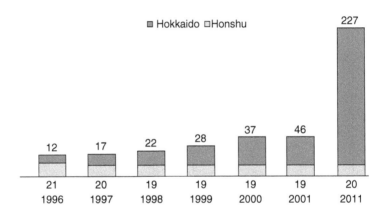

Figure 4.5 Number of stores in Hokkaido and Honshu (source: Nitori homepage www.Nitori.co.jp, accessed 11 March 2011).

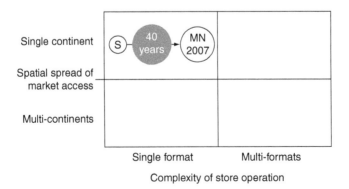

Figure 4.6 GPS map of Nitori.

Back system by Nitori International Group

The group Nitori Holding Co., Ltd has overseas subsidiary companies, collectively called Nitori International, which undertake Nitori's product procurement from several countries in South East Asia and its store development in Japan and Taiwan. Nitori International is composed of 15 companies in total, mainly manufacturing, importing and selling furniture and interior products. Nitori groups these companies into three categories as shown in Table 4.2.

In 1981, Nitori started importing products directly from abroad and subsequently expanded this activity. As its procurement network expanded, Nitori established its own foreign subsidiary companies in 1989 and established its own factories in Indonesia and in Vietnam in 1994 and in 2004. Furthermore, Nitori established its own distribution centre in China to make it possible to function as a warehouse, and so reduced its costs associated with logistics. The share of foreign manufactured products increased substantially in the late 1990s and by 2011 had reached 80 per cent (Figure 4.7).

Table 4.2 Nitori International Group

Product items	Subsidiary companies engaged in each business
Furniture	Nitori Co., Ltd
	Home Logistics Co., Ltd
	Nitori Furniture Co., Ltd
	P.T. Nitori Furniture Indonesia
	Nitori Furniture Vietnam EPE.
	Nitori (Thailand) Co., Ltd
	Nitori (Malaysia) SDN, BHD
	Nitori (China) Co., Ltd
	Shanghai Liqiao Industrial Co., Ltd
	Nitori Taiwan Co., Ltd
	Nitori Huizhou Logistics Co., Ltd
	Nitori India Private Limited
	Decohome Co., Ltd
	Minying Commercial Shanghai Co., Ltd
Interior goods	Nitori Co., Ltd
	Home Logistics Co., Ltd
	Nitori (Thailand) Co., Ltd
	Nitori (Malaysia) SDN, BHD
	Nitori China Co., Ltd
	Shanghai Liqiao Industrial Co., Ltd
	Nitori Taiwan Co., Ltd
	Nitori India Private Limited
	Decohome Co., Ltd
	Minying Commercial Shanghai Co., Ltd
Other (advertisement)	Nitori Public Co., Ltd

Source: Nitori Annual Report 2012.

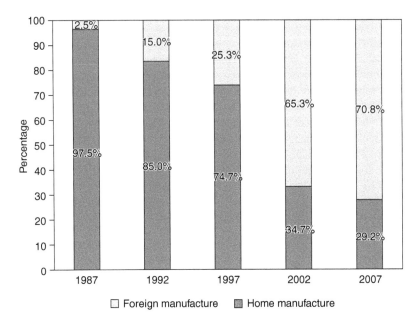

Figure 4.7 Share of home and foreign manufacturing of Nitori products (source: company internal reports).

Products developed in-house are procured from 350 companies around the world and the sales of these accounted for 75 per cent of total sales, in the year ending February 2008 (www.Nitori-intl.com).

The current sourcing network is shown in Figure 4.8 and the logistics support for this network is shown in Figure 4.9. Of the eight distribution centres in Japan four are dedicated to furniture and four to home furnishings. Nitori has transferred warehousing functions from Japan to China, taking higher distribution costs into account.

Critical events

Global sourcing network

Nitori needed to enhance its supply network in order to apply its business concept of 'high quality and low price'to consumers. Even though Nitori had imported products directly from abroad since 1986 and established a foreign subsidiary, it was critical that Nitori speeded up its rate of global sourcing. Nitori, originally specializing in the sale of furniture, had to fill the gap of a speciality store with a private label. Since Nitori had no know-how for designing and producing its own private label, it combined with Marumitsu Woodwork, a furniture manufacturer and wholesaler.

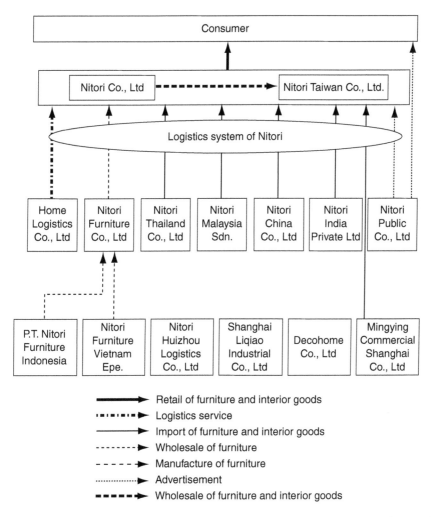

Figure 4.8 Global sourcing network of Nitori Holding Co., Ltd. (source: Nitori Annual Report 2012; company internal material).

Nitori acquired 30 per cent of the stock of Marumitsu Woodwork in 1987 and the president of Nitori assumed the position of chairman of the board and representative director. Manufacturing companies of Nitori's own furniture in Taiwan and Singapore were guided by the expertise of Marumitsu Woodwork in producing better quality and lower priced furniture. Whilst beginning to manufacture its own goods, it relied on imports from the United States, South Korea and Malaysia, Taiwan, Singapore and other countries with the aim of expanding sales in the domestic market.

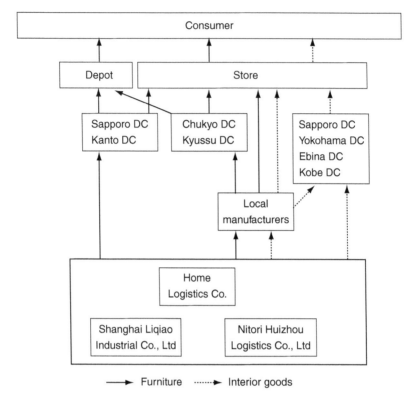

Figure 4.9 Logistics system of Nitori (source: Nitori Annual Report 2011, p. 5; company internal material; Distribution Design 21, September 2004, p. 104).

Marumitsu Woodwork assembled materials and parts imported from foreign countries, advised overseas furniture manufacturers and imported the final products. Nitori and Marumitsu Woodwork increased their imports of dining sets, sofas, beds and so on. Nitori sources local manufacturers to produce the furniture suitable for Japan through the technical guidance of Marumitsu Woodwork.

The Marumitsu Woodwork factory in Medan, Indonesia was started in April 1994 and completed in February 1995. Previously imported materials and parts were sent to Hokkaido, but were now sent to Indonesia, which began assembling these in July 1995. Subsequently, the assembled products were sent to Japan on an experimental basis. 150 single beds with drawers (made of rubber-tree wood) were sent to Japan in September1995 and were sold in each store of Nitori in December 1995. They were all sold in one week, because the price was only ¥29,800, approximately ¥10,000 cheaper than comparable products. Because of the lower production costs the gross margin, at 45 per cent, was the same as the higher priced.

The main reason for the cost reduction is the lower labour cost. The average income of a worker was reported at ¥7,500 per month at that time. The cost of distribution was also cheaper. When furniture is produced in Asahikawa and carried to any store of Nitori around Tokyo, it costs as much as ¥4,000 for one cabinet (120 cm in width) because domestic truck rates are high. However, the cost to ship the equivalent product from Medan to Tokyo is only ¥2,500. Moreover, most of the raw materials used in the furniture, such as rubber-tree wood, are locally sourced in Indonesia, resulting in an improvement in the efficiency of the production process from materials to assembly. Since the Plaza Accord in 1985, the president of Nitori foresaw that the low cost of overseas procurement would become a key factor that would give him the edge over competitors. Consequently, imports increased considerably over the next ten-year period, to 25 per cent of sales in 1995 and subsequently to 80 per cent in 2011.

Nitori joined with a timber company in North America in 1988 and constructed a saw mill processing oak in Russia because of the low labour cost. The lumber was shipped from Russia to the Medan factory and manufactured into chests of drawers and cupboards, and sold in its stores in Japan. The oak cupboards were very popular for ¥99,800, and Nitori could save ¥20,000 on the manufacturing process at the Medan factory.

Nitori acquired all the remaining stock of Marumitsu in August 2000 for ¥135 million to create a wholly owned subsidiary. This move enabled better decision making and strengthened the link between manufacturing and sales. The name of Marumitsu was changed to Nitori Furniture in 2011.

Importance of quality control

Nitori has been developing its own original business model in Japan, building a global sourcing network with vertical integration. Controlling the technological processes of various manufacturers in many countries has been central to the success of the model. It has been essential for Nitori to manage the manufacturing process and to impose its technological expertise. Although coming from a background with limited knowledge of mass production Nitori has succeeded in managing the integrated processes. To achieve this Nitori recruited two experts from major manufacturing companies and used their knowledge of logistics system and quality control in manufacturing processes in its consignment factories. The first employee from an outside major company was Kiyoshi Sugiyama who joined Nitori in 2005: previously he had been president at Honda China. He was an expert in operations management in manufacturing and had experiences in many operations in automobile manufacture and in personnel management of Chinese employees. Controlling the logistics system went to Naoki Kodama, formerly a director at IBM Japan. He was well-versed in systems and promoted the in-house development of systems rather than using outside contractors in order to enhance efficiency.

Sugiyama and Kodama advised Nitori and its consignment factories on the value of total quality control. As a result of learning and implementing total quality management and control, which Nitori never had before, the rate of defective furniture that previous to 2004 was 3 per cent reduced by half to 1.5 per cent in one year. This method was then applied to the total organization of the company.

Risk management of environmental changes

Pursuing global sourcing and supply networks based on lower labour costs and operating costs was a high-risk gamble, because the development of the company depended on foreign exchange rates. There was for example a slowing of earnings because of the rising materials and crude-oil prices and the yen weakness in 2005, and the improvement of the gross profit margin because of a stronger yen since 2008.

The improvement of a delivery system, the standardization of an administrative system for logistics centres, and the rationalization of operating systems offset the cost increases associated with a weaker yen. Subsequently, a strong yen offset the cost growth. The economic recession and financial crisis of 2008 meant that Nitori could not expect to expand market share under the existing marketing approach and so an aggressive price reduction policy was introduced. Although Nitori reduced the gross margin, it actually acquired several benefits, for example, a stronger underlying support from customers in 2008 when business conditions turned severe and an improvement in the business mix and systems, without any of the extended delays seen in the past.

Historical analysis of phases

We can consider the historical evolutionary path of Nitori as divided into three phases:

1   1967–1985: establishes Nitori Furniture Store as the business format. Changes name from Corporation Nitori to Home Furnishing Nitori. Realizes need to have a private label for its imported products.
2   1985–2004: reaches the target of sales of ¥100,000 million.
3   2004–2011 aggressive price cutting.

For each of these phases it is useful to consider critical events, timing of developments and also the social, economic and political factors that created these phases.

Phase 1: 1967–1985

Nitori launched a furniture business during the period of strong economic growth and the emerging consumer spending boom. It started as a small local store in Hokkaido where the traditional Japanese furniture businesses had developed. At that time, in Hokkaido, there were many manufacturers and wholesalers, but the number of retailers was small with most of the production going to stores on mainland Japan. The wholesalers usually exercised leadership in furnishing distribution and marketing. A combination of a relative absence of competitors at the retailing level and a location where it could be very easily source products enabled Nitori to establish itself quickly.

The consumer demand patterns were changing, however, and a new design development was needed to meet the increasingly diversified needs of the consumers, and simultaneously adapt to the growing demand of furniture that was functional and integrated within an overall design of a room. At first, Nitori established direct dealings with manufacturers, bypassing wholesalers. However, Nitori's direct dealing system was not successful in a domestic market because of the traditional power structure in the channel, and so it began to import products directly from abroad.

Nitori had a problem in deploying its new business concept. In order to sell its imported products it needed to differentiate them from the home-produced products. It therefore launched its private label for its products. However, Nitori had been buying furniture from wholesalers and selling to consumers and so, it had no know-how about designing and producing its own private label.

Phase 2: 1985–2004

As the sales in the domestic market expanded rapidly, Nitori had to be more dependent on overseas manufacturers in order to design and produce its own private label. But again Nitori lacked know-how for design and production, so finally, Nitori made a decision to solve that problem by establishing a joint venture with the manufacturing company Marumitsu Woodwork to provide the necessary expertise.

Marumitsu Woodwork is a furniture manufacturer and wholesaler from Hokkaido. Nitori already had consignment manufacturing companies in Taiwan and Singapore and these companies were advised by Marumitsu Woodwork and expertise in producing better quality and lower priced furniture transferred from Marumitsu. However, since 1995, imported materials and parts have been sent to Indonesia where a factory of Marumitsu woodwork is located. There, Marumitsu Woodwork has assembled them and finished the final products in its own factory. Nitori and Marumitsu Woodwork could therefore provide their own products at a lower price to the Japanese consumers. Nitori made Marumitsu a completely affiliated company in 2000. This move enabled Nitori to make better decisions and strengthen the link between manufacturing and sales. Nitori reached the sales target of ¥100,000 million for this period.

Phase 3: 2004–2011

The success of Nitori might not have been possible were it not for managing and controlling technological processes of various manufacturers located in different countries. It was essential for Nitori to manage the manufacturing process and to input its technological expertise. It was at this time that Nitori hired external experts formerly with Honda and IBM to support the logistics and quality management programme. The creation of an integrated production facility allowed an emphasis on low-cost production so placing Nitori in a strong position when the recession of 2008 began to have an effect on consumer demand. The price reduction policy could be implemented to grow sales in the recessionary period.

The factors associated with the three phases are summarized in Table 4.3.

Table 4.3 Summary of the characteristics of the phases of development of Nitori

	Phase 1	*Phase 2*	*Phase 3*
Environmental factors	• Reduction of the sale of the Japanese traditional high quality furniture • Rise in the demand which needs the Western style of furniture with four legs	• Lacks expertise for for designing and procuring its own private label	• Impact of the quality control of IKEA • The rising materials and crude-oil prices and the yen weakness in 2005 • The stronger yen since 2008
Critical dates and decisions	*June1981* • Imports products directly from abroad	*January 1987* • Acquires 30% of the stocks of Marumitsu Woodwork, a furniture manufacturer and wholesaler	*2005* • The rationalization of operating system • The first senior manager from an outside major company appointed *October 2007* • Second external senior manager appointed *June 2008* • Introduction of aggressive price reduction policy
Results	• Begins to manufacture its own goods	• A factory of Marumitsu Woodwork in Indonesia begins assembling in July 1995, to supply lower priced furniture	• The rate of defective furniture that was 3% until 2004; reduces to 1.5% in one year

Conclusion

Nitori has developed from a traditional furniture retailer into a speciality chain-store retailer of private label of home furnishing over 45 years. A number of key events have facilitated this growth and transition.

Two major functions which it accomplished were developing stores and building a global sourcing network. Alongside enlarging its scale to that of a national chain Nitori strengthened its off-shore sourcing network. The success of Nitori has been built on managing and controlling technological processes of various manufacturers in many countries. However, initially Nitori did not have the necessary technological expertise about quality control and logistics. It was essential for Nitori to acquire these skills before it was able to manage the manufacturing and logistics processes necessary for an integrated company. This was achieved by appointing external experts to senior positions.

Nitori has successfully operated a business model of high quality and low price through its retail operation with an off-shore sourcing and supply network. This has enabled it to become the largest furniture and furnishings retailer in Japan.

Appendix

Nitori timeline of development

Year	Events
December 1967	Nitori Furniture Store is opened.
March 1972	Corporate Nitori Furniture Warehouse is established and opens two stores.
June 1978	The company's name is changed to Corporation Nitori Furniture.
August 1980	The distribution centre is moved to Teinei-ku, Sapporo-shi, and a three-dimensional auto-warehouse opens and is set up as headquarters.
June 1981	Imports products directly from abroad.
July 1986	The company's name is changed to Nitori Co., Ltd from Corporation Nitori Furniture, the store's name is changed to Home Furnishing Nitori.
March 1989	Establishes foreign branch, N. T. Singapore Pte., Ltd.
February 1990	Builds a new headquarters office.
July 1990	Builds a distribution centre in Kyusyu.
1994	Upgrades to the latest system in three-dimensional auto-warehouse in its fourth expansion of a distribution centre.
October 1994	Establishes foreign branch, P. T. Marumitsu Indonesia.
February 1995	Completes the factory in Medan, Indonesia.
September 1995	Upgrades to the latest system in three-dimensional auto-warehouse in its fifth expansion of a distribution centre.
November 1995	Establishes Kanto distribution centre in Funabashi-shi, Chiba-ken.
January 1997	Introduces open system operation by PC.
September 1999	Establishes foreign branch, Nitori Thailand Co., Ltd.
June 2000	Establishes foreign branch, Nitori Shanghai International Trade Co., Ltd.

continued

Year	Events
July 2000	Moves Kanto distribution centre from Funabashi-shi, Chiba-ken into Shirooka-cho, Saitama-ken.
August 2000	Makes Marumitsu a completely affiliated company.
August 2001	Establishes Chukyo distribution centre in Komaki-shi, Aichi-ken.
October 2001	Constructs the extension of the eastern distribution centre.
August 2002	Extends the eastern distribution centre.
February 2003	Reaches the top of sales in home furnishing retail in Japan (with ¥88.2 billion)
June 2003	Establishes Nitori Malaysia Sdn., Bhd.
July 2003	Establishes Nitori (HK) Co. Ltd. in collaboration with Nitori (Singapore).
October 2003	Establishes Marumitsu-Vietnam EPE.
November 2003	Constructs Kansai distribution centre in Chuo-ku, Kobe-shi, Hyogo-ken
December 2003	Constructs a factory in Hanoi, Vietnam.
January 2004	TARGET's visiting the eastern distribution centre of Nitori.
March 2004	Reaches the target of ¥1,000 billions in sales.
March 2004	Establishes Nitori China Co., Ltd. (Shanghai Pudong) in collaboration with Nitori (HK), and a distribution centre in Shanghai.
October 2004	Starts manufacturing in its factory in Vietnam.
November 2004	Operates the western distribution centre in Chuo-ku, Kobe-shi, Hyogo-ken.
February 2005	Cut ties with NT Singapore Pte. Ltd shifting its import base to China.
March 2005	Starts on the advertising agency as Nitori Public Co.
2005	Opens Nitori China Co., Ltd. Huizho Branch and Huizho Logistics Centre construction starts.
November 2005	Acquired certificate of ISO9001:2000 as the international standard of quality management system.
June 2006	Constructs a distribution centre in Keisyu, China.
July 2006	Relocates a section of the headquarters office to Tokyo, on the 6/7th floors in Akabane.
August 2006	Opens Nitori China Co. Ltd. Shenzhen branch.
	Nitori China Co. Ltd acquires Shanghai Liqiao Industrial Co., Ltd. and makes it a completely affiliated company. Shanghai Logistics Centre construction starts.
October 2006	The regular meeting for management rule of foreign correspondent is held for the first time in Japan.
December 2006	Establishes Nitori Taiwan as an affiliated retail company in Taipei, Taiwan.
December 2006	Cut ties with Nitori Shanghai International Trade Co., Ltd. by reorganizing the foreign branches.
February 2007	Established Nitori China Co., Ltd, Guanzhou Branch and Nitori Huizhou Logistics Co., Ltd, and opens Representative Office of India.
May 2007	Opens the first foreign store in Kaohsiung, Taiwan.
November 2007	Cut ties with NT Hongkong Ltd., by reorganizing the foreign branches.
November 2008	Opens the second foreign store in south of Taiwan, as a smaller road store.
December 2008	Opens the third foreign store in Taoyuan, a road store $(1,500\,m^2)$, 6,000 items.
January 2009	Opens the fourth foreign store in Taipei as a tenant of a shopping mall, 4,000 items.

Year	Events
February 2009	Has 14 offices in six countries in total in the fiscal year ended February 2009.
January 2010	Representative Office of India was scaled up to overseas subsidiary as Nitori India Private Ltd.
May 2010	Another 'Price Reduction Declared' conducted. Reduced the prices of 3,400 items.
August 2010	Reorganizes to a holding company. The corporate name and organization are changed Nitori Co., Ltd to Nitori Holdings Co., Ltd.
October 2010	Constructs new Kyussu distribution centre.
February 2011	Opens three home fashion stores called Decohome.
March 2011	Has stores in 47 prefectures with opening of Matsue store in Shimane.
	Changes Marumitsu Co., Ltd to Nitori Furniture Co., Ltd.
May 2011	Changes Marumitsu-Vietnam EPE to Nitori Furniture Vietnam EPE.
June 2011	Changes P. T. Marumitsu Indonesia to P. T. Nitori Furniture Indonesia.
February 2012	Opened 28 stores, and closed seven stores in Japan, and opened three stores abroad in the fiscal year ended February 2012. Operates 258 stores in Japan and ten stores abroad.

Bibliography

Asahikawa Shinkin Industrial Information Center (1985) *Problem and proposal of Asahikawa Furniture Industry* (in Japanese).

Baek, Jung-Yim (2009) The growth tracks of Nitori made SPA establish in the Japanese furniture industry: the global sourcing strategy in Asia. *Izumiya General Laboratory Quarterly*, 77, 36–43 (in Japanese).

Cooperation of labour union of Asahikawa furniture industry (1994) *Research report on the marketing and distribution problems of Asahikawa furniture* (in Japanese).

Diamond Homecenter, various issues.

Each *Annual Security Report.*

Hokkaido Newspaper, various issues.

Hoppo Journal, various issues.

Innovations in Sales, various issues.

Management Council of Asahikawa as a Source of Furniture (1997) *Evaluation report on Asahikawa as a source of furniture* (in Japanese).

Nikkan Sangyo Newspaper, various issues.

Nikkei Finance Newspaper, various issues.

Nikkei Industry Newspaper, various issues.

Nikkei Marketing Journal, various issues.

Nikkei Newspaper, various issues.

UBS Investment Research, *Nitori*, various issues.

5   President Chain Store Corporation

Globalization through business diversification

Masao Mukoyama

Uni-President Enterprises Corporation (UPEC) is the biggest food conglomerate company in Taiwan with operating revenue of NT$388,028 million in fiscal year 2011. Many food manufacturers in Taiwan use a very particular business strategy which involves not only food manufacturing but also retailing and physical distribution. President Chain Store Corporation (henceforth PCSC) comprises the retail business division of UPEC. PCSC is the only distribution company in the world with the unusual business style drawn from its parent company. The general merchandise retailers in Japan aimed, in the past, at being conglomerate merchants, and have a history of operating a retail business and the other businesses that relate to lifestyle. However, this strategy is now completely overturned as a result of reorganization of the structure of their businesses. PCSC, however, not only continues in the retail sector but also moves into other sectors, and so is reminiscent of past activity of the Japanese merchant conglomerate. This diversification strategy has succeeded to the extent that PCSC has sustained growth over many years. In the 2000s, the overseas market became a target for this strategy and moves to internationalize began. This chapter considers the strategy of PCSC, exploring why such a unique business style was feasible and how the business style constructed in Taiwan has a profound effect on the development in overseas markets.

Background

PCSC consists of a group of distribution companies within UPEC. UPEC was established in 1967 as a milling company and fodder manufacturer but quickly began manufacturing processed food moving into instant noodle manufacture in 1969 and cooking oil in 1971. Its position as a general food processing company including the beverages, dairy products, soy sauce and seasoning, etc. was established within the first ten years of existence. To achieve further growth as a full-line processed food manufacturer, it became necessary to secure its own marketing channel. To secure a retail channel there was a move into the convenience store format with a focused assortment in processed food (Chung 2005). PCSC was established in 1978, opening simultaneously eight stores in Taipei, two in Tainan and two in Kaohsiung. A licence to operate as a franchisee was obtained from Southland Corporation in the United States in 1980, and the first 7–11 Taiwan store was established. The chain operated at a loss for two years because the managerial knowledge imported directly from Southland Corporation was not effective in the Taiwanese market. As a result, UPEC absorbed PCSC and decided to reconstitute PCSC as a business division of the parent company. After considerable efforts to adjust the convenience store to the Taiwanese market, 7–11 Taiwan reached 100 stores and was able to recover accumulated losses by 1986. At this point PCSC was converted from being a business division of UPEC to being an independent company in 1987.

The turnaround of PCSC is attributed largely to President Hsu who after a long period in the position retired in 2012. The turnaround and subsequent growth was on the basis of diversifying operations beyond convenience stores to the development of other retail formats, diversifying into new related sectors and investing to enable rapid expansion of activities. PCSC developed in five related sectors: retailing; consumer services; physical distribution and information; food services; and manufacturing. Table 5.1 summarizes the progression of activity in the five sectors.

The first investment of PCSC was in Carrefour in 1987. After a brief respite President Drugstore Business Corp. was established in 1995 to develop drugstore Cosmed. The Uni-President Yellow Hat Corp. was established in 2001 to sell tyres. A number of other new retail businesses followed. However, development was not limited to retailing with investments in non-retail sectors more active. In the service sector for instance, the Tong-Ho Development Corp. for resort development was established in 1994, Duskin Service Taiwan the rental of cleaning equipment in 1995, Mech-President petrol stations in 1997 and the spa and fitness club management BEING Sports in 2003. In addition, Starbucks (1998), Uni-President Oven Bakery Corp. (2000), Mister Donut (2004) and Cold Stone Creamery Taiwan Ltd (2006) were established in food service. In the physical distribution and information sector, Retail Support International was established in 1990, and Wisdom Distribution and Uni-President Cold-Chain were established in 1999, so that PCSC constructed its own physical distribution system to support the various subsidiary companies. Moreover, in manufacturing the President Pharmaceutical Corp. was established in 1993 to make medicine and cosmetics. In 1999 Uni-President Organic Corp. that processed organic food and the President Musashino Corp. that manufactured the box lunch for convenience stores were established. As a result of this rapid diversification programme by July, 2012 PCSC comprised 47 subsidiaries in five business sectors: 17 in retailing, five in the service sector, ten in physical distribution and information, 12 in food service, and three in manufacturing. Within the retail group of subsidiaries multiple formats were operated with convenience stores, drugstores, the department stores, supermarkets, hypermarkets, variety stores, online shopping and speciality stores for example pet shops, the car accessory shops and bakery shops. The wide base of its diversified activity, established over 34 years, makes PCSC unique as a distribution company

Table 5.1 PCSC subsidiaries

Year of foundation	Name of company	Business area	Business contents	Foreign location	Share of investment (%)	No. of stores
1978	President Chain Store Corp.	Retail	7–11 convenience store	—	100	4,821
1987	Carrefour Taiwan	Retail	Carrefour	—	40	60
1990	Retail Support International	Physical distribution and information processing	Room temperature physical distribution	—	25	—
1993	President Pharmaceutical Corp.	Manufacturing	Drug/cosmetic supplier	—	73.74	—
1994	Tong-Ho Development Corp.	Service	Resort development	—	59.50	4
1994	Duskin Service Taiwan	Service	Rental of cleaning products	—	51	—
1995	President Drugstore Business Corp.	Retail	Drug store (Cosmed)	—	100	355
1997	President Information Corp.	Physical distribution and information processing	Consulting service	—	56	—
1997	Mech-President	Service	Petrol station	—	99.76	111
1998	President Starbucks Coffee Corp.	Food service	Coffee shop	—	30	270
1998	Capital Inventory Service Corp.	Physical distribution and information processing	Inventory auditing service	—	100	—
1999	Uni-President Organic Co.	Manufacturing	Organic food supplier	—	93.33	—
1999	Wisdom Distribution	Physical distribution and information processing	Physical distribution	—	100	—
1999	Uni-President Cold-Chain	Physical distribution and information processing	Physical distribution	—	60	—
1999	President Musashino Corp.	Manufacturing	Fresh food supplier	—	40	—
1999	President Transnet Corp.	Physical distribution and information processing	Delivery service	—	70	—
2000	President Chain Store Corp.	Retail	7–11 Convenience store	Philippines	56.59	759
2000	Uni-President Oven Bakery Corp	Food service	Bakery shop	—	100	11
2000	President Starbucks Coffee Corp.	Food service	Coffee shop	Shanghai	30	271
2000	President Logistics International	Physical distribution and information processing	Physical distribution	—	49	—

Year	Company	Category	Business	Location	%	No.
2000	Bank Pro E-Service technology Co., Ltd.	Physical distribution and information processing	E-commerce	—	53.33	—
2001	Uni-President Yellow Hat Corp.	Retail	Tyre selling Yellow Hat	—	100	5
2001	Beijing Tongjie Fabao	Retail	Supermarket	Beijing	48.87	9
2001	Book.com Co., Ltd	Retail	Online shopping	—	50.03	—
2002	President Collect Service Co., Ltd	Physical distribution and information processing.	Payment collection service	—	70	—
2003	MUJI Taiwan Co., Ltd	Retail	Lifestyle store MUJI	—	41	26
2003	21Century Enterprise Co., Ltd	Food service	Fast food	—	20	34
2003	BEING Sports	Service	Spa and fitness centres	—	100	17
2004	President Drugstore Business Corp.	Retail	Drug store	Shenzhen	65	14
2004	Mister Donut Taiwan Corp.	Food service	Doughnut shop	—	50	71
2004	President YiLan Art & Culture Corp.	Service	Club Health	—	100	1
2005	Vietnam Uni-mart	Retail	Supermarket Uni-Mart	Vietnam	51	172
2005	Shandong Uni-mart	Retail	Supermarket Uni-Mart	Shandong	55	4
2005	Sichuan Uni-mart	Retail	Hypermarket Uni-Mart	Sichuan	100	16
2005	Uni-President Oven Bakery Corp.	Food service	Bakery	Wuhan	100	2
2006	Uni-President Department Stores Corp.	Retail	Department store	—	70	37
2006	Cold Stone Creamery Taiwan Ltd	Food service	Ice cream store	—	100	57
2007	Cold Stone Creamery Taiwan Ltd	Food service	Ice cream store	China	100	—
2007	Q-ware System & Service Corp.	Physical distribution and information processing	iban platform and digital service provider	—	23.07	7
2007	Pet Plus Co., Ltd	Retail	Pet shop Pet Plus	—	70	14
2007	Afternoon Tea Taiwan Corp.	Food service	Household items, gifts, team room	—	51	—
2008	Taiwan RAKUTEN	Retail	Online shopping mall	—	49	100
2009	President Chain Store Corp.	Retail	7–11 convenience store	Shanghai	100	—
2009	President Chain Store Tokyo Marketing Corp.	Retail	Brand marketing, market research	—	100	20
2009	Mister Donut Taiwan Corp.	Food service	Doughnut shop	Shanghai	50	2
2009	Afternoon Tea Taiwan Corp.	Food service	Household items, gifts, team room	Shanghai	51	1
2010	Sato Restaurant Systems Corp.	Food service	Japanese fusion restaurant	—	81	

The GPS map of PCSC

The internal development of PCSC in the retail sector is shown on the GPA map (Figure 5.1) and summarized in Figure 5.2. The 7–11 convenience store in Taiwan began the store expansion in 1979. This is plotted in the second quadrant (single continent – single format) on the map. The first entry into an overseas market was the Philippines in 2000, 21 years after the initial convenience store development in Taiwan. The overseas developments were all limited to the continent of Asia and this has continued with entry to China in 2009. On the other hand, the convenience store, that was the first retail format operated by PCSC, was the basis of rapid diversification to other formats. It began to develop Carrefour hypermarkets in 1987 after eight years, and drugstore Cosmed was begun in 1995 eight years later. Moreover the tyre shop was begun six years later, followed by the development of MUJI (2003), the department store (2006), and the pet shop (2007), all in Taiwan. PCSC opened a drugstore in Shenzhen (China) during the period of diversification in the domestic market. Retail formats other than the convenience store began to enter foreign countries but in all cases they were restricted to the Asian continent.

Figure 5.2 indicates that it took 21 years to develop the convenience store in a second country within Asia. However in 1987, 13 years before the first convenience store opening outside Taiwan, PCSC started to develop hypermarkets in Taiwan. Thus, PCSC shifted first from single continent–single format to single continent–multi-format, and eight years were required for this move. In addition, 18 years were required to develop the hypermarket, that was not PCSC's original retail format, in another Asian country with the development of Uni-Mart in China.

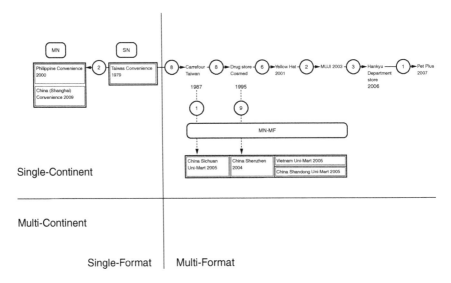

Figure 5.1 GPS map of PCSC.

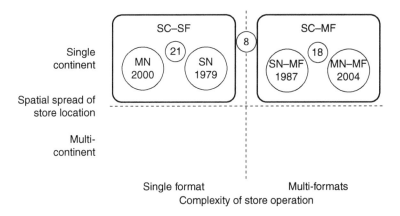

Figure 5.2 GPS position shift of PCSC (summary).

From single-format to multi-format

The positional shift of PCSC on the GPS map in Figure 5.2 is from a situation where only one retail format is developed in a single continent to where many retail formats are developed in a single continent. In order to understand this diversification pattern it is necessary to consider activities in the other four business sectors of PCSC.

The PCSC growth process. At the start of the process of growth is the 7–11 convenience store that was the original retail format of PCSC. Figure 5.3 shows the growth of sales and number of stores. The number of 7–11 stores increased after 1980 with rapid growth beginning from the after early 1990s until 2008 after which it slowed. Store numbers reached 4,803 in 2011. Sales increased in line with store numbers and continued to increase even after 2008.

Figure 5.4 shows the number of group subsidiaries operating in PCSC and the number of stores of 7–11 convenience stores. Figure 5.5 shows the increase in group-level sales. The increase in the number of stores and the increase of the number of subsidiaries show a very similar overall growth trend. The number of stores has increased through the process of corporate growth and the subsidiaries also have increased. The stores provide a solid platform that both has to be serviced by subsidiaries and provides opportunity to diversify through subsidiaries. As store numbers increase so also do sales (Figure 5.3) providing this platform for the creation of subsidiaries. The relationship between the growth of 7–11 stores and the consequential growth of subsidiaries is key to understanding the development of PCSC.

Purpose of diversification. PCSC classifies subsidiaries as vertical and horizontal subsidiaries. Physical distribution, information processing and the financial subsidiaries belong to the former, and the subsidiaries that relate to retail, food service, internet shopping and manufacturing belong to the latter. In

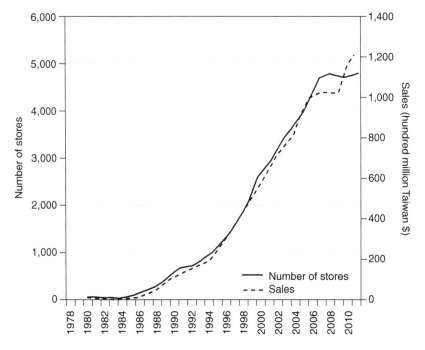

Figure 5.3 Number of PCSC stores and its sales.

interview (for details see the interview list at the end of the chapter), Vice President Lai argued that the subsidiary groups support successful diversification in the following ways:

- Establishment of a new company within the company. The presence of a subsidiary provides the possibility that an excellent employee can be promoted on an inter-company career track. This would not be possible if PCSC only operated a convenience store chain. The possibility for an employee who has ambition and motivation is promotion to a directorship or presidential position in one of the several subsidiaries.
- Specialization. For some business functions special and higher levels of knowledge and technological competences are needed that are beyond the expertise available is all the subsidiaries. Having one subsidiary that acts as a service provider to others for these functions increases efficiencies and also allows a very high level of specialist expertise to be built in the service subsidiary. For example in physical distribution, information processing and finance these high-level specialisms can be developed in one subsidiary, often a vertical subsidiary, and then used to service other, often horizontal, subsidiaries.
- Pursuit of economies of scale. The Taiwanese market is relatively small in population and land area. It has 23.43 million people which is small

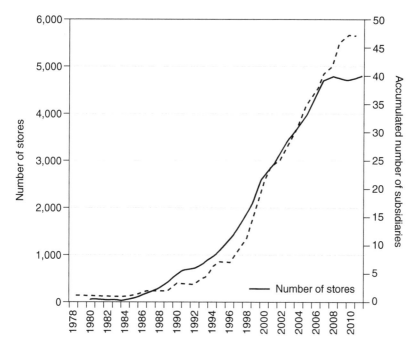

Figure 5.4 Number of PCSC stores and number of its subsidiaries.

compared with many surrounding Asian countries. In area it is $36,000\,km^2$, about one-tenth the size of Japan. The small domestic market means that the growth limit for a business comes early. For instance, the convenience store market is very close to saturation with, in 2011, 9,788 operated by the top four companies giving a ratio of 2,400 people per store compared with Japan with a ratio of 3,400 people per store which many believe has already reached saturation. In order to avoid the limitation imposed by market size diversification is necessary and if business functions can be shared amongst subsidiaries then scale economies can be obtained by diversification. This has been the approach of PCSC group.

The factors that have enabled successful diversification. The model of vertical and horizontal subsidiaries is central to the success of the PCSC diversification strategy. The system of physical distribution for the 7–11 convenience store became inadequate when the number of new stores per year exceeded 100. It was not possible to respond to rapid store expansion with the existing physical distribution system. There was no retailer with a chain store system in Taiwan at that time, and it was small-sized forwarding agents that were providing physical distribution services. A modern physical distribution system did not exist and the know-how to construct a system could not be got from within Taiwan. PCSC,

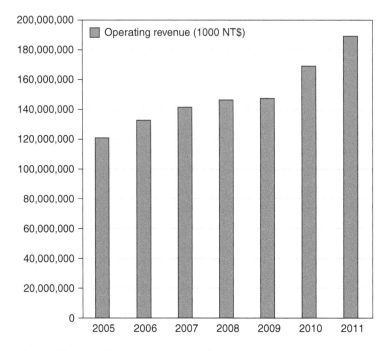

Figure 5.5 Operating revenue of PCSC Group.

therefore, consulted Mitsubishi Corp. general trading company in Japan, and established a joint venture company Retail Support International. The joint venture comprises PCSC, Mitsubishi Corp. and Japanese wholesaler Ryoshoku, a company with close links to Mitsubishi. Retail Support International became responsible for the physical distribution in 1990. This subsidiary, which operates the ambient temperature physical distribution of miscellaneous goods, had a big influence on the subsequent growth of PCSC.

The improvement in the physical distribution system was effected through the know-how offered by Ryoshoku and the dispatch of employees to Japan for training. The number of delivery vans per store per day decreased from six to one or two, the value of store inventory decreased from 1,000,000 Taiwanese dollars to 80,000 Taiwanese dollars whilst the stock turnover rose from two to three. Store-level out-of-stock decreased and the waste ratio of merchandise decreased drastically. Uni-President Cold Chain, to operate the low temperature physical distribution, and Wisdom Distribution (a tie-up with Tokyo Shuppan Hanbai Co., Ltd a book wholesaler in Japan), to operate the physical distribution of books, were established in 1999. A substantial distribution efficiency improvement resulted. PCSC, therefore, had three physical distribution companies and it was equipped fully with its own physical distribution services. The growth of 7–11 convenience stores and the facility to establish subsidiaries increased rapidly by the presence of the physical distribution subsidiaries. The rapid increase in number of 7–11 stores (Figure 5.6) through the 1990s reflects the establishment of Retail Support International in 1990.

The growth of store numbers related to the introduction of Uni-President Cold Chain and Wisdom Distribution is less dramatic but they enabled high levels of store growth to be sustained to 2007, although figures fluctuated from year to year. Comparing the average annual number of store increase: in the period of rapid expansion 1991 to 1999 it was 185 and for the period of maintained growth from 2000 to 2008 it was 284. The new physical distribution subsidiaries also enabled other subsidiary companies to be established, particularly after 2000, but providing them with shared services. This is clearly seen in Table 5.2. Thirty-one subsidiaries are established after 2000 in the total of 47 PCSC subsidiaries. Table 5.3 shows the number of physical distribution and information processing subsidiaries established before and after 2000. The six established before 2000 accounted for 37.5 per cent of the subsidiaries established during the period but these provided the infrastructure for the development of subsidiaries in other sectors after 2000. After 2000 there were only four distribution and information processing subsidiaries established but 31 in other sectors.

Implications of the vertical subsidiaries

Vertical subsidiaries became the drivers of growth through the infrastructure support activity to PCSC group companies, including the horizontal subsidiaries that developed various businesses. When a new retail format is developed, the

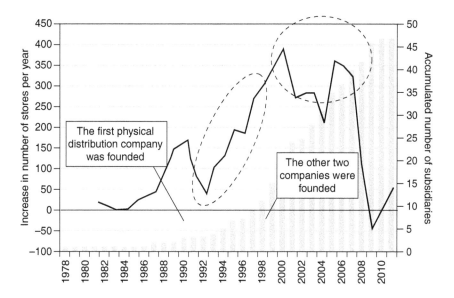

Figure 5.6 Number of increased stores per year and its number of subsidiaries.

Table 5.2 Number of subsidiaries by decade of establishment

	Number	Share (%)
1970s	1	2.1
1980s	1	2.1
1990s	14	29.8
2000s	31	66.0
Total	47	100

Table 5.3 Number and share of physical distribution and information processing subsidiaries

Year of foundation	Number of subsidiaries	Number of physical distribution and information processing	Share (%)
Before 2000	16	6	37.5
After 2000	31	4	12.5

vertical subsidiaries are responsible for the integrated physical distribution and the information processing activity. The new horizontal subsidiary can develop the business rapidly by depending on the vertical subsidiaries that provide specific support. In respect of physical distribution and information services, Table 5.4 shows the relation of Retail Support International to the horizontal subsidiary companies in the group depending on the characteristics of products.

The horizontal subsidiaries dependency on the vertical subsidiaries for physical distribution and the information processing function has another effect. Being relieved of the need to develop their own physical distribution the horizontal subsidiaries can focus more effectively on building knowledge and investing in new technologies relevant to their horizontal market.

PCSC enhanced the role of vertical subsidiaries progressively and, after 2000, elaborated a plan for overseas deployment. The concept of vertical subsidiaries

Table 5.4 Examples of horizontal subsidiaries supported by Retail Support International

	Ambient product	Chilled product	Frozen product
7–11 convenience store	○		
Cosmed	○		
MUJI	○		
Starbucks	○	○	
Cold Stone		○	○
Mister Donut	○	○	○
Afternoon Tea		○	○
President Pharmaceutical Corp.	○		
Uni-President Organic Corp.	○	○	

as specialists to provide infrastructure services for corporate growth led, with the help of a consulting firm, to the design of a shared service centre. The idea behind this centre is to reduce the costs of diversification cost by consolidating the services which are common to each subsidiary in the shared service centre.

Specifically, functions of store development, advertising, human resource management and legal affairs that each subsidiary requires individually are provided to subsidiaries by the shared service centre. For example, when a new food service is started the shared service centre will be responsible for the sourcing of store equipment and design of the interior, preparing the advertising plan and the necessary legal procedures to facilitate opening. The store operation and marketing remain with the food service subsidiary. PCSC, with the shared service centre, has established a way of efficiently promoting diversification. The horizontal subsidiaries concentrate on the operation of the business and PCSC supports the basic aspects of each business by the vertical subsidiaries and the share service centre. This method of growth in domestic diversification can be applied also to the development in foreign countries. Figure 5.7 summarizes this support system of diversification.

Key characteristics of development

As of 2012, the internationalization level of PCSC remains modest and the operational area has stayed the Asian continent. The shift in quadrants on the GPS

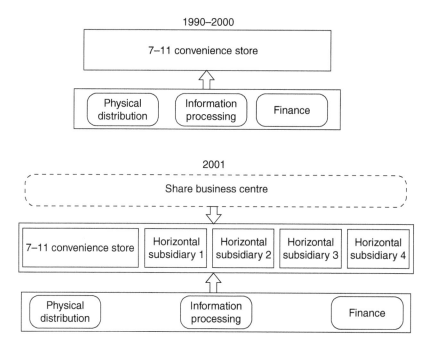

Figure 5.7 PCSC and the supporting system.

map in Figure 5.2 represents the total of internationalization activity. PCSC, however, begins to develop its business not only in Taiwan but also in other countries in Asia. Figure 5.8 illustrates the reasons for the shift in the GPS map.

The first turning point

The first turning point was the establishment of a horizontal diversification mindset within senior management in PCSC. PCSC started with the development of 7–11 convenience stores in Taiwan in 1979. PCSC soon began to develop retail formats other than the convenience store in Taiwan. A retailer with a single format, the convenience store in Taiwan, changed to a multi-format retailer with drugstores, department stores and hypermarkets. An important point in the subsequent internationalization process was the acceptance of the idea that horizontal diversification, not only within retailing but also in other sectors, could provide a viable growth for the firm. This acceptance resulted from and generated a number of synergistic factors.

Establishment of Retail Support International. PCSC perceived that the construction of the physical distribution system holds the key to chain-store expansion and a specialist subsidiary was required. Retail Support International was established. This enabled substantial expansion of 7–11 and also provided the opportunity to provide physical distribution services to support other subsidiaries. Physical distribution is required in some form whatever the sector of business. By addressing a central provision of service, diversification of operations was made more easily and the physical distribution subsidiaries became the core of diversification activity.

Identification of opportunities. The acceptance by PCSC of the fact that the total domestic market of Taiwan is small but that market sectors provided opportunities was a major factor in accepting diversification as a way of growing. President Hsu recognized that the identification of sectoral opportunities held the key to business growth. Many subsidiaries listed in Table 5.1 were established by joint venture with foreign partners, particularly ones from Japan. Retail Support International was established with a Japanese general trading company and wholesaler, President Musashino Corp., Yellow Hat Corp., MUJI Taiwan, Mister Donut Taiwan Corp., Uni-President Department Stores Corp., Pet Plus Co. Ltd, President Transnet Corp. and Afternoon Tea Taiwan Corp. are all joint with Japanese companies. In addition the drugstore Cosmed, although PCSC established it as their first wholly owned retail subsidiary, owes much to transfers of knowledge from Japan where the drugstore format was evolving rapidly at that time. An important factor in the success of the diversification was sensing opportunities for rapid horizontal diversification into a format which was not present in Taiwan but was seen as having market potential. A factor in this market sensing was the experience of President Hsu in studying at a graduate school in Japan and so being a frequent visitor there with many contacts in the social and commercial networks. The direct role of President Hsu in sensing and seizing opportunities was an important aspect of the diversification strategy.

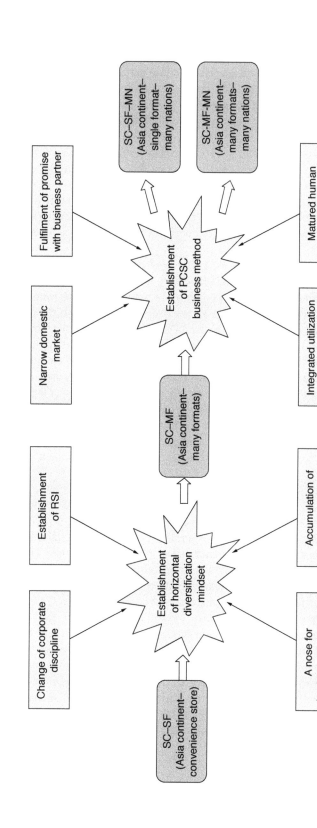

Figure 5.8 Turning point and crucial events in PCSC.

Change of corporate discipline. After finding that the 7–11 operating systems provided in manuals brought from the United States were useless in Taiwan, PCSC concentrated on adapting operations for Taiwan. Therefore, PCSC started putting the concept of 'Convenience' into all aspects of operations to reinforce the values that the convenience store should deliver. It aimed to be the 'Best Retailer of Convenience'. The 7–11 convenience stores achieved rapid growth under this dictum. However, it began to notice that all the needs of consumers are not able to be fulfilled by a convenience store alone. As a result, PCSC thought that a focus solely on 'convenience' was inadequate so it widened its perspective on consumer needs to encompass other lifestyle needs. The concept to which PCSC aimed was changed to being the as 'Best Retailer for Supporting Total Human Life'.

Accumulation of know-how in 7–11. The 7–11 chain grew to have 100 stores in 1986 and began to make a profit following several years of losses. In 1987 it became an independent subsidiary company. The move into profit resulted from a programme to adjust the stores, often on a trial and error basis, to better reflect Taiwanese consumer purchasing behaviour. This experience of transferring to the home country an unknown business that succeeded in an overseas market and making adaptions for its success in Taiwan gave PCSC substantial confidence in its competence as a retailer. Knowledge had been gained not only in chain store management systems, a management style largely absent from Taiwan at that time, but also the knowledge associated with store design and store development to create a retail business. This accumulation and application of knowledge was important as a basis for future diversification and internationalization.

The second turning point

The establishment of the PCSC strategic business model is a second turning point in the development of the company. In the GPS map, 7–11 stores are developed in countries other than Taiwan, PCSC develops new retail formats by diversification and begins to launch these in countries other than Taiwan. An important point that enabled the advance to other countries was the establishment of the particular business model based on diversification and central services. Four factors underpin and characterize the business model.

Narrow domestic market. Because of the limited size of the Taiwanese market, PCSC tried to secure the scale necessary for growth by diversifying into multiple sectors. It is often the case that retailer internationalization takes place in firms with a narrow domestic market. In the case of PCSC, whilst the home market is relatively small it is not saturated but growth prospects were starting to be limited so international moves were a logical response. PCSC recognized that staying in the domestic market would restrict the growth. PCSC moved to the Philippines in 2000. President Hsu, when interviewed, explained,

> I wanted to go to foreign countries from an early time. As to China, we entered in Shanghai for the first time in 2009, but I wanted to go to China

earlier than that. The background was that the Chinese government put severe restrictions on foreign capital and there were circumstances that the licence was not able to be got from 7–11 in the United States easily. At that time there was information from the owner who had the area licence of 7–11 in the Philippines that he was looking for a business partner in Philippines 7–11 and I wanted to experience foreign countries as soon as possible. Therefore PCSC entered the Philippines.

Using network contacts. PCSC has many subsidiaries through its diversification strategy. Many of the subsidiaries are joint-ventures. The experience of diversification based on joint-venture cooperation has brought access to new networks for PCSC and also information on new markets. For example, PCSC established a supermarket (Uni-Mart) in China (Santo) in 2005 and now has 172 stores. The creation of this business is linked to the network established it invested in Carrefour in 1987. The origin of Uni-Mart is that President Hsu spoke with the president of Carrefour Taiwan when he retired, and they agreed that in the future there was a great opportunity for the neighbourhood supermarket format in China rather than large-scale hypermarkets. As a result the Uni-Mart development was started. Similarly, when Uni-Mart was started in 2005 in Vietnam, in a joint venture with Mitsubishi Corp., The Seiyu Ltd, and Hanoi foods, the previous network links involving the Mitsubishi Corp. were important. PCSC needed to learn about the market in Vietnam and the joint venture provided an entry mechanism of relatively low risk and modest investment. The internationalization method of PCSC is to seize a business opportunity using contacts in personal and business networks generated through the subsidiaries.

Building on network partnerships. For PCSC, China is one of their target markets. This is also the case for other firms in the business network that PCSC has created through its subsidiaries. Being based in Taiwan gives PCSC good insights and information on the market in China that are potentially useful to joint-venture members in the network of subsidiaries. PCSC therefore, in several cases, has proposed to a partner 'Let's experiment first in Taiwan, and then both aim at China after that'. This has been the case with Starbucks, Cold Stone, Mister Donut and Afternoon Tea who all have moved to mainland China after first entering Taiwan. PCSC therefore has first gained knowledge and expertise in specialist operations from their partner and applied this in a joint venture in Taiwan and then at a second stage has used the expertise developed in Taiwan to enable transfer of the venture into mainland China. In this way both partners of the joint venture gain benefits making the joint-venture arrangement more stable.

Integrated utilization of resources. The shared service centre is a support system launched when PCSC diversified in the domestic market. A similar arrangement is in place for entry into foreign markets. The policy of providing shared functions through the shared service centre is adopted irrespective of whether entry is domestic or in a foreign country. One aspect of the shared function of location analysis is the 'clumping' of PCSC stores such that several subsidiaries locate stores close together in the same neighbourhood. Thus a We drugstore may locate adjacent to a 7–11 store with a Starbucks and Mister Donut close by. This concentration or 'clumping' strategy strengthens competitive positioning, provides some cost economies of agglomeration for shared logistic services and enables joint promotional activity at a local level. This practice has been used not only in Taiwan but also is now used in Shanghai. It is a strategy only made possible by having the business model of diversified horizontal subsidiaries.

Conclusion

The internationalization level of PCSC is not extensive because the several retail formats are developed in only four countries including the home country within the Asian continent. However, the following three conclusions can be drawn from PCSC case study.

First, we see internationalization of a vertical integrated company. UPEC, the parent company of PCSC, is a vertical conglomerate company that develops the overall business from manufacturing to physical distribution and retailing. It has five business groups of provisions; instant food; dairy and beverage; general foods; and health all linked to food, and additionally has a logistics group. It has 236 consolidated subsidiaries. PCSC is a core company within UPEC covering the distribution sector. PCSC started from the convenience store business with the purpose of expanding the marketing channel in UPEC. This meant that PCSC had a tight relationship with the parent company from the beginning. The relationship continues still. The existing physical distribution company of UPEC supports the development of convenience stores in Shanghai. The internationalization of PCSC was realized using the relationship with the parent company. PCSC is unique because there is almost no firm in which the retail subsidiary of a conglomerate company is internationalized. This internationalization model that is unified with the parent company is specifically an Asian type of retail internationalization.

Second, there is synchronization of vertical diversification and horizontal diversification within internationalization. PCSC advanced the vertical and horizontal diversification simultaneously in a short period in Taiwan. Moreover, it diversified horizontally not only to the retail sector but to the service and food service sector, and was vertically diversified to physical distribution, information processing and financial services. It should be noted here that vertical subsidiaries supported the horizontal diversification. In addition, what has been important is that the supporting system which was constructed in a domestic market was also used in the international market. This meant that a system that inclusively supported the internationalization of retailer was constructed. PCSC proved the effectiveness of a unified support system of experienced specialist functional management teams in comparison to making a support system for every retail format and country independently.

Third, the strength of the strategy of PCSC depends on charismatic leadership in senior management and a strong link with Japan. The domestic and international growth by simultaneous horizontal diversification and vertical diversification was realized by President Hsu. Over periods of study and work in Japan he built and maintained an extensive network with Japanese executives. The network with Japan was used actively in implementation of the strategy. The business was diversified by discovering a sequence of promising businesses in Japanese market and bringing them into Taiwan. The partnership with Japan and the transplanting of a Japanese model were big factors enabling the rapid growth of PCSC.

These three features have implications for the future development of PCSC. Following the retirement of President Hsu it will be essential to maintain the momentum of growth with a new executive group. The next stage of development will require the support system that has been developed for the domestic market to be extended to support the internationalization of PCSC potentially beyond Asia. In this next stage of development will the strategy of linking to and monitoring the Japanese market continue to provide the required pointers for development? How these issues are addressed will determine the move of PCSC to the next position on the GPS map and whether, or not, it can become a multi-format, multi-continent global retailer.

Bibliography

Chung, S. (2005) *The birth of vertical integrated company: business history of UPEC in Taiwan.* Tokyo: Hakuto-Shobo (in Japanese).

Hsu, C. J. (2007) *A chance encounter changed my life*, Taipei: Taiwan Kadokawa (in Japanese).

Nikkei Business (1997) Ryoshoku: the counterattacking wholesaler. *Nikkei Business*, 29 September1997 (in Japanese).

PCSC (2008) *7-ELEVEN 30 Years*.

PCSC Annual Report, 2006, 2007, 2008, 2009, 2010, 2011.

Interview list (title is correct at the time of interview)

Victor Lai, vice-president, PCSC, 11 May 2010.

Masaaki Kawaguchi, general manager, Pet Plus Co., Ltd, 12 May 2010.

Po-Ming Yang, vice general manager, Pet Plus Co., Ltd, 12 May 2010.

Kuo-Hsuan Wu, president, Retail Support International, 22 December 2010.

Ho Hsin, business planning team manager, Retail Support International, 22 December 2010.

Chien Wen Ho, chief operating officer, President Drugstore Business Corp., 23 December 2010.

Hsu Chung Jen, president, PCSC, 15 June 2011.

6 Lotte Shopping

Transforming a Korean retailer towards being global

Sang Chul Choi

The East Asian region is steadily changing from being primarily the production centre of the world economy to additionally being a huge consumer market. The big retailers from around the world have rushed into the region as the potential of this transition has become apparent. The OECD Development Centre (Kharas 2010) expects that by 2020 half the world's middle class, defined as households with daily per capita incomes of between US$10 and US$100 in purchasing power parity terms, could be living in the region.

The representatives of the big retailers from the developed countries, however, have changed over recent decades. Initially, from the 1960s till the 1980s the Japanese big retailers, i.e. the department store and GMS (general merchandise store) companies, were involved as the first movers investing outside their home market (Mukoyama 1996) due not only to geographic proximity but also the societal and cultural similarities of the markets (Treadgold and Davies 1988; Burt 1993). The weakening of the Japanese economy after the collapse of the bubble economy forced Japanese retail companies to reconsider their strategies and they reallocated their limited marketing and management resources to the home market resulting in withdrawal or reduced commitment to foreign operations. Replacing the Japanese retailers and following the steady deregulation and opening of Asian retail market (Yahagi 2007) since the 1990s, the Western global retailers have attempted to build positions of leadership in Asian markets.

During this more recent period of competitive advance by retailers of the advanced countries for the position of the leader in the Asian retail market, a new trend has occurred. Some Asian local retailers have become strong by investing in retail technology and also gaining knowledge from the foreign retail companies, through competition and cooperation with them. These retailers have themselves invested outside their own domestic retail markets to become significant international retailers in the region (Choi 2003). One such retailer is Lotte Shopping Co. which is the focus of this chapter. Although Lotte Shopping has been a late entrant to Asian markets outside Korea, having only begun in 2007, its business performance deserves close attention (Choi 2009).

Historically, Lotte Shopping has been well-known for its conservative management style since its establishment in 1979, so the pace of aggressive globalization of the company represents a major change of strategy for the firm. In this chapter, first we explain about the maturation of the main retail formats in the Korean retail market. Next, we outline Lotte Shopping in terms of the globalization of the company focusing on the department store and hypermarket formats. Finally we analyse the factors that brought about the paradigm shift from a traditional local retailer to an aggressive global retailer.

Maturation of retailing in Korea and rush to market

Saturation of the hypermarket and department store formats

Each retail format in the Korean retail market reflects the cycle of general business conditions, although for each format total sales have been rising throughout. Table 6.1 shows the trend of the sales and share of the retail formats from 1996, when the Korean retail market opened to foreign capital, until 2010.

The hypermarket has reached saturation stage in recent years. In 1996 the sales of hypermarkets businesses reached 2.1 trillion Korean Won with 2.3 per cent market share. By 2010 sales were 33.7 trillion Korean Won with a market share of 17.3 per cent. Growth, however had slowed in the late 2000s with compound annual growth rate (CAGR) at 5.3 per cent for the period 2007–2010 compared with 12.4 per cent from 2000–2010. The decline in CAGR suggests saturation has been reached. As of the end of 2011 there were 444 hypermarkets. Moves now are towards higher market concentration with the big three hypermarket companies, E-mart, Samsung-Tesco (company name changed to 'Homeplus' since March 2011), and Lotte Mart watching for merger and acquisition (M&A) opportunities amongst the few smaller firms involved in the format (Choi 2009).

Meanwhile, the department store, the biggest retail format for a long time with 12.5 trillion Korean Won and 13.8 per cent share in 1996, was usurped for the top position in 2003 by the hypermarket. The market share of department stores had fallen to 12.5 per cent in 2010 and the number of department stores fell from 140 in 1997 to 82 in 2011. Market concentration remains high with three firms; Lotte (29 stores), Hyundai (13 stores), and Shinsegye (nine stores) having a combined market share of 82 per cent.

Korean retail companies' rush abroad

The major retail companies are moving rapidly to other Asian countries. Underpinning these moves is the well-established push–pull framework of changed circumstances encouraging moves out of the home market with department store and hypermarket saturation and the high growth in Asian target markets providing the pull to new host country (Alexander 1990; Treadgold and Davies 1988; Dawson 1994; Mukoyama 1996; Kawabata 2000). For example, Vietnam, following China, has opened the retail market to foreign capital completely and both are exhibiting rapid growth in consumer retail spending.

Table 6.1 Trend of sales by retail format in Korea: 1996–2010

	1996		2000		2001		2010		2000–2010 CAGR[3]	2007–2010 CAGR[3]
	sales[2]	share	sales	share	sales	share	sales	share		
Department stores[1]	12.5	13.8	15.1	12.8	18.7	11.7	24.3	12.5	4.9	6.9
Hypermarkets	2.1	2.3	10.5	8.9	28.9	18.1	33.7	17.3	12.4	5.3
Supermarkets	5.6	6.2	6.3	5.4	11.6	7.3	23.8	12.2	14.2	27.1
Convenience stores	1.0	1.1	1.3	1.1	5.5	3.4	7.0	3.6	18.3	8.4
Non-store retailing	–	–	3.2	2.7	20.6	12.9	31.1	15.9	25.5	14.7
Other retail sales	69.7	76.7	81.3	69.1	74.3	46.7	75.2	38.5	-0.8	0.4
Total	90.9	100.0	117.7	100.0	159.6	100.0	195.1	100.0	5.2	6.9

Sources: adapted from various years of Economic Statistics Bureau of the Statistics Korea and Korea Chainstores Association (www.koca.or.kr).

Notes
1 Includes wholesale clubs.
2 Trillion Won.
3 Compound Annual Growth (%).

Lotte Shopping has been active in these international moves, although the company's first move was after that of E-Mart of Shinsegye group which opened its first hypermarket in China in Shanghai, 1997 (see Table 6.2). Lotte Shopping, however, has been more active since the decision was made to move internationally and it has developed both hypermarkets and department stores in several countries by direct investment and M&A activity.

Brief history of Lotte Shopping and problems of format portfolio

Origins of Lotte Shopping and the rapid expansion of Lotte Department Store

In order to understand the origins of Lotte Shopping, it is important to appreciate that the Korea Lotte Group is the fifth largest Korean industrial and service conglomerate (*zaibatsu*) in terms of group total sales in the 2010 fiscal year.

The start of the Korea Lotte Group was the Lotte Confectionery Co., Ltd that was established in 1967 with the purpose of investing in Korea by the general food manufacturer Japan Lotte Group. Lotte Confectionery progressed to be the biggest general food manufacturing group in Korea in a short period through the launch of other food-associated companies and an M&A strategy. Japan Lotte Group judged that there was a limit in the growth and development for a manufacturer in the confectionery sector in Korea. A diversification strategy was therefore adopted with new investment in tourism and retailing and the creation of Hotel Lotte division (Lotte Shopping 2009). The choice of tourism and retailing was taken because while the tourism industry could earn foreign currency with the possibilities of high added value, the retail industry had yet to be modernized and so there was considerable potential returns on future investment.

The first Hotel Lotte opened in the centre of Seoul in 1973. Subsequently, a shopping centre development division was established in 1976 for the purpose of entering the department store business. Hotel Lotte formed a collaboration with

Table 6.2 Foreign entry by Korean retail companies

Format	Company (store)	Host country	Entry date
Hypermarket	E-Mart	China	February 1997
	Mega Mart	China	January 2001
		USA	October 2010
	Lotte Mart	China	December 2007
		Indonesia	October 2008
		Vietnam	December 2008
Department store	Lotte Department	Russia	September 2007
		China	August 2008

Takashimaya of Japan and requested their support for the operation of the department store, training of employees and guidance regarding merchandizing (Kawabata 2000, 2011). In 1979, the shopping centre division was separated from Hotel Lotte and changed into the local corporation, Lotte Shopping. Thus the origin of Lotte Shopping dates officially from this year with the use of the store brand, Lotte Shopping Centre. In 1988, the store brand of Lotte Shopping Centre was changed to Lotte Department Store following the deregulation of the sector by the government (Lotte Shopping 2009). It was designated as the official department store of the Seoul Olympics in 1988. In 1993, it became the first Korean department store to record an annual sale of one trillion Korean Won.

Lotte Shopping established a network strategy with multiple department stores to maintain its dominant position and drive the modernization of retailing. At the end of 2011, Lotte Department Store had 29 stores in Korea and retained its prime position in the market. The second and third positioned firms, Hyundai Department Store (13 stores) and the Shinsegye Department Store (nine shops) are not large enough to be a major competitive challenge. Although the Lotte Department Store has built the overwhelming position domestically (Lotte Shopping 2012), maturity of the domestic market is unavoidable. It is inevitable that the company, in order to grow, has to go abroad.

Entry into the hypermarket business

In 1993, Shinsegye Group, the rival of Lotte Shopping, entered the Korean hypermarket business – which had not existed in Korea – by opening the first store in suburban Seoul, with the store brand of E-Mart. The opening of the entire Korean distribution market in 1996 encouraged the global hypermarket retailers Carrefour, Wal-Mart and Tesco to consider expansion into Korea. The synergistic effect of the simultaneous entry of both domestic and Western power retailers into hypermarket development and customer acceptance of the new format generated rapid growth (Choi 2003). By 2003 the hypermarket business surpassed the department store in terms of annual total sales.

Because Lotte Shopping focused its management resources overwhelmingly on the department store format, they delayed their entry to this promising new hypermarket format (Choi 2009). As price competition increased in the Korean retail industry, however, Lotte Shopping set up a project team for the new format in 1995. After three years of research, it joined the hypermarket business by opening the first store in the suburbs of Seoul with the store name of Magnet. The store brand of Magnet was changed to Lotte Mart in 2002 and was separated into an independent management organization in 2003 (Lotte Shopping 2009).

As Lotte Shopping had the ambition to become the largest firm in the hypermarket sector, similar to the department store sector, so it attempted the purchase of the stores of Carrefour and Wal-Mart when they left Korea in 2005 and 2006. However, it did not succeed with these purchases and its rivals, Samsung-Tesco and E-Mart eventually took ownership of these stores (Choi 2009). As a result, Lotte Mart remains in third place in the hypermarket sector. In order to grow in the hypermarket industry there was no alternative but to go abroad.

Format portfolio of Lotte Shopping

Since Lotte Shopping began with its department store format, it has pursued a format diversification strategy, into hypermarkets, convenience stores and super-markets. In addition, the company has entered non-store retailing. As a result, the company has been able to benefit from scale economies as it has expanded presence in a format and scope economies across the formats. The multiple format portfolio strategy with several formats developed simultaneously pro-vides consumers with variety of assortments, entertainment and amenity (Lee *et al.* 2010; Lotte Shopping 2009).

Although there has been diversification of formats Lotte Shopping operations remain dominated by department stores and hypermarkets. Sales in 2011 were 22,253 billion Korean Won with gross profit of 7,002 billion Won and net profit of 1,013 billion Won and the divisional contribution to sales was: department stores (36.2 per cent), hypermarkets (37.3 per cent), finance (5.9 per cent), super-markets (7.4 per cent), home shopping (3.1 per cent), cinemas (1.4 per cent), convenience stores (8.7 per cent). The dominance of the two formats is clear and both are in a mature stage in Korea.

Rapid shift toward a global retailer

After being listed in the Seoul stock exchange in February, 2006 Lotte Shopping has expanded rapidly inside and outside Korea. This expansion is shown in Table 6.3.

The dominant position in department stores has been maintained in Korea and steady expansion of hypermarkets has taken place. International expansion has opened up new markets and the traditional Korean based strategy of Lotte shop-ping has been replaced by a more international strategy.

Lotte Department Store's foreign entry

At year end 2011, Lotte Department Store had one store each in Beijing and Tientsin in China and in Moscow. This modest development is the result of the difficulty in transferring the distinctive Korean-based culture and history of Lotte Department Store into new markets (Lotte Shopping 2009). Lotte Department Store organized a business team to research internationalization in 2006 with specific task forces related to Russia, China, Vietnam and India. Simultaneously, it opened representative offices in Beijing, Ho Chi Minh City and New Delhi, which took charge of market research and business area analysis. It also pre-pared a personnel training programme focusing on English and local languages and enhancement of a global perspective in its head office in Seoul.

Table 6.3 Store network of Lotte Shopping: domestic stores and overseas stores (year end total)

		2006	2007	2008	2009	2010	2011	2012(E)
Domestic stores								
Department Store	full-line store	20	21	22	23	23	24	25
	franchise store	3	3	3	3	6	6	6
	young plaza	1	3	3	3	3	3	3
	outlet mall	–	–	2	3	4	6	8
Hypermarket		50	56	63	69	90	95	102
Overseas stores								
Department Store	Russia	–	1	1	1	1	1	1
	China	–	–	1	1	1	2	3
	Indonesia	–	–	–	–	–	–	–
Hypermarket	China	–	8[1]	8	79[3]	82	94	110
	Vietnam	–	–	1	1	2	2	3
	Indonesia	–	–	19[2]	19	22	28	33

Sources: Lotte Shopping (2011, 2012).

Notes
1 Acquired eight CTA Makro stores in Beijing and Tianjin.
2 Acquired 19 Makro stores in Indonesia.
3 Acquired 68 Times stores in China (including 11 supermarkets).

Entry to Russia

In 1997, Lotte Department Store established a joint venture (L&L Limited) with the Logovaz Group of Russia. It took total control in 2002, because Lotte Group planned to undertake a large-scale development including not only department store but also office and hotel buildings. L&L changed its corporate name to Lotte Shopping Rus in 2006 and immediately began work on establishing a department store. Lotte Plaza, the first overseas store of the Lotte Department Store opened in Moscow in 2007. As this store was also the first overseas venture of any Korean department store, it received considerable publicity as an Asian retailer entering a Western market.

This new department store was a full-line department store in the Korean style with categories including foods, imported brands, fashion apparel, electric appliances and furniture. It had an open styled interior in the Korean trend, unlike shopping malls of Moscow with their shop-in-shop layouts. It therefore highlighted many imported brands, particularly Korean brands, and emphasized the image of a global department store. Lotte Plaza had a merchandizing concept that involved the coexistence of inexpensive and high quality goods, so there were big differences from the existing department stores (Lee *et al.* 2010). As a result, it experienced a slow start with adaptions being made as more was learnt about consumer demand, but gradually sales have improved. Lotte Department Store has plans to open an additional store in Moscow or in Petersburg.

Entry to China

Lotte Department Store's entry to China was stimulated by both the opening of the retail market in 1992 and the aggressive entry of global retailers. So after it agreed a strategic Memorandum of Understanding with Intime Department Store (Group) Co. Ltd, a large Chinese retailer, it established the joint venture on a 50 per cent to 50 per cent basis.

Lotte Department Store established the Beijing office in 2006 and the Shenyang office in 2007. It opened the first store of Intime Lotte at Wangfujing, one of the biggest shopping centres in Beijing. The initial Intime Lotte store was a full-line department store similar to Lotte Plaza, Moscow. While it attracted many imported brand shops that were already the tenants of the shopping malls, it also included both local and Korean brand shops. It established anchor shops, premium mega shops and the special edition shops of imported watches, sunglasses and perfume, fur counters, special event dress counters, a VIP lounge, special skincare room, and culture events including presentations by notable lecturers. The aim was to differentiate the store from the local department stores.

Lotte Department Store changed the joint governance structure (50 per cent to 50 per cent) to take full control because the first jointly operated store had exposed critical communication problems between the two firms (ChosunBiz. com, 4 October 2011). The second store opened in 2011, Tientsin Dongmalu store, was fully owned by Lotte Department Store. The Tientsin Dongmalu store benefited from the knowledge, often gained by trial and error, of the Beijing store operation. While Lotte Department Store utilizes the retail know-how that it has accumulated in Korea, it intends to adapt this to create a differentiation with locally established department stores of Tientsin (ChosunBiz.com, 30 August 2012). Lotte Department Store opened Weihai store in 2012 also located in Tientsin city and is scheduled to open a fourth store in Santou prefecture in 2013.

Direction of foreign entry in the near future

Lotte Department Store is considering opportunities in countries other than Russia and China. It was scheduled to open a department store in Djakarta, Indonesia by the end of 2013, although the original plan has been delayed because of economic recession. It had also planned to open in Hanoi, Vietnam by the end of 2013.

Lotte Department Store has set the goal to build a network of 23 stores in China, four in Vietnam, five in Indonesia and six in Russia by 2018 making in total 38 stores abroad (*Nihon Keizai Shinbun* 31 May 2011). This goal implies that the company has to open five stores abroad every year, which seems very difficult to accomplish. Lotte Department Store, however, has continued to try to reach the goal, by establishing, in 2011, the vision of being a 'Global Top 5' department store and by establishing a target of raising the percentage of the sales generated in overseas markets from 2 per cent in 2011 to 25 per cent in

2018. Considering that 'The Global 2000' 2011 edition of *Forbes* ranked the company in sixth place in their world department store ranking, it is possible for Lotte Department Store to realize the vision of being in the global top five in 2018.

Lotte Mart's foreign entry

At year end 2011 Lotte Mart had 127 stores outside Korea. The number of Lotte Mart's hypermarkets abroad is greater than the domestic stores (95 stores). The Lotte Mart division, therefore, is seen as the globalization nucleus of Lotte Shopping.

The foreign expansion results from changes in the structure of the Korean market. The hypermarket business of Korea was characterized by intense competition among the domestic retailers and global retailers from the late 1990s until the mid-2000s. The decisions of Carrefour and Wal-Mart to leave Korea in 2005 and 2006 effectively put on sale their respective store portfolios. The 32 stores of Carrefour eventually, in 2008, were transferred to Samsung-Tesco, trading under the Homeplus brand. The 16 stores of Wal-Mart were acquired by the Shinsegye Group, trading under the E-Mart brand (Choi 2009). Thus the hypermarket industry of Korea was consolidated by E-Mart and Homeplus. Lotte Mart attempted to purchase both Carrefour and Wal-Mart stores. However, it failed, although it had more substantial managerial resources and a more distinguished corporate brand in Lotte Shopping than its two rivals. The hypermarket market of Korea was already about to reach saturation point making organic growth in Korea very difficult (Choi 2009; Lim 2010). In losing out in the acquisitions Lotte Mart had no option but to go abroad.

Entry to Vietnam

The first target of Lotte Mart in the emerging markets of Asia was Vietnam. In 2005, Lotte Mart concluded a joint venture agreement with Minh Van Manufacture Trade Private Enterprise. Lotte Mart applied for investment permission to the Vietnamese government in early 2006 and obtained the retail investment permission in late 2006. This enabled establishment, in late 2006, of Lotte Vietnam Shopping Co., Ltd, in which Lotte Mart has 80 per cent ownership.

In late 2008, Lotte Mart opened the first Vietnamese store, the Nam Saigon store in Ho Chi Minh City, although the opening was behind schedule because of extensive market surveys. Lotte Mart offered not only its own hypermarket, but also the various related retail facilities such as a food court, bookstore and bowling alley in order to satisfy the cultural needs of local consumers. It also provided promotional consumer services such as the frequent buyer programme, fresh food guarantee system and the lowest price security system that were not common aspects of the Vietnamese traditional shopping practice. Lotte Mart contributed to the emerging modernization of Vietnamese distribution (Lotte Shopping 2009; Lim 2010).

Lotte Mart opened the second store in July 2010. This was again delayed a little from the original schedule due in this case to opposition from the anti-hypermarket movement and lobbying by local retailers. Since then it has opened stores steadily and plans to extend its store network to 30 stores by 2018 with locations mainly around the major cities of Ho Chi Minh and Hanoi (*Nihon Keizai Shinbun* 2 March 2012).

Entry to China

In late 2007, only a little later than the entry into Vietnam, Lotte Mart entered China by purchasing 49 per cent of CTA Makro, which was the local corporation of Makro, Netherlands. This was the first M&A in a foreign country by a retailer from Korea. Lotte Mart, by this move, immediately gained a market presence in the Chinese market. Lotte Mart had been monitoring opportunities in the hypermarket business of China, through the Shanghai office established in 2004, and the Shenzhen office in 2005. In 2008, a year after the acquisition, Lotte Mart bought the remaining 51 per cent share CTA Makro. Thus, Lotte Mart became the first Korean retailer operating stores in Beijing, through a totally owned subsidiary. This provided the platform for aggressive growth (Lotte Shopping 2009).

As CTA Makro's eight stores (six in Beijing, two in Tientsin) taken by Lotte Mart were managed as membership wholesalers, it changed the business model to the consumer-oriented hypermarket business with higher retail service to more local customers. Furthermore, Lotte Mart purchased a store site in 2009 in Tsingtau for organic growth of the ninth store in China. Two additional stores by the same method followed quickly.

A second acquisition was made in 2009 with the purchase of 68 Times stores in 2009 which belonged to Lianhua Supermarket Holdings Co., Ltd, one of the biggest retail groups in China. The Lotte Mart chain grew to 79 stores. Thus, Lotte Mart, although it was the second mover from Korea in the Chinese market established the scale to enable competition with the global retailers in a store network covering the north-east to the middle-east of China. After the acquisition of the Times stores, Lotte Mart added a further three stores in 2010 and 12 in 2011, continuing the aggressive attitude to Chinese market. Plans for opening 12 stores in 2012 (Lotte Shopping 2012), will give it a hypermarket network with more than 100 stores.

Entry to Indonesia

Lotte Mart became the first Korean retail corporation to enter Indonesia, through the acquisition in 2008 of PT Makro Indonesia that was operating with the store brand Makro. Indonesia Makro started its business in 1991 but failed to adapt sufficiently to the local market, although it was operating 19 cash and carry wholesale club units in several cities including Djakarta. These stores were available for purchase and Lotte Mart won them in competition with Carrefour and Metro. Lotte Mart acquired all 19 stores giving it an immediate market presence.

Lotte Mart continued to operate as a conventional cash and carry style business, while adding sophisticated merchandizing and retail services. At the same time, Lotte Mart undertook a separate store development strategy opening, in 2010, the Gandaria City store, a hypermarket with 100 per cent direct investment, located in Djakarta's central commercial area. This store was widely reported by the mass media of Korea as the hundredth store of Lotte Mart abroad. After only four years, 100 foreign stores were in operation.

After 2010, Lotte Mart speeded up the store opening programme and added seven stores by the end of 2011. In addition, it opened a store of the hybrid concept of both wholesale and retail business in November, 2011. Lotte Mart also opened its twentieth store in Java, which is the first wholesale cash and carry addition to the Makro chain.

The distribution policy of the Indonesian government is favourable to Lotte Mart. The distribution policy limits the opening of new stores by Carrefour, which has 68 hypermarkets and 17 supermarkets as at the end of 2011, due to the size of its market share. Lotte Mart has no problem for new store opening at its current stage of development. Although Lotte Mart has 28 stores, it is planning the expansion of its store network through direct store development and M&A as opportunities become available.

Direction of foreign entry in the near future

On 31 August 2011, Byeong-Yong Noh, CEO of Lotte Mart, announced an ambitious goal in the ceremony to commemorate the opening of Changchun store, the eighty-third store of China and also the two-hundredth store of the whole Lotte Mart. His goal is for 1,000 hypermarkets by 2018 consisting of 300 in Korea and 700 abroad (*Korea Financial News* 30 August 2011). He expressed the goal in detail as a store network of 500 in China, 100 in Indonesia, 30 in Vietnam, and even 70 in India where Lotte Mart has not yet entered. There are questions over whether the goal is realistic given that the foreign deployment of Lotte Mart has been too fast and beyond its competence, and the difficulties in entering the Indian market because of the continuing regulation of foreign retailers.

Initial condition and turning point of global shifting

Culture of the Lotte Group's founder

Lotte Shopping's global shift is different from those of the other big retailers in Korea, for example, Shinsegye Group or GS Retail Group. Lotte has moved more quickly and in a more determined way.[1] In order to understand this difference we have to understand the personal history of the CEO, Kyuk-Ho Shin (Takeo Shigemitu in Japanese), officially now Lotte Group Executive Chairman since 2011. He has transformed the Group, from a small food business starting in Japan in the colonial period to become the Lotte *zaibatsu* (*Konzern*) which is a major company group of food, distribution, leisure and petrochemicals in both Korea and Japan, and moreover has absolute influence even now in family management at the age of 90.

Mr Shin, the founder of Lotte Group, was born in 1922 in the southern part of Korea. He went to Japan in 1942 and began studying while delivering newspapers and milk. A Japanese investor who saw his potential, invested for Mr Shin to start a cutting oil manufacturing factory in 1944 to begin his career as a businessman. The factory was bombed and burned during the Second World War. In 1947, he started the production of chewing gum and established Japan Lotte Co., Ltd in 1948. In 1964 he started the production of chocolate which was a major change in production technologies. The company grew into a general sweets manufacturer familiar to consumers with the sales message of 'the sweetheart of your mouth' not only through chewing gum and chocolate, but also through a wide variety of confectionery products including cookies.

Though Mr Shin started his business career in Japan, his dream was to start a business in Korea and it came true when he established Lotte Confectionery in 1967. Since then, he has diversified from various manufacturers to retailing (Lotte Shopping 2009; Lim 2010).

What should be emphasized is that Mr Shin has spent his business life as the marginal businessman on the boundary of Korea and Japan. Due to the historically unhappy relationship between the two nations, he has experienced a distinctive career. Mr Shin has been occasionally criticized because he does not belong completely to the business societies of either country where nationalism has frequently become a critical issue. While experiencing a business 'identity crisis', he has avoided exposure to the mass media. For this reason he is sometimes called 'the hidden manager' (Lim 2010).

Thus his distinctive career and character have created in both Lotte Group of Korea and Japan a culture of conservatism and managerial stability. This particular corporate culture is a defining feature of Lotte Shopping and the way it has become a nuclear enterprise in the Korea Lotte Group.

It is important to understand that almost all the companies of Korea Lotte Group have adopted various kinds of technology and knowledge from Japan in addition to capital transfer. Lotte Shopping in particular had to adopt the advanced know-how of the department stores and also general merchandise stores of Japan (Kawabata 2000, 2011) because the retail industry of Korea was anachronistic at that time. This duality of operations between Japan and Korea and the various knowledge exchanges has facilitated the existence of both a domestic-oriented management style and an international mindset for Lotte Shopping and as such has defined the initial conditions for more extensive international activity.

Turning point towards aggressive global retailer with the two formats

Many of the Korean large enterprises that experienced the economic crisis in 1997 and the IMF intervention realized that entry to emerging markets is an inevitable strategic direction for them. The department store and hypermarket divisions of Lotte Shopping went abroad in 2007 and 2008 after Korea Lotte Group's declaration in December 2005 that 2006 is the 'first year of global management' and that its longer-term intention was to enter Vietnam, Russia, India and China (VRICs) *Maeil Business Newspaper* 11 January 2006; *Korea Financial News* 23 January 2006).

Figure 6.1 shows establishment with a single format in one country in 1979 and the development 19 years later of a second format in the same country. After eight years of building knowledge in multi-format operation, this multi-format approach was then taken to multiple markets within the one continent in 2007.[2]

In May, 2009 Lotte Group announced their 'Vision of 2018 Asia Top 10 Global Group' (*Vision 2018* hereinafter). The stated aim is to move to being a global business group and in this to be one of the top ten global business groups in Asia. According to the stated goals of the *Vision 2018*, Lotte Group aimed at total sales of 200 trillion Korean Won (about 200 billion dollars) by 2018 (www.lotte.co.kr; *Chosun Monthly Economy Plus*, May 2010) by expanding the scale of the group by an active M&A strategy and aggressive foreign entry and expansion.

A major issue is the need to increase the percentage of sales attributable to non-Korean operations. In 2008, the year previous to the *Vision 2018* document, this was only 4.5 per cent (sales of two trillion Won) within the total sales of

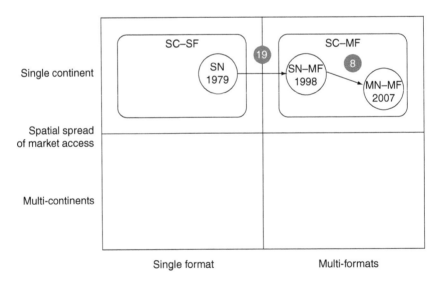

Figure 6.1 Global portfolio strategy map of Lotte Shopping.

Note
In this figure, the one department store of Lotte Shopping opened in 2007 in Russia is not included. So, in this chapter, its spatial coverage is considered as only one continent.

approximately 41 trillion Won. According to *Vision 2018*, the percentage has to be raised to 30 per cent by 2018, which means the sales in foreign countries have to grow to 60 trillion Won by that year within planned sales of 200 trillion Won. To have any chance of achieving these targets the requirement is for a massive expansion of activity in many foreign markets.

Lotte Group's top management thought Lotte Shopping should take the lead in the global mission of *Vision 2018* by entry into VRICs (*Chosun Weekly* 30 June 2009; Lee *et al.* 2010). In accordance with this, Lotte Shopping established 'Lotte Shopping 2018 Vision' separately, recognizing the inevitable role of Lotte Mart and Lotte Department Store at the forefront of globalization mission of *Vision 2018*. The company declared it would aim to be 'Asia Top 3' in 2018 and do its best to achieve *Vision 2018*. In terms of the percentage of sales in the foreign countries, it should reach 30.3 per cent from its 10.5 per cent in 2009. This requires a 16.6 per cent compound annual growth of foreign sales during the period. Lotte Shopping has to change its stable and conservative corporate culture if it is to succeed in being regarded, for *Vision 2018*, as the symbol of 'New Lotte' (*Chosun Monthly Economy Plus* March 2012).

Crucial events for the turning point

The 'Asia Top 3' declaration in the Lotte Shopping *Vision 2018* is a critical turning point for Lotte Shopping strategy on its way to becoming a global retailer. Several crucial events occurred before or after this turning point. These crucial events are illustrated in Figure 6.2 as:

- *Initial Public Offering* of Lotte Shopping
- Aggressive M&A activity to overcome the economic crisis
- Change of a global target: from BRICs to VRICs, and now to VRICI
- Passing the baton to the transformational leader
- Synergy effect of retail formats portfolio
- Use of Group power of Lotte Zaibatsu
- Construction of global sourcing network
- Cultivation of a global manpower

Initial public offering of Lotte Shopping

In February 2006, Lotte Shopping was listed simultaneously on both the Korea Exchange and London Stock Exchange. Through this Initial Public Offering, the company was valued at 3.6 trillion Won. Thus, the company in April, 2006 was positioned as the eleventh largest enterprise in Korea in terms of aggregate stock value and now had a transparent governance system. The listing provided the finance for international expansion. Furthermore, because of the increase of the capital, improvement of the debt to equity ratio and an AA+ credit rating on its bonds, Lotte Shopping could improve the financial flexibility through the paid-in capital increase and issue of bonds. As a result, the company could obtain finance for M&A of foreign retailers in the target countries and it became possible to quicken the speed of the foreign entry (*Chosun Monthly Economy Plus* May 2010).

Aggressive M&A strategy to overcome the economic crisis

At the time of the IMF economic crisis in 1997, most of the Korean big companies that belonged to *zaibatsu* group had a huge debt because of the investment in plant and equipment of the heavy industry divisions to promote foreign trade. The headquarters of *zaibatsu* groups had to separate the affiliate companies to reduce the debt, because of the compulsory demands of the government at that time. However, only Lotte Group was exceptional because it held typically domestic-demand oriented companies in the light industries, such as the manufacturers of confectionery and drinks, and retailing with department stores and duty-free shops. It had the corporate culture with family management of non-listed companies and did not rely on loans from financial institutions.

Lotte Group with such a conservative and diligent corporate culture was able to buy the companies that the *zaibatsu* groups gave up at a very cheap price. It can be said that resulting from the M&A strategy in the IMF era, Lotte Group stood out from the Korean *zaibatsu* groups' society. Furthermore, the same

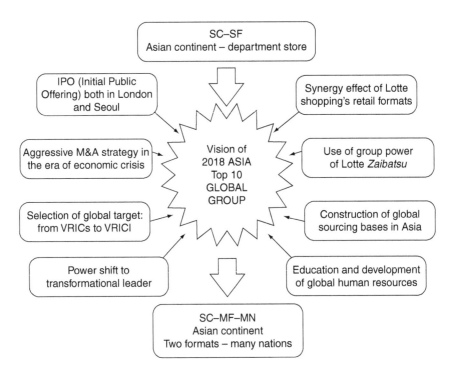

Figure 6.2 Turning point and crucial events of Lotte Shopping.

situation happened in the economic downturn precipitated by the Lehman Brothers' bankruptcy in 2008. At that time, the objects of M&A strategy was not only Korean companies but also foreign companies. It is important that Lotte Shopping among the companies of Lotte Group purchased several companies. The fact that Lotte Mart entered Indonesia and China by purchasing local companies is the reflection of such a M&A strategy (*Choongang Economist* 17 August 2010; *Chosun Monthly Economy Plus* May 2010)

From BRICs to VRICs, and now to VRICI

Lotte Group determined VRICs (Vietnam, Russia, India and China) as the future target markets (*Maeil Business Newspaper*, 11 January 2006; *Korea Financial News*, 23 January 2006; *Chosun Monthly Economy Plus*, October 2006). The concept of VRICs resembles that of BRICs (Brazil, Russia, India and, China) which the O'Neill (2001) report of US Goldman Sachs indicated as the emerging nations. Lotte Group put in 'V'ietnam, which shows rapid economic growth with a large population in Asia, instead of 'B'razil which is distantly located. Furthermore, Indonesia took the place of India. Lotte Group judged Indonesia had, like Vietnam, the potential for rapid economic development. This decision of Lotte Group was beneficial to Lotte Shopping because India has not opened its retail market. However, the Lotte Group recognizes the importance of the so-called 'Chindia strategy' (Sheth 2008) which considers both China and India as the big two emerging nations, and so proposes VRICI (Vietnam, Russia, Indonesia, China and India) strategy that again includes India as a target (Shin 2011).

Passing the baton to the transformational leader

Mr Dong-Bin Shin (Shigemitsu Akio in Japanese), the present chairman of Korea Lotte Group, directed the simultaneous listing in Seoul and London and aggressive M&A strategy of Lotte Shopping. The new chairman of Korea Lotte Group is of Japanese nationality and is the second son of the founder, Mr Kyuk-Ho Shin who is the present Lotte Group Executive Chairman. He is said to be a transformational leader (Bass 1990) with the remit to bring about the change of the corporate culture.

Mr Dong-Bin Shin acquired an MBA majoring in the finance at Colombia University in the USA and worked for five years in London after joining Nomura Securities Co. in 1980. After working in Lotte Trading in Japan from 1988, he moved to Korea from 1990 to work at Korea Lotte Group. He had worked as a managing director of Honam Petrochemical Corp. and executive director of Korea Seven Co., Ltd and became the vice president of Korea Lotte Group in 1997.

In 2004, when the strategy headquarters of Lotte Group was established, he became its general manager. Consequently he was at the centre of the strategic management of Korea Lotte Group and Lotte Shopping. He forced Lotte Shopping to be listed. He said that listing of Lotte Shopping offered the opportunity to change the culture of Lotte Group (Chosunbiz.com 21 July 2010). He also urged adoption of the *Vision 2018* strategies of Lotte Group and Lotte Shopping. Finally he became chairman of Korea Lotte Group in February 2011. Thus, Lotte Group changed to successor's management from founder's management. It is expected that the new chairman is going to accelerate the globalization of Lotte Shopping.

Synergy effect of retail formats portfolio

In addition to its main store based formats Lotte Shopping also operates non-store online retail formats, while it holds all kinds of offline retail formats. It is the only firm in Korea with the full range of both online and offline formats (see Table 6. 4). The range of formats enables benefits of a powerful synergy effect in foreign entry of the company. This synergy effect will be demonstrated in the emerging markets such as Indonesia and Vietnam where Lotte Mart is initially operating but other formats will enter in the next few years.

Use of group power of Lotte Zaibatsu

The foreign entry and development of Lotte Shopping is of several types. One type involves first undertaking extensive market research. Lotte Department Store needed over ten years to open its first store in Moscow, with a detailed survey undertaken by many staff including top management. Initial market research was followed by the building of market share with the creation of a store network through M&A. Lotte Mart secured 19 stores from Makro in Indonesia and purchased 79 stores from Makro and Times in China.

A second type of entrance method is also evident that uses the synergy effect between the various affiliates in Lotte Group including Lotte Shopping. Lotte Group has affiliated companies in several sectors including hotels, theme parks, construction, cinemas, restaurants and finance, in addition to the various retailer

Table 6.4 Format portfolio of the major retail companies in Korea (at year end 2010)

	Lotte Shopping	Shinsegye	Hyundai Depart	GS Retail	Samsung-Tesco
Department store	◎	◎	◎		
Hypermarket	◎	◎			◎
Supermarket	○				○
Convenience store	○			◎	○
Home shopping	○		○	○	
Internet shopping	○	○	○	○	○

Sources: adapted from company data and Lee *et al.* (2010).

Notes
◎ means main format for each company;
○ means new entry format for diversification strategy, though it is not main format.

formats. The Group creates a development that is a multi-use complex with various affiliates involved in the final scheme. For example, the project of the Shenyang theme park complex now under construction is of this type. Lotte Group secured the rights to land of about 194,000 m² from the Shenyang City authority in Liaoning province in north-east China in 2008. The project involves a total investment of two trillion Korean Won. It is planned that it will involve the main retail formats of both Lotte Department Store and Lotte Mart as the key tenants, but also Lotte World as theme park, Lotte Cinema, and Lotte Hotel as the entertainment-related tenants. Completion is scheduled for 2014. The *Vision 2018* strategy involves similar schemes in Indonesia and Vietnam as well ones additional to Shenyang in China.

Construction of global sourcing network

The purpose of the aggressive entry to Asian countries by Lotte Shopping is not only to establish stores abroad, but to adapt to the local needs and gain knowledge from these overseas markets that can be used through the group (Yahagi 2007). In this respect, Lotte Shopping, particularly Lotte Mart, has recognized the importance of global sourcing. Lotte Mart has been constructing strategic global sourcing bases, since the company developed store networks in the emerging markets. Lotte Mart established five buying offices in China, since it opened the Shanghai and Shenzhen office in 2004. In October 2010 the Lotte Global Procurement Centre was established in Shanghai as an official corporation to coordinate these buying offices. The aggregate global sourcing is expected to amount to 350 billion Won in 2012 (*Chosun Weekly* 30 June 2009). By the establishment of a global sourcing network, Lotte Mart has the potential also to introduce the small- and medium-sized manufacturers of Korea to the new overseas market (*Korea Economic Daily* 20 January 2012), enabling these suppliers to gain scale economies that could result in lower prices in Korea.

Cultivation of a global manpower

The more Lotte Shopping establish stores abroad, the more it requires global staff. The company faces the problem of a shortage of excellent staff, because it has established its international store network very rapidly. Therefore, it is essential to train a cadre of international managers. Lotte Group had opened a global school from 2008, before the start of the *Vision 2018* and VRICs study meeting in 2009, for the purpose of developing this managerial expertise. The Global Lotte Expert programme (GLEP) began in 2008. It aims to create programmes to discuss the politics, economy, society and culture of host countries by bringing together the global staff and local residents of Lotte Group abroad (*Korea Economic Daily* 5 July 2010). In the future it will be essential for Lotte Shopping to obtain the benefits from such global personnel training programmes in order to sustain the development of the international store network.

Conclusion

The entry and growth strategy of an Asian-rooted retailer like Lotte Shopping, as a latecomer to internationalization, has to be executed differently from that of a Western retailer who is a first mover in the Asian market. In general, Asian countries hold in high regard social commitments in commercial relationships in addition to profit-related aspects of the relationship. Knowledge and use of these socially constructed business practices in the Asian countries can provide Asian retailers with the capability to make speedier and bolder decisions than competitors, from Western countries, who have already entered and developed stores.

Lotte Shopping's strategic change resulting from the *Vision 2018* moved onto an irreversible path towards being a global retailer. The company has been entering overseas markets with the main retail format or a portfolio of retail formats often being supported by affiliated companies of the Lotte Group that have already entered to Asian countries. Therefore, the synergy effect associated with the power of Lotte Group and format portfolio of Lotte Shopping works to facilitate international expansion. In the Asian market with economic uncertainty in local environments and the existence of strong competitors, the transformational leadership (Bass 1990) of the new president of Lotte Group is critical to gaining the full synergy effects from the Lotte Group.

Mr Dong-Bin Shin, Korea Lotte Group chairman, also as the young leader of Lotte Shopping, is recognizing the Asian markets as the 'low-trust societies' of Fukuyama (1996) in business (*Nikkei Business* 26 September 2011). Undoubtedly, he and Lotte Shopping will face many barriers: for example a working capital problems associated with opening many stores abroad and local adaption problems from the rapid and large M&A strategy toward local retailers (Xun 2010), and inevitable problems of financial losses in the early stage of foreign entry. The road for Lotte Shopping to become a global retailer will be full of such barriers. Therefore, the management capability of the new chairman who inherits the DNA of the founder of Lotte Group is going to be tested from now on.

In this chapter, the rapid foreign entry strategy and individualistic business model of the Lotte Shopping as an emerging new global retailer has been analysed. However, because the history of the globalization of the company is so short, it is difficult to judge whether the globalization model adopted by Lotte Shopping will be successful in the long term.

Notes

1 The discussion hereinafter follows the theory of historical path dependence after David (1985) that the customs or system of the present and the future are restricted and influenced by the historical path. Also refer to Aoki (2001) and Kojima (2002).
2 It could be said that Lotte Shopping also moved to be multi-continent, after 29 years of existence, in a single format when it opened the department store in Moscow. However, in this chapter, its spatial coverage is considered as only one (Asian) continent, as its business deployment in Russia is restricted as just one store.

References

Alexander, N. (1990) Retailers and international markets: motives for expansions. *International Marketing Review*, 7(4), 75–85.

Aoki, M. (2001) *Toward a comparative institutional analysis*. Cambridge, MA: MIT Press.

Bass, B. M. (1990) From transactional to transformational leadership: learning to share the vision. *Organizational Dynamics*, 18(3), 19–31.

Burt, S. (1993) Temporal trends in the internationalization of British retailing. *International Review of Retail, Distribution and Consumer Research*, 3(4), 391–410.

Choi, S. C. (2003) Moves into the Korean market by global retailers and the response of local retailers. In J. Dawson, M. Mukoyama, S. C. Choi and R. Larke (eds) *The internationalization of retailing in Asia*. London/New York: Routledge Curzon, pp. 49–66.

Choi, S. C. (2009) Retail internationalization in Korea. In: M. Mukoyama and S. C. Choi (eds) *New development of retail internationalization*. Tokyo: Chuo Keizaisya (in Japanese), pp. 49–66.

Choongang Economist, issue of 17 August 2010 (in Korean).

ChosunBiz.com, issues of 21 July 2010, 4 October 2011 and 30 August 2012. Available at: http://biz.chosun.com (in Korean).

Chosun Monthly Economy Plus, issues of October 2006, May 2010 and March 2012 (in Korean).

Chosun Weekly, issue of 30 June 2009 (in Korean).

David, A. (1985) Clio and the economics of QWERTY. *American Economic Review*, 75(2), 323–337.

Dawson, J. (1994) Internationalization of retailing operations. *Journal of Marketing Management*, 10(4), 267–282.

Economic Statistics Bureau of the Statistics Korea *The wholesale and retail trade survey*, various years. Seoul: Economic Statistics Bureau of the Statistics Korea.

Forbes (2011) The Global 2000, 9 May issue. Available at: www.forbes.com/ global2000/ list.

Fukuyama, F. (1996) *Trust: the social virtues and the creation of prosperity*. New York: Touchstone Books.

Kawabata, M. (2000) *The internationalization of Japanese retailers: locations and strategies*. Tokyo: Shinhyouron (in Japanese).

Kawabata, M. (2011) *Open the Asian market: 100 years of retailing internationalization and market globalization*. Tokyo: Shinhyouron (in Japanese).

Kharas, H. (2010) The emerging middle class in developing countries. *OECD Development Centre Working Paper*, 285, Paris: OECD.

Kojima, K. (2002) Comparative trade institutional analysis: an introduction. *Kokumin Keizai Zassi*, 185(6), 29–36.

Korea Financial News, issues of 23 January 2006and 30 August 2011 (in Korean).

Korea Economic Daily, issues of 5 July 2010and 20 January 2012 (in Korean).

Lee, J. Y., Kim, C. K. and Joo, Y. H. (2010) Lotte Shopping's marketing strategy for achieving the goal of becoming a global leader. *Korea Marketing Journal*, 12(1), 81–101.

Lim, J. W. (2010) *Lotte and Kyug-Ho Shin*, Seoul: Cheongrim Publishing (in Korean).

Lotte Shopping (2009) *Lotte Shopping 30th Anniversary: 1979–2009*. Seoul: Tara TPS.

Lotte Shopping (2011) *Investor Relations*, Lotte Shopping Co., Ltd, January.

Lotte Shopping (2012) *Investor Relations*, Lotte Shopping Co., Ltd, August.

Maeil Business Newspaper, issue of 11 January 2006 (in Korean).

Mukoyama, M. (1996) *Towards the emergence of pure global*. Tokyo: Chikurashobo (in Japanese).

Nihon Keizai Shinbun, issues of 31 May 2011 and 2 March 2012 (in Japanese).

Nikkei Business, issue of 26 September 2011(in Japanese).

O'Neill, J. (2001) Building better global economic BRICs. *Goldman Sachs Global Economics Paper* No. 66.

Sheth J. N. (2008) *Chindia rising: how China and India will benefit your business.* New York: McGraw-Hill Professional.

Shin, D. B. (2011) Lotte: Challenge and vision to distribution. Presentation to Nakauchi Seminar, University of Marketing and Distribution Sciences, Kobe, Japan (in Japanese).

Treadgold, A. and Davies, R. L (1988) *The internationalization of retailing*. London: Oxford Institute of Retailing Management, Longman Group.

Xun, J. (2010) Retail internationalization through M&As: a study of the talent challenge in a British-retailer in mainland China. *International Review of Retail, Distribution and Consumer Research*, 20(5), 469–493.

Yahagi, T. (2007) *Retail internationalization process*. Tokyo: Yuhikaku (in Japanese).

Interview list

Mr Lee Chul Woo, president of Lotte Shopping, 2 February 2011.

Mr Park Keum Soo, director of overseas business division, Lotte Department Store, 2 February 2011.

7 IKEA

The making of a global giant

Ulf Johansson

People in general have more time than money.
Ingvar Kamprad

IKEA is an abbreviation using the two initials of the founder Ingvar Kamprad, as well as the names of the farm where he grow up (Elmtaryd) and the parish in which the farm was located (Agunnaryd). Ingvar Kamprad founded IKEA in 1943 when he was 17 years old (Björk 1998; Torekull 1998). At first he operated IKEA as a mail-order business but by 1953, a store was opened and finally the first big store, similar to the ones we now know, was opened in Älmhult, in Småland in southern Sweden, in 1958.

IKEA, the home furniture business, is part of a complex organization of foundations and businesses, all controlled by the Kamprad family. The IKEA conglomerate also includes a bank, IKANO bank, as well as a real estate business, owning land and also opening and operating shopping centres across Europe, and a food wholesaling business, selling mainly through IKEA stores around the world. IKEA is a franchise-type of business where Inter IKEA Systems is the owner of the 'IKEA concept', comprising brands and other immaterial rights, which is mainly licensed to the IKEA group, owned by Ingka Holding B.V. Inter IKEA Systems main revenue is a royalty of 3 per cent of the sales of the stores. This structure is shown in Figure 7.1

As at January 2013, IKEA has 338 stores (www.ikea.com 2013). The IKEA group is the main franchise holder and operates 298 stores, the rest are operated by other franchisees, with four operated by IKANO group. The growth of sales and the number of stores opened each year is shown in Figure 7.2.

The first period of IKEA's existence, roughly 1953–1974, comprised establishing operations of stores in Sweden and of starting the first international operations, both in retail and in sourcing. International growth was extensive in the following period, 1975–1981/1982, with also a big leap in the beginning of the 1990s. Substantial expansion started around the mid-1990s and has continued since with some slowdown in number of stores opened each year between 2008 to 2012, compared to the high figures at the beginning of the 2000s.

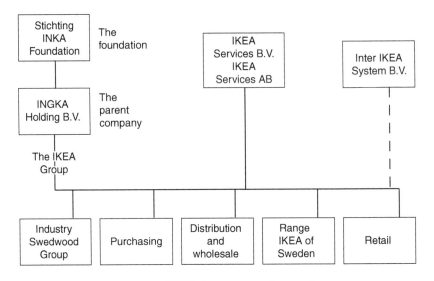

Figure 7.1 The organization of IKEA (source: www.ikea.com).

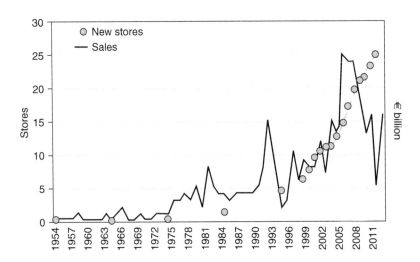

Figure 7.2 IKEA store expansion (number of new stores annually) and sales revenues (billon euro) 1954–2012 (selected years 1954–1998) (source: compiled from various data sources at www.ikea.com 2007–2012).

IKEA operations

IKEA is known for operating a standardized business concept (Figure 7.3). The base for that concept is the assortment and the stores, which basically look the same around the globe, although adaptions occur for different markets (see below). It is important to note that the big assortment, of approximately 10,000 available articles, is the assortment from which products in the stores are sourced. The assortments actually presented in stores draws from this total. For example, IKEA in Japan in response to the small room-sizes of consumers will choose products that suit the particular situation of Japan and will not include in the assortment items that will not fit with that particular situation, while Australia, with big room sizes will include products that Japan will not source. So adaption is undertaken but within the standardized assortment. A third dimension of standardization is the IKEA unique catalogue which is the backbone of IKEA marketing. This has also been standardized but now is increasingly adapted to local markets as IKEA moved into countries like the US, China and Japan where the voluminous catalogue was not efficient and leaner versions have been developed. Additionally, IKEA Family is a loyalty programme that was developed for Sweden but is now rolled out across the IKEA world. The main areas for adaption are advertisements and sales promotion where different countries are, within limits, able to decide on an approach that is suitable for the country in question (Burt *et al.* 2007, 2011a, 2011b; Johansson and Thelander 2009).

The formulation of the IKEA business idea is probably one of the best-known ones in the retailing industry:

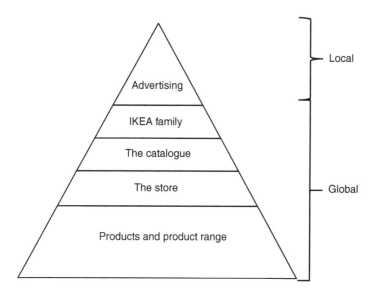

Figure 7.3 Global vs local focus of marketing activities (source: Burt *et al.* 2011b, p. 4).

The IKEA vision is to create a better everyday for the many people. We make this possible by offering a wide range of well-designed functional home furnishing products at prices so low that as many people as possible will be able to afford them.

(www.ikea.com 2013)

IKEA's business model

Central in IKEA is the private brand (IKEA) and the in-house designed and branded products, with a particular Scandinavian style (Aitken 2004; Bjarnestam 2009). These are supplied by a unified supply structure in order to reduce prices through high volumes. Long-term relationships with suppliers exist and suppliers are selected on the basis of performance in manufacturing certain parts of furniture. The furniture is then packaged in flat packages for low-cost transportation, storage and home-transportation by customers. Last but not least, the model involves customer participation in collecting and assembling the products in a form of DIY home furnishings. These are the key characteristics of the IKEA business model (Dahlvig 2010; Porter 1996) and are shown in Figure 7.4.

IKEA's competitive advantages

IKEA's competitive advantages focus around five areas (Figure 7.5). The logic is that while there might be competitors that can beat IKEA on immediate price, none will be able to do this over a longer period so providing sustained

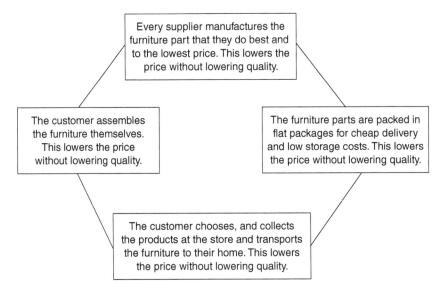

Figure 7.4 Important parts of the IKEA business model (source: Bruzelius and Skärvad 2012, p. 63).

The price
To give value for money and be competitive considering quality and design
Inspiration
To be considered innovative, i.e. the products and the way they are displayed
in stores, catalogue and web should give inspiration in home furnishing
All in one place
To have a broad offer of home furnishing products, all under one roof
Products and assortment
To have a unique assortment with unique products
Shopping experience
To give a pleasurable experience in the store

Figure 7.5 The five competitive advantages of IKEA.

competitive advantage. In areas other than price IKEA there is both short- and long-term advantage. Providing inspiration is an important part, for example the room settings that are typical of IKEA are planned to provide inspiration. Compared to competitors the offer, all in one place, of a wide range of home furnishing products is unmatched. Also, the assortment of private brand products under the IKEA brand is unique in design. Lastly, the IKEA store is supposed to give a special shopping experience, where also the restaurant provides a special touch, and encourages customers to stay longer than would otherwise be the case.

The pattern of the internationalization of IKEA

IKEA has during the nearly 60 years of existence gone from a local mail-order supplier to a global, multi-continent retailer, operating 338 stores in one format on four continents (Table 7.1). At least at first it follows, based on the 'prescriptions' of most textbooks on international marketing, a predictable internationalization pattern. The first country to be entered outside Sweden was Norway which is in the same region and in the same language area, as is Denmark and to some extent Germany. The pattern after these early excursions is of more continuous expansion in Europe and also a 'wild globalization' into Canada, Australia and Japan in the mid-1970s. This global expansion, in several cases according to senior managers in the company, was a result of spontaneous interest from individuals and companies that wanted to sell IKEA products to consumers on a franchise basis. Thus, it was not based on any systematic analysis of available and interesting markets but more opportunistic and based on others contacting IKEA.

In several of these cases the business was not successful and eventually proved to be a hindrance to further expansion. For example there was competition between IKEA group stores and other IKEA franchisees in Australia until quite recently when a re-launch was made in competition with the original franchise holders. Japan was originally based on a franchise outside the IKEA Group, leading to the first withdrawal, in 1984, from a country in the company's history.

Table 7.1 IKEA's moves within and outside original continent (Europe)

SINGLE FORMAT and CONTINENT	SINGLE CONTINENT, MULTI-FORMAT
1 Sweden 1958 (17) 2 Norway 1963 (6) 3 Denmark 1969 (5) 4 Switzerland 1973 (9) 5 Germany 1974 (46) 6 Austria 1977 (7) 7 Spain 1980 (18) 8 Iceland 1981 (1) 9 Netherlands 1982 (12) 10 France 1983 (29) 11 Belgium 1984 (6) 12 UK 1987 (18) 13 Italy 1989 (20) 14 Hungary 1990 (2) 15 Czech Republic 1991 (4) 16 Poland 1991 (8) 17 Slovakia 1992 (1) 18 Finland 1996 (5) 19 Russia 2000 (14) 20 Greece 2001 (5) 21 Portugal 2004 (3) 22 Turkey 2005 (5) 23 Romania 2007 (1) 24 Cyprus 2007 (1) 25 Ireland 2009 (1) 26 Bulgaria 2012 (1) Total of 245 stores in 26 countries	
MULTI-CONTINENT, SINGLE FORMAT	MULTI-CONTINENT, MULTI-FORMAT
1 Australia 1975 (7) 2 Canada 1976 (11) 3 Japan 1976 – Exit 1984, re-entry 2006 (6) 4 Singapore 1978 (2) 5 Saudi Arabia 1983 (3) 6 Kuwait 1984 (1) 7 USA 1985 (38) 8 United Arab Emirates 1991 (2) 9 Malaysia 1996 (1) 10 Taiwan 1998 (4) 11 People's Republic of China 1998 – first store opened in Hong Kong 1975; mainland China, first store in Shanghai 1998 (14) 12 Israel 2001 (2) 13 Dominican republic 2010 (1) 14 Thailand 2012 (1) Total of 93 stores in 14 countries	

Source: compiled from www.ikea.com 2013.

The next big global move by IKEA was the entry into the US in 1985. Expansion on this market was slow with only three stores in the first five years, but growth became more rapid and the USA is now one of IKEA's most important markets. The USA is IKEA's second market in terms of sales 2012 with 38 stores, mainly on the west and east coasts. Asia was entered initially with Japan in the 1970s but the more significant entries into Asian markets were China in 1998 and the re-entry into Japan in 2006. With these market entries, together with the other already existing ten stores in East Asia, IKEA now has a major retail hub in East Asia.

The phases of the internationalization of IKEA

The analyses of the phases of internationalization of IKEA is summarized in Table 7.2. In general, IKEA illustrates the process of a domestic retailer moving to become a global giant while transforming itself from a heavily entrepreneur-reliant firm, controlled by and influenced through many years by founder Ingvar Kamprad, who also acted as CEO for many years, to a professional global retailer. Time-periods have been added to the different phases providing an approximation to the date of entry of each new phase of IKEA's internationalization.

The early years of IKEA were characterized by a truly entrepreneurial spirit, a style personified by the founder Ingvar Kamprad. His un-academic approach, based on trial-and-error rather than a formal business plan, characterized the first decade of IKEA's internationalization. For example, while initial international moves were into neighbouring countries Denmark and Norway, the early global moves into Australia and Japan were initiated by unexpected opportunities and offers from actors in those markets, rather than a carefully constructed business plan. These moves also later turned out to have a number of negative consequences for IKEA in terms of binding and constraining a growing IKEA for many decades to come in these markets. For example, the Japanese partner for the first entry created a lot of bad will in the market, damaging the IKEA brand name for years to come by actions that associated the brand with an image that runs contrary to what IKEA wanted. In the Australian case, stores are actually still operated by the original, outside IKEA group, franchisee and by IKEA group, making a unified position on the Australian market difficult to achieve.

The main reasons for spreading globally, the more controlled globalization of Phases 3 and 4, are in IKEA's case several, ranging for the conventional ones to the more subjective and, from a company perspective, irrational. One major reason cited in interviews with senior managers is risk reduction.

> Part of why IKEA has spread internationally and indeed globally is due to reducing business risk. IKEA is still, but has been even more in the past, dependent on Europe, the cyclical business situation and business conditions there. It would not be professional as a senior manager at a company with IKEA's ambition to not want to spread the risk and get a few more 'legs' in the business.
>
> (From interview with a former senior manager at IKEA group)

Table 7.2 The phases of IKEA internationalization

Dimension of activity	Phase 1	Phase 2	Phase 3	Phase 4
Style	Initial phases very much driven by founder Ingvar Kamprad and individuals close to him	Indeed opportunistic as globalization starts early through opportunities	More strategic but opportunism still evident in some cases	Strategic. Strong top level commitment
Market selection	Countries closest to Sweden	Continued border hopping – including some long jumps	First real global move	Multi-continent. Focus on large markets
Key activity	Sourcing is the main concern in the early phases	Still very entrepreneurial driven, with focus on expansion	Continued learning by doing but increasing 'structured' entrepreneurship	Creating new markets. Building market share in key markets
Format transferred	Existing format	Existing format	Existing formats (with adaptions)	Existing formats (with adaptions). Emerging multi-channel very slow
Approach	Very much pioneering and entrepreneur driven	Still pioneering and bagging more countries. Learning as they go along	Increase number of markets, spread risk. Build scale in selected markets	Building scale in key markets, spread risk. Identify new key markets
Entry and growth modes	Direct investment through franchising	Franchising but both within IKEA group and outside	Franchising but both within IKEA group and outside (key markets inside IKEA group). Increasing embeddedness	Franchising but both within IKEA group and outside (key markets inside IKEA group). Increasing embeddedness
Role in firm	Marginal but soon increasing	Increasing focus on internationalization but self-financed making growth harder	Increasing focus on internationalization requires more back-office knowledge and know-how	International is core part of firm
Impact on firm	Internationalization was an early option as growth was part of the aim	Increasingly strategic and long term	Increasingly strategic and long term	Strategic and long-term
Buying and sourcing	International sourcing was early part of the plan due to domestic conditions	Existing sources of supply	Inter-continent move necessitates change of supply chain towards local and regional sourcing	Global supply chains to support global sales presence

Being very dependent on Europe means a risk in the case of a regional economic downturn. Having a second leg in terms of a large continent like the US or a large market like China or Japan, is understandable from a risk reduction perspective. The logic of this approach is evident currently (2012) with the economy in USA and Europe in recession but with Asia still showing good rates of growth.

There is of course also present the perspective of market opportunity and it is true for both the USA and for China and Japan (*Business Week* 2005, 2006; ECCH 2006a–f, 2007; Lewis 2005; *The China Business Review* 2004; *Guardian* 2004). The USA, by far still the largest market in the world, with a growing home furnishing market where Scandinavian products have a good standing, is of course tempting. As for China, in 1998 IKEA was the first big box retailer to enter, giving it access to a market of more than one billion people. While nobody can argue the market size of China, in 1998 it was still very undeveloped in terms of Western retail and in many respects a daring move to move into China. One major challenge for IKEA when opening the first store in Shanghai was how to set prices:

> When we had decided to enter China, I went there several times in the build up. I also went there quite close to the opening of the first store with the mission of trying to get some grasp on what price level we were going to use in China. But that was not an easy task as there was – you have to remember that this was in 1998 when the market looked very much different from the way it looks today – nothing to compare with. And then I mean there were no other big-box retailers present that could give us a hint as to what price level would be suitable. All the competition was local and could not be used – at least that is what I thought – as guidance for what prices to set. So we ended up setting prices based on what we thought would be right. And of course, we put exactly the wrong prices on everything as we came from markets where the living standard was so much higher and it is very easy to find price references.
>
> (From interview with former senior manager at IKEA group)

What became a trick question in the China market seems almost trivial: what should the prices of different items be? Answering this is not easy in a country with a low but growing disposable income and no retailers with which to compare. All existing retailers in the broad sector were Chinese and operating totally different, more traditional concepts of tailor-made furniture. Eventually prices where set guessing what would be a reasonable price-level. These turned out to be too high, leaving the store with a lot of non-buying customers for the first period of time. In a new opening market like China there is also, alongside the pricing conundrum, the challenge that IKEA, due to its unusual concept, often has of teaching consumers what retailing Western style is about. The IKEA way with providing show rooms on the top floor and market hall, where you collect the products you want, on the lower floor was very different from existing practices in the country.

In many ways the China entry is the 'last' of IKEA's old-style entry into new markets. By that is meant entry without very much analysis and with a low level of knowledge management that you can expect from an experienced and successful retailer like IKEA (Jonsson 2008). Until after China, and very clearly when re-entering Japan, entry decisions and entry plans were not built on extensive planning and analysis. Rather it seemed to be done in the true entrepreneurial spirit that has built IKEA. Let us do something (rather than not do something) and then learn from that. It is also in the spirit of the founder Ingvar Kamprad that acting is better than sitting around waiting (Kamprad 2007). The entry into Japan is in stark contrast to this. In its four-year build up to entry, IKEA interviewed thousands of Japanese customers about the home and how they viewed the home. Furthermore, an important IKEA management principle was ignored, namely that you pick experienced IKEA managers for top positions around the world. The person chosen for the position was someone totally new to the IKEA world but someone who had a lot of experience in working in Japan and helping foreign companies enter Japan.

In the case of the entry into Japan, other adaptions never heard of in the IKEA world were made. The YPP-programme is an example. The Young Professional Programme was launched and used as a recruitment platform twice in preparation for Japan. In the first programme 50 people were involved and there were 35 in the second programme. In YPP, people in Sweden speaking Japanese and/or people particularly familiar with Japanese culture where recruited, sent to work in the IKEA world for a period of time to learn IKEA culture, and then sent to Japan to manage the work of setting up and opening stores in Japan, in 2006.

In the case of the entry into the US market, interviews with senior IKEA managers that were directly involved when the decision to enter the US was made, and also present in the subsequent launch, explained how the reasons for the US entry and the process of entry were not those as advocated in text books on internationalization. While such views are difficult to validate, as is inevitable with interviews related to post hoc events, these views appeared in interviews several times. Again, the US market is the biggest consumer market in the world, a market that, at least until recently, has set the pace and the launched trends for other markets in the world.

> If you want respect (from other business people) you have to be active on the US market. It may seem silly but that is the case. You are not anyone and have not achieved anything until you put your foot – or in this case our stores – in the US market. This explanation is not found in any textbooks but it is rational from a different perspective (my status as a senior manager) than the company rational.
>
> (From interview with former senior manager at IKEA group)

To be active in the USA market thus carries in itself a lot of status – this is the market that really makes or breaks a concept. It is not just any market, it is *the* market and if you are not active there and not successful there, all the other markets and efforts do not count when you measure the status of the senior management team of a company. In IKEA's case this could also explain why the entry into the USA, and even the years after entry, was such a mess and littered with mistakes that could be seen as beginners' mistakes. Examples include: offering beds and kitchen cabinets which did not fit US sheets and electrical appliances; beds measured in centimetres not described as king, queen and twin; sofas too firm and too small for American preferences; product dimensions displayed in centimetres not inches; and kitchenware too small for American preferences etc. The mistakes were many and varied but corrections were made and processes and products were eventually adjusted.

It can be argued that the entrepreneurial style of early IKEA is still present and important for the international expansion. The company culture of IKEA is well documented and dominated by a preference for simplicity and doing rather than complexity and analysis (see, for example, Salzinger 1998; Edvardsson and Enquist 2002, 2011; Edvardsson *et al.* 2006). While it still may be important internally in IKEA, it is no longer a small international retailer but a business with more than 150,000 employees, with annual sales of over €20 billion. Thus, some of the entrepreneurial spirit has certainly had to make way for other, more managerially oriented, ways of doing business. Indications are that re-entry into Japan, preparations starting 2002, was the real start of a change of approach. Hence, the processes linked to market selection and building scale become more and more important. This was clear with the entry into China and Japan, with subsequent growth in these markets making Asia an important hub in the IKEA world. Also, for a niche concept such as IKEA's the international, and indeed global, aspects of the business came naturally very early. This was also driven by the supply situation in Sweden in the early years where international relations and growth become important well before stores were opened in foreign markets.

IKEA is a retail company that through the years, and even in its current phase of internationalization, has kept to a single format strategy. This needs some explanation as some might argue that IKEA uses different store formats. The typical IKEA store is a big blue–yellow, being the colours of the Swedish flag, box, located in the outskirts of a city and/or in a retail park/shopping centre setting. Normally consumers need cars to go to the store and to bring home items from the store, hence the big car park that many IKEA stores have in front of the store. On entering the store you have the IKEA typical room settings on the second (top) floor and market place area, with smaller home furnishings, with the storage space for products in flat packages to be picked up by customers on the ground (first) floor. That is the basic and the generic IKEA store. There are, however, variations to this theme. One variation present for most of IKEA's latter expansion from the 1990s onward, is variation in store sizes. The stores have been built of varying size according to the proportion of the assortment they carry. Stores have been characterized as small, medium and large stores. The difference between them is roughly 2,000 items, with the large category carrying around 9,000 of the 10,000 items in the IKEA assortment. Here the main difference has been the size of the assortment the different stores carry, nothing else differs in the format. Moreover, these differences will disappear, if current strategies persist, as the ambition for the future is to build only the large type of store and hence removing this variation amongst stores.

In China and the UK where building and planning laws have been very restrictive, IKEA has adapted in some cases by changing the structure of the store. In the existing Shanghai stores, the parking space is under the store and hence the second floor is market place and the third is room settings and heavier furniture. This type of store layout is also seen in other places in the world, for example in the UK and in Sweden. However, the format is in other respects unchanged and the same around the world. The space needed for the two-floor layout compared to that for the three-floor layout is exactly the same, while the latter fits better with planning restrictions in some countries.

There is limited adaption in the store to local conditions. These do not concern the different products as these are the same around world, being based on the 10,000 articles in the assortment. The adaption concerns the first five rooms on the second floor where the rooms are supposed to be of the size and layout that dominates the local national market. For example, in Japan it is often 75 m² flats with an earthquake beam going through the apartment. This is the design of millions of flats in urban areas in Japan. The challenge here then becomes one of furnishing this typical Japanese apartment with IKEA furniture, to show local customers that IKEA also has furnishing items that fit your specific conditions and tastes.

Moving beyond space and assortment, service levels differ somewhat across markets. Moving into service-oriented Asia where the DIY concept is quite alien to consumer culture, was as a surprise to IKEA. This is especially true in China where, it was pointed out repeatedly in interviews, screwdrivers are a foreign concept and the DIY culture is at a very early stage. In order to sell products in this consumer culture, the service concept of IKEA had to be developed. Services such as home delivery and assembly were added for an additional price. Later these services spread to other IKEA markets around the world.

Globalization of both store operations and sourcing is increasing in IKEA but Europe still dominates in both areas. The sourcing part of the business is still based in Europe to a large extent This is changing as China continues to grow and has become the single biggest sourcing country accounting for over 20 per cent of total sourcing in IKEA. While trading offices were opened in Asia quite early in the 1970s sourcing grew quite slowly here with only a share of 5 per cent in 1986, growing to 19 per cent in 1996 (Hultman and Hertz 2011). In North America, sourcing increased during the 1990s with only 1 per cent sourcing here prior to that. Volumes sourced in North America have since increased and a trading office opened in Mexico 2001 (Hultman and Hertz 2011). Concentration of sourcing in Europe has historical reasons but it has often been considered a major asset as the focus on one region creates a knowledge base as well as a concentration of efforts and from that emerges financial as well as other benefits.

The major challenge is to re-align the supply chain and sourcing to fit with an increasingly global strategy. This has for example been the case in the US, in China and, to a lesser extent in Japan. In all these cases, the IKEA supply chain has had to change as a result of expansion.

When Ingvar Kamprad started the IKEA business and it grew, the Swedish furniture manufacturing sector rejected him and his business, refusing to sell its products through IKEA. Hence, IKEA could not source its products in Sweden (Hultman *et al.* 2012), prompting Ingvar Kamprad to look for other sourcing options. He went abroad and found sources in Poland, among other countries, and thus started what has become one of the main streams of sourcing to this day in IKEA, i.e. sourcing in former Eastern and Central Europe. Since then this part of the supply chain has been developed and extended but the development of this stream of sourcing has been crucial for building IKEA into the retail company it is today. The move to the US challenged the supply chain and sourcing also prompting a major development on the supply side for the North American market. The same was the case for China, and later Japan, but for different reasons. The high price level of IKEA hampered the China entry; prices are low from a European perspective but not an Asian perspective. China was a virgin supply market at the time of the entry. The use of Chinese sources increased with around 60–70 per cent of what is sold in Chinese stores sourced in China. This made it possible to lower prices in China to the lowest in the IKEA world. Also, increased sourcing in China overall has meant the possibility for low-price sourcing for the entire IKEA world of stores. The increased sourcing globally from markets where IKEA operate stores, Russia, China and the USA particularly, has increased the firms' embeddedness in the markets where it operates.

Conclusions

From a local mail order firm, started by entrepreneur Ingvar Kamprad, IKEA has turned into a global niche retailer operating in more than 30 countries across four continents, mastering different consumer and business traditions. While starting as a local retail business, international expansion was an early part of IKEA's operations. This was, at least initially, driven by the problems Ingvar Kamprad and IKEA had sourcing products for its stores from Swedish furniture manufacturers. That drove IKEA abroad for sourcing, something that was followed in the 1970s with the stores.

The entrepreneurial nature is also seen throughout the history of IKEA in the early international moves in the 1970s and 1980s. These seemed to be driven, according to interviews made with senior managers at IKEA, by entrepreneurial spirit and individual motives rather than managerial consideration and analysis. However, by the 2000s, IKEA has become more textbook-like in its preparation and management of knowledge in the organization. There is more strategy and more of a plan to the international moves than before, marking clearly a move to a fourth phase in the IKEA internationalization.

Being a niche retailer with a very marked business model around DIY, flat packaging and supplier selection, IKEA has to a certain degree been able to maintain its standardized business model around the world. But, there is adaption (Burt *et al.* 2007, 2011a, 2011b) and that seems to be increasing as IKEA turned to Asia for growth. One of the key features for IKEA has been its ability to make changes without changing the business model, for example in the increasing service focus, starting in Asia. This adaption has proved a challenge but as it does not change the overall business model, this adaption creates embeddedness without endangering the business model.

In their development internationally IKEA has been and still is a one-format retailer. Some argue that not changing the format has been one of the major ingredients in IKEA's success. Through the years it has varied its size of store, with a preference for increased size to make way for holding as much as possible of the total assortment, and one can only speculate as to whether or not IKEA will be a single format retailer in the future. When entering China, the first Shanghai store was deliberately located close to subway and bus lines to make up for low levels of car ownership, at that time. But that is, in general, as far as adaptions in terms of location has gone. IKEA has not so far shown very much interest in e-tailing, as the brick-and-mortar store is a big part of the success story. While e-tailing may not be another format in the traditional sense, increasingly IKEA is pressured by the increasing trend of consumers wishing to buy on the internet.

References

Aitken, L. (2004) The world: Ikea: chucking out the chintz around the world. *Brand Republic*, 10 December, 9–12.

Bjarnestam, E. A. (2009) IKEA Design och Identitet. Malmö: Bokförlaget Arena.

Björk, S. (1998) IKEA entreprenören, affärsidén, kulturen. Stockholm: Svenska Förlaget.

Bruzelius, L. and Skärvad, P. H. (2012) *Management*. Lund: Studentlitteratur.

Burt, S., Johansson, U. and Thelander, Å. (2007) Retail image as seen through consumers' eyes: studying international retail image through consumer photographs of stores. *International Review of Retail, Distribution and Consumer Research*, 17(5), 447–467.

Burt, S., Johansson, U. and Thelander, Å. (eds) (2011a) *Consuming IKEA: different perspectives on consumer images of a global retailer.* Lund: Lund University Press.

Burt, S., Johansson, U. and Thelander, Å. (2011b) International retail image: a comparative study in three countries. *Journal of Retailing and Consumer Services*, 18(3), 183–193.

Business Week (2005) 14 November.

Business Week (2006) 26 April.

Dahlvig, A. (2010) *The IKEA edge: building global growth and social good at the world's most iconic home store.* New York: McGraw Hill.

ECCH (2006a) *Case 306-164-1 IKEA in 2005: Evolution of global marketing strategy.* Available at: www.ecch.com/educators/products/view?id=67993.

ECCH (2006b) *Case 306-189-1 IKEA's Globalisation strategies and its foray into China.* Available at: www.ecch.com/educators/products/view?id=68076.

ECCH (2006c) *Case 306-270-1 IKEA in China: competing through low cost strategies.* Available at: www.ecch.com/educators/products/view?id=68568.

ECCH (2006d) *Case 306-569-1 IKEA: re-entering the land of rising sun.* Available at: www.ecch.com/educators/products/view?id=70200.

ECCH (2006e) *Case 506-045-1 IKEA's global marketing strategy.* Available at: www.ecch.com/educators/products/view?id=68070.

ECCH (2006f) *Case 506-120-1 IKEA: the furniture giant reawakens in Funabashi.* Available at: www.ecch.com/educators/products/view?id=69156.

ECCH (2007) *Case 306-377-8 IKEA in Japan: the market re-entry strategies.* Available at: www.ecch.com/educators/products/view?id=69145.

Edvardsson, B. and Enquist, E. (2002) The IKEA saga: How service culture drives service strategy. *Service Industries Journal*, 22(4), 153–186.

Edvardsson, B. and Enquist, E. (2011) The service excellence and innovation model: lessons from IKEA and other service frontiers. *Total Quality Management*, 22(5), 535–551.

Edvardsson, B., Enquist, E. and Hay, M. (2006) Values-based service brands: narratives from IKEA. *Managing Service Quality*, 16(3), 230–246.

Guardian (2004) 17 June.

Hultman, J. and Hertz, S. (2011) Exploring the dynamics of global sourcing development over time: the case of IKEA. *International Journal of Integrated Supply Management*, 6(2), 109–126.

Hultman, J., Johnsen, T., Johnsen, R. and Hertz, S. (2012) An interaction approach to global sourcing: s case study of IKEA. *Journal of Purchasing and Supply Management*, 18(1), 9–21.

IKEA (2013) corporate webpage: www.ikea-group.ikea.com/2013-01-12.

Johansson, U. and Thelander, Å. (2009) A standardised approach to the world? IKEA in China. *International Journal of Quality and Service Science*, 1(2): 199–219.

Jonsson, A. (2008) Knowledge sharing across borders: a study in the IKEA world. University of Lund doctoral dissertation, Lund University Press.

Kamprad, I. (2007) The testament of a furniture dealer. A little IKEA® dictionary. Inter IKEA Systems B.V.

Lewis, E. (2005) *Great IKEA! A brand for all the people.* London: Cyan Books.

Porter, M. (1996) What is strategy? *Harvard Business Review*, 74, (November–December), 61–78.

Salzinger, M, (1998), *Identity across borders: a study in the 'IKEA-World'*, Linkoping Studies in Management and Economics, Dissertations No 27, Linkoping University.

The China Business Review (2004) IKEA with Chinese characteristics. July–August, 36–38.

Torekull, B. (1998) *Historien om IKEA.* Stockholm: Wahlstrom and Widstrand (reprinted in English: (1999) *Leading by design: the IKEA story*. New York: Harper Business).

8 MUJI

The evolution of a local private label to a global retailer

Tatsuro Toba

The issue of 'standardization' and 'adaption' has been at the centre of a long-standing controversy in the research of international marketing. This dichotomy has been applied in the research of international retailing. In standardization, retailers replicate their operations on a world scale making only modest adaptions to the local market. On the other hand, retailers that make substantial adaption embrace local needs and pursue distinct operations in each of their different markets.

In the literature on international retailing, several types of strategy have been proposed in the conceptual ground that exists between 'standardization' and 'adaption' (Salmon and Tordjman 1989; Treadgold 1990/1991; Helfferich *et al.* 1997; Alexander and Myers 2000). For example, Salmon and Tordjman (1989) extracted two types of fundamental strategies. The first one was called 'Global Strategy' in which retailers try to replicate a retail concept faithfully in international markets. The other one was called 'Multinational Strategy'. In this type, retailers adapt their original format to fit local market conditions while keeping its basic concept. However many studies lack a clear understanding of what global standardization and local adaption might mean in a retail perspective (Burt *et al.* 2011).

It was believed that a retailer with a unique offering could operate in a niche market on a world scale and expand by replicating in standardized manner (Salmon and Tordjman 1989; Treadgold 1990/1991). Actually, it was observed that most global retailers, especially small- and medium-sized retailers, offer unique products that are tailored to specific consumers who appreciate a particular value or lifestyle (Simpson and Thorpe 1995, 1999). In many cases, standardization has been considered to be an easier approach than adaption. Even if operating in a standardized manner, however, retailers are placed in different surroundings or social contexts. That is, retailers could not expect the same performance from its international business as in its domestic market. Even if a retailer replicates its operation faithfully in foreign markets, the evaluation for it varies according to the retail environments of each country formed by the diverse factors like consumer preference and retail competition. There is relatively little literature on the standardization approach to international retail strategy with the notable exceptions of Burt and Carralero-Encinas (2000) and Burt and Mavrommatis (2006).

This chapter considers standardization behaviour through the case study of MUJI. This Japanese retailer has built considerable brand awareness in the global market despite its modest size. The sales in 2010 fiscal year ranked at sixty-eighth place in the Japanese retail market (Nikkei Inc. 2011, p. 72). MUJI was a relatively small retailer at the time of its initial international venture, but has succeeded in growing incrementally on a world scale. Some studies have identified strong concepts, formats and products as the main driving forces of smaller retailers that make successful international expansion (Hutchinson *et al.* 2005, 2007; Hutchinson and Quinn 2011) and these are relevant for a study of MUJI.

The internationalization of retailing has been considered as a continuous process (Whitehead 1992; Dawson 1994; Vida and Fairhurst 1998; Alexander and Myers 2000; Dawson and Mukoyama 2006; Jonsson 2010). Retailers have opportunities to learn in the process of extending their operations to foreign markets (Palmer and Quinn 2005; Palmer 2006). In this case study, we focus on some important experiences including positive and negative ones as crucial events and examples of continuous learning which have promoted subsequent international expansion. The historical development of MUJI is considered by a case-study approach based on company publications including annual reports, an archive of news release, annual securities reports and the company history books. In addition, use is made of secondary materials such as Japanese newspapers and commercial journals, whose coverage is rich in description and executive interview.

Historical background

Ryohin Keikaku is a Japanese global retailer that at the end of 2012 operates 535 stores in 21 countries including Japan, selling a range of 7,413 products and employing 5,197 people. Nearly one-third of its total stores are operated outside Japan (Ryohin Keikaku 2012). MUJI is an abbreviation of Mujirushi Ryohin, which in Japanese means a non-branded product with high quality. This brand is known as 'MUJI' in foreign countries outside Japan. MUJI was born as a private label of the Japanese General Merchandise Store (GMS), Seiyu, in 1980 and started with 40 product items.

Following the oil shocks in the 1970s, Japanese consumers were beginning to voice their concerns about sustainability. In those days, GMS chains made remarkable progress and took leading positions in in the Japanese retail market. This retail format comprises many categories of food, household goods and apparel with low to congruent pricing and operating by self-service. In the accelerating intra-type competition among GMS chains at that time, they started to develop private labels to differentiate their offerings while coping with the vertical pressure for the control of retail prices by manufacturers of national brands. After Daiei, the largest GMS at that time, started to carry a private label home electric appliances under the name of BUBU as the pioneer in early 1970s, other leading GMS chains including JUSCO (later renamed AEON) and Seiyu followed the movement.

Seiyu opened the first stand-alone MUJI store in the Aoyama district of Tokyo in 1983. This district had a concentration of designers so there was an atmosphere of creativity and emergent ideas. In addition, Aoyama was one of the most popular shopping areas with many fashionable boutiques. MUJI tried to incorporate the image of the culturally sophisticated location into its store design. MUJI positioned the first store not only as an antenna shop for customers, but also a showroom for buyers at the same time, and actually succeeded in attracting enormous attention and media coverage (Mujirushi Ryohin White Paper Project Team 1986: 61–62, 176; Yui 1991: 167–168).

At that time, Seiyu used to be a member of the Saison Group which was a large conglomerate with interests in retail, food, finance, real estate, entertainment and other areas. The Saison Group's major retail investments included Seibu department store and Seiyu. MUJI took advantage of the link created by the Saison Group, and expanded its store network rapidly by opening its shop-in-shop formula in Seibu department store and Seiyu (see Table 8.1).

During the period of the asset-inflated economy in the late 1980s in Japan, designer brands were flaunted as badges of good taste. However, Japanese consumers in the recessionary period in 1990s put priority on function rather than to appearances. They began to pursue a more frugal lifestyle and were more aware of the trade-off between quality and price. Many consumers came to select products that were suited to their own individual needs and lifestyles.

MUJI was operated by Seiyu for about a decade following its birth. After achieving great success in this period, MUJI was spun off from Seiyu and established Ryohin Keikaku as the operational base in 1989. Furthermore, Ryohin Keikaku (hereinafter referred to as MUJI) gained independence from the parent company, Seiyu, in the following year. This transition means an evolution of a store brand into a corporate brand. Six years later, in 1995, the stock of the company was placed on the over-the counter-market. Then in 1998, the stocks were listed on the Tokyo Stock Exchange Second Section. Through these steps, MUJI built the foundation for independent growth. MUJI carries more than 7,000 products in categories supporting the core areas of daily life including clothing, household goods and food. The wide assortment of inexpensive and minimalist products includes stationery, cosmetics, kitchen equipment, clothing and furniture. The number of products has grown by 18 times over the past three decades (see Figure 8.1). This enormous increase has reflected its strategy of presenting a total life style toward consumers.

Uniqueness as a brand

When MUJI was created as a private label, luxury brands from Western countries were gaining popularity within an economic bubble in Japan's economy. When flashy and expensive brands were all the rage, the newcomer's clothing and household products were free of labels and moderately priced. This fresh approach turned MUJI into something of a legend in Japanese retailing.

Table 8.1 Number of MUJI stores in the Japanese market

Type/year	1991	1992	1993	1994	1995	1996	1997	1998	1999	2000	2001	2002	2003	2004	2005	2006	2007	2008	2009	2010	2011
DM[1]	35	43	48	47	45	47	59	70	83	110	105	100	123	141	153	172	181	197	212	238	256
LS[2]	34	37	40	46	53	59	66	65	68	69	72	65	63	65	67	68	68	72	70	64	60
Seibu	38	34	29	28	28	27	26	23	22	18	18	20	0	0	0	0	0	0	0	0	0
Seiyu	95	95	94	97	96	95	93	93	78	80	79	80	80	79	78	78	79	75	57	57	56
Total	202	209	211	218	222	228	244	251	251	277	274	265	266	285	298	318	328	344	339	359	372

Source: Ryohin Keikaku, Business Review and Mukoyama (1996), Table 5–6, p. 151

Notes
1 DM are directly managed stores.
2 LS are licensed stores.

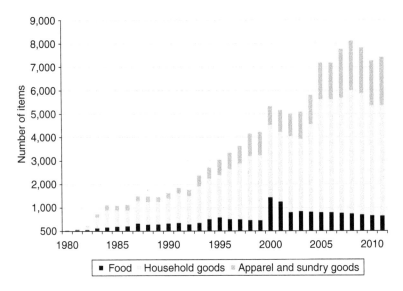

Figure 8.1 Number of product items carried by MUJI (source: Ryohin Keikaku: http://
ryohin-keikaku.jp/corporate/history).

The concept of MUJI is not to be a distinctive brand, but to be a no-brand
brand or anti-brand brand. It pursues simplicity, nature, moderation, humanity
and self-restraint, and does not communicate like any other brands. This attitude
to eliminate self-assertion generated its uniqueness. MUJI appeals to simplicity
and functionality in the products. This brand was introduced with the aim of providing the best value for consumers while maintaining higher quality. The
natural and simple design proposes rational lifestyles for today's world. In
modern society, consumers have been confused by the active promotion undertaken by abundant brands. Consumers are overloaded with self-assertive mes-
sages from those brands. While most brands communicate through a loud-hailer,
MUJI whispers its message to consumers.

The basic concept of MUJI is to provide simply designed products that people
need in their daily lives. To realize this, materials are carefully selected, the production process is arranged, and packaging is reduced. MUJI products have a
limited colour range, and are displayed with minimal packaging on shelves. Its
concept resulted in simple and beautiful products which meet the requirements
of the present day.

Product development and sourcing

The products of MUJI are characterized by functional and simple designs. The
unique brand has been developed by a unique production policy. Its uniqueness
is present in the attitude of seeking simplicity and functionality in product

development. MUJI is a retailer with vertical control over the suppliers. That is, this retailer has the functions of planning, development, production, distribution and sale of the products. The company's basic principle is to develop novel and simple products at reasonable prices by making the best use of materials while being environmentally conscious.

There are several reasons why this retailer can provide such good quality products at reasonable prices. MUJI established a slogan that says 'Lower Priced for a Reason', and continues to use it. Through the careful selection of materials, streamlining the manufacturing processes, and simplifying packaging, MUJI has successfully provided high quality products at reasonable prices. The secret of its success can be summarized in the following three points.

First, MUJI has made a point of using industrial materials and materials not commonly used by other companies because of their plain or simple appearance. These materials are available at low cost and in bulk. Using these materials keeps prices low, but it also enables the creation of distinctive and simple designs. Second, MUJI utilizes efficient production processes by paying close attention to its manufacturing process, and continues to closely monitor the production process. In this respect, some processes that have no negative influences on the product's quality, such as sizing and polishing, have been eliminated. Third, MUJI keeps packaging to a bare minimum to seek the natural qualities and minimize cost and waste. When packaging its products, MUJI tries to highlight their natural colours and shapes without much decoration. For this reason, all products appear in simple packaging with minimum information and a price tag.

MUJI has sourced practical and suitable materials internationally since the early 1980s, and began to shift its production base overseas in 1986 (*The Nihon Keizai Shimbun* 6 September 1984; *The Nikkei Marketing Journal* 31 July 1986). The procurement on a global scale was consistent with its goal of cost reduction and making quality products. These efforts have underpinned its ability to create low priced and high quality products. Currently, MUJI procures about 75 per cent of the products from foreign suppliers (*The Nikkei Marketing Journal* 5 June 2006).

International expansion

MUJI has two decades experience in its international business, and currently operates 134 stores in 21 foreign countries in Europe, Asia, and North America (see Table 8.2). There are few Japanese retailers with as wide an international expansion as MUJI. Its overseas business has grown incrementally, and accounted for 17.2 per cent of net sales, 15.8 per cent of operating profit and 23.2 per cent of net profit respectively in 2011 (see Table 8.3).

MUJI could be categorized as a type of speciality store format in that it provides a single private label with a specific concept (Mukoyama 1996, pp. 137–138). Since the brand concept has universal appeal, MUJI has responded to these universal needs in a standardized manner. Its offerings, which are represented by store design, layout, ambience, assortment and customer service,

Table 8.2 Number of MUJI stores in foreign markets

Region/country	1991	1992	1993	1994	1995	1996	1997	1998	1999	2000	2001	2002	2003	2004	2005	2006	2007	2008	2009	2010	2011
Europe																					
UK	1	3	3	4	3	4	5	9	13	15	16	16	17	15	16	17	16	14	14	13	13
France	–	–	–	–	–	–	–	1	4	7	4	4	4	5	7	8	7	7	8	7	8
Belgium	–	–	–	–	–	–	–	–	–	(1)[1]	–	–	–	–	–	–	–	–	–	–	–
Ireland	–	–	–	–	–	–	–	–	–	–	–	–	–	(1)	(1)	(1)	(1)	(1)	(1)	(1)	(1)
Italy	–	–	–	–	–	–	–	–	–	–	–	(1)	–	1	2	3	3	5	5	6	6
Sweden	–	–	–	–	–	–	–	–	–	–	–	–	–	(3)	(5)	(6)	(6)	(7)	(6)	(7)	(7)
Germany	–	–	–	–	–	–	–	–	–	–	–	–	–	–	1	2	2	3	4	5	5
Norway	–	–	–	–	–	–	–	–	–	–	–	–	–	–	(2)	(4)	(6)	(8)	(7)	(6)	(5)
Spain	–	–	–	–	–	–	–	–	–	–	–	–	–	–	–	(2)	(3)	(4)	(4)	(4)	(5)
Turkey	–	–	–	–	–	–	–	–	–	–	–	–	–	–	–	–	–	(1)	(2)	(2)	(2)
Poland	–	–	–	–	–	–	–	–	–	–	–	–	–	–	–	–	–	–	–	(1)	(1)
Portugal	–	–	–	–	–	–	–	–	–	–	–	–	–	–	–	–	–	–	–	(1)	(1)
Subtotal	1	3	3	4	3	4	5	10	17	23	20	21	21	25	34	43	44	50	51	53	54
Asia																					
Hong Kong	1	2	4	8	8	6	4	–	–	–	2	3	3	4	5	6	6	8	9	9	10
Singapore	–	–	–	–	3	3	3	–	–	–	–	2	2	2	2	3	3	3	4	4	4
Taiwan	–	–	–	–	–	–	–	–	–	–	–	–	–	(4)	(6)	(9)	(11)	(14)	(17)	(19)	(23)

	1	2	3	4	5	6	7	8	9	10	11	12	13	14	15	16	17	18	19	20	21
Korea	–	–	–	–	–	–	–	–	–	–	–	–	(1)	(1)	3	5	6	8	9	8	11
China	–	–	–	–	–	–	–	–	–	–	–	–	–	–	1	1	1	5	13	26	38
Thailand	–	–	–	–	–	–	–	–	–	–	–	–	–	–	–	(2)	(4)	(6)	(7)	(8)	(10)
Indonesia	–	–	–	–	–	–	–	–	–	–	–	–	–	–	–	–	–	–	(1)	(1)	(5)
Philippines	–	–	–	–	–	–	–	–	–	–	–	–	–	–	–	–	–	–	–	(2)	(4)
Subtotal	1	2	4	8	11	9	7	0	0	0	2	3	6	11	17	26	31	44	60	77	105
America																					
USA	0	–	–	–	–	–	–	–	–	–	–	–	–	–	–	1	1	4	4	4	4
Subtotal	0	0	0	0	0	0	0	0	0	0	0	0	0	0	0	1	1	4	4	4	4
Total																					
DS[2]	2	5	7	12	14	13	12	10	17	22	22	23	26	28	37	45	45	57	70	82	99
LS[3]	0	0	0	0	0	0	0	0	0	(1)	0	(1)	(1)	(9)	(14)	(24)	(31)	(41)	(45)	(52)	(64)
TS[4]	2	5	7	12	14	13	12	10	17	23	22	24	27	36	51	69	76	98	115	134	163

Sources: Ryohin Keikaku (1996–2012); Annual Securities Report 1995–2011.

Notes

1 Numbers in parentheses are licensed stores.
2 DS are directly managed stores.
3 LS are licensed stores.
4 TS are total stores.

Table 8.3 Performance of international department of MUJI (million Yen)

Performance measures		2002	2003	2004	2005	2006	2007	2008	2009	2010	2011
Total	Net sales	114,324	119,189	127,836	140,185	156,204	162,060	162,814	163,733	169,137	177,532
	Operating profit	6,750	8,790	11,478	15,234	16,582	18,579	17,223	14,134	13,900	15,438
	Net profit	2,350	4,695	6,347	9,344	9,313	10,689	6,936	7,506	7,859	8,850
International	Net sales	7,085	7,600	9,652	12,866	16,817	19,332	16,908	21,226	24,297	30,499
	Operating profit	204	395	693	541	700	1,573	1,172	1,172	1,826	2,442
	Net profit	159	335	597	423	606	925	572	343	1,234	2,057
Ratio of	Net sales	6.2	6.4	7.6	9.2	10.8	11.9	10.4	12.9	14.4	17.2
International	Operating profit	3.0	4.5	6.0	3.6	4.2	8.5	6.8	8.2	13.1	15.8
	Net profit	6.8	7.1	9.4	4.5	6.5	8.7	8.2	4.5	15.7	23.2

Source: Ryohin Keikaku (2005–2008, 2009–2012).

are almost totally standardized in every market. If we apply the classification of strategies for cross-border expansion by Salmon and Tordjman (1989), the approach taken by MUJI could be categorized as a 'Global Strategy'.

Motives for international expansion

International expansion of MUJI began in the two years after its founding. There were some important factors that motivated MUJI to undertake international expansion. First, MUJI had to expand its sales channels. While increasing the number of product items, MUJI needed to secure a certain size of production order to maintain the profitability of the each product. As a countermeasure for this challenge, MUJI decided to make inroads into foreign countries in pursuit of sales opportunities and enable these scale economies to be effective. Second, MUJI conducted its sourcing through the 'develop-and-import scheme' (*kaihatsu yunyu*). In this scheme, MUJI consigns the production to its affiliated factories in foreign countries, but does not allocate all of it to them. MUJI has become closely involved in the production process, and sources materials from around the world. In this process, MUJI became aware of the possibility of marketing activities in overseas markets. Third, MUJI had inquiries for supplying products from many foreign buyers who visited Japan since shortly after its debut. Such inquiries brought about the positive attitude toward its international business (Mukoyama 1996: 149–152; Ryutukigyou Kenkyukai 1996: 167–168).

Initial experience in foreign markets

The initial international expansion was made when it was still one of the private labels of Seiyu. MUJI opened shop-in-shops in Daimaru, a Japanese department store, in Singapore in 1983, and opened a store in a shopping centre in Thailand in the following year. However, these stores were closed within a few years because of their poor sales. The actual international expansion started when MUJI made inroads into the UK in 1991 by establishing a joint venture with local department store, Liberty plc. The arrangement was made through the business relationship of the Saison Group with Liberty plc. MUJI also expanded into Hong Kong in the same year. MUJI established Mujirushi Ryohin Bermuda by setting up a joint venture with Wing On department stores in Bermuda, which is a British overseas territory, and placed its subsidiary in Hong Kong through this joint venture.

International joint venture is an attractive entry mode into unfamiliar foreign markets. It reduces the time, cost and business risk of entry by working with a local partner who is familiar with the market. This entry mode provides retailers with chances to access the resources of the partners, and creates opportunities to learn from them in the new market. Partners can provide helpful knowledge about local consumers or ways of doing business (Palmer 2006; Palmer and Owens 2006).

MUJI has been welcomed with open arms in European markets, especially in the UK since its initial international adventure. According to a survey conducted by MUJI in 1998, many customers in London reported impressions of 'modernity', 'creativity' and 'novelty' for MUJI (*Nikkei Business* 1999). As one of the main factors, there is the positive effect of being an 'Oriental or Japanese' brand in foreign markets. MUJI was featured as a brand that embodies the spirit of 'Zen' in European newspapers and magazines (*The Nikkei Marketing Journal*, 13 February 1999). 'Zen' is a Japanese form of Buddhism that emphasizes the importance of controlling or concentrating the mind, and pursues simplicity as one of own aesthetic principles. The bland concept of MUJI that emphasizes the intrinsic appeal of objects through rationalization and elimination is closely connected to the Japanese traditional aesthetic. The concept of 'quietness', 'emptiness' and 'intangibility' lies at the centre of Japanese culture as seen in the tea ceremony and flower arrangement. There is a traditional Japanese aesthetic that sees the utmost richness in what is extremely plain.

Retailers conduct their business by manipulating its creative retailing mix (Lazer and Kelley 1961: 37–39). Retailing mix is the composite of all efforts that embodies the adjustment of the retail store to its market environment. Although MUJI stores in foreign markets might have a slightly different assortment from those in the home market, the overall offering that is created by its retailing mix including basic assortment, price and store environment has kept uniformity in every market. Nevertheless, MUJI makes adaptive actions by adjusting its assortment from the wide product range for each market. Its brand identity has been preserved by exercising tight controls over basic merchandizing, distribution and pricing strategies. The products were designed and developed in Japan, and have been introduced to foreign markets without making adaptions. As one of few exceptions, MUJI adapted the size of clothing for the European market after a few years of experience (*The Nikkei Marketing Journal*, 15 May 2004).

Crucial events

Minor crucial events in foreign markets

There are issues of control and communication in international joint venture. Problems might arise simply from the slow or complex decision-making process that involves local and central organizations. Maintaining the sound relationships with partners can be time consuming. Conflicts may be generated frequently in the relationship with partners having incompatible goals, different opinions of the decision-making process, and different perceptions for the local market. It is not easy to share common vision and profit with the local partner (Owens and Quinn 2007).

First, MUJI suffered from a slow decision-making process in the joint venture with Liberty plc, which impeded the rapid progress of the business (*The Nikkei Marketing Journal*, 6 October 1998). In the end, MUJI was forced to dissolve the relationship (*The Nikkei Marketing Journal*, 3 April 1997). Since then, MUJI made it a rule to hold the majority share even when establishing international joint ventures for such reasons as regulations in host countries. Second, MUJI had shipped its products to the UK and Hong Kong from Japan during the early stages of international business. It was extremely inefficient for each supplier to deliver a variety of products with small quantities to stores in foreign countries. At the same time, such an approach gives rise to a troublesome procedure for foreign stores when they receive products from many suppliers (Mukoyama 1996: 160). As a result, the pricing for products sold in foreign markets has been much higher than the pricing in the Japanese market. In its initial store operations in London, the price of MUJI products was about 80 per cent higher than the price in Japan (*The Nikkei Marketing Journal* 28 January 1992). Thereafter, on average, 30 per cent or more has been added on the price to cover import costs for store operations in European countries (*The Nikkei Marketing Journal* 1 October 1992, 16 January 2001).

What is worse, MUJI had bitter experiences in Asian markets in the early stage of its internationalization process. This international expansion had considerable problems and was in deficit for several years. Its product designs were not accepted favourably in comparison with local flashier designs in Hong Kong and Singapore. MUJI evaluated that these markets were too immature to appreciate its own brand concept, and learned from the experience that a brand would not be evaluated in the same way in every market (*The Nihon Keizai Shimbun* 12 January 1999; *The Nikkei Marketing Journal* 13 February 1999). As a result, MUJI made a decision to dissolve the joint venture in 1998, eight years after its entry, and closed down all stores in both markets.

As indicated in other studies, slump in the home country often leads to a divestment decision of foreign markets (Alexander and Quinn 2002; Jackson *et al.* 2004; Jackson and Sparks 2005). There seems to be some relation between the decision to withdraw from Singapore and Hong Kong and crucial events described in the following sections.

Major crucial events in the home market

MUJI faced a sharp decline of business in the early 2000s (see Figure 8.2). This company had considerable growth in sales and profit every single year between its debut and fiscal 1999. After these record-breaking years, however, its sales and profit declined and a first-ever year-on-year drop in annual sales was reported in the 2000 fiscal year. Its consolidated operating profit fell 14 per cent in this year.

There were several causes for this slump. First, MUJI faced a problem in procurement. MUJI had tripled the number of product items since early 1990s (see Figure 8.1). This increase required MUJI to produce each item in quantities large enough to secure scale economies in procurement. However, the number of stores did not grow sufficiently to allow the required increases in procurement volumes. The products are deliberately designed to be not susceptible to fashion trends so products unsold in a season could be held and sold again in the following season. As a result, MUJI did not take the sourcing problem seriously for a

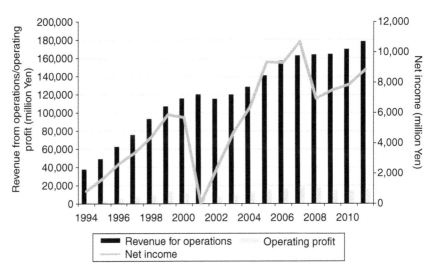

Figure 8.2 Financial performance of MUJI (source: Ryohin Keikaku 1996–2012; Annual Securities Report 1995–2011).

long time but the amount of unsold stock increased steadily. In consequence, MUJI had excess stock and tried to avoid creating a negative impression in the stock market by reporting a loss resulting from disposing of excess inventory at the same time. In reality the issue was not a problem with store inventory but with lack of sourcing scale. Second, MUJI faced growing competition with emerging speciality stores in the 1990s. Large-scale speciality stores in some categories became successful: in casual apparel (for example, UNIQLO and Shimamura), consumer electronics (for example, Yamada Denki and Kojima), furniture (for example, Nitori), and 100-yen sundries (for example, Daiso and CAN DO). MUJI lost sight of market trends and also failed to stay true to the original brand concept. That is, MUJI pursued greater sales volume by expanding the number of stores and product items, and also cut prices to avoid losing customers to these competitors. In this process, MUJI made a transition toward chasing trends, and started to lose its uniqueness as a brand (*The Nihon Keizai Shimbun* 29 March 2001).

Renovations as turning points

The bitter experience gave a wake-up call to MUJI. MUJI disposed of ¥3.8 billion worth of dead stock, and booked its extraordinary loss in 2001 and 2002 as the first step to recovery. Since then, MUJI has tried to survive the growing competition by improving the function and quality of the products. Figure 8.3 shows the GPS map of MUJI. As we can see in the map, MUJI had reached the position of 'Home Multi-Nations and Away Single-Nation' (HMN–ASN) in

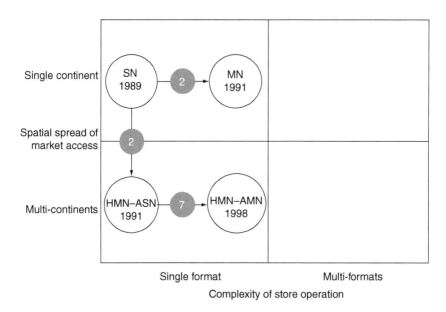

Figure 8.3 GPS map of MUJI.

only two years from its birth. However, its international expansion progress was slow. MUJI had spent no less than seven years to reach the position of 'Home Multi-Nations and Away Multi-Nations' (HMN–AMN).

Renovation of the organization

MUJI reconsidered its well-developed business formula and decided to bring in external knowledge for its organizational renovation. MUJI appointed two outside directors (*The Nikkei Sangyo Shimbun* 2002). One was Hidejiro Fuji-wara, president of Shimamura which is one of the Japanese leading apparel retailers, and the other was Shuji Abe, president of Yoshinoya which is the largest beef bowl restaurant chain in Japan. MUJI learned from them not only the importance of standardization in its business operations, but also the neces-sity of continual improvement. As a result of those efforts, MUJI has built a series of manuals, which are called 'MUJI GRAM', in order to achieve efficient and effective management through greater standardization. This manual covers every aspect from store operation to labour management (Ikeda 2008: 47–48; Metsugi 2008: 58).

In addition to overhauling its organization and operations, MUJI reviewed the strategy, and went back to the basics that originally attached greater importance to quality and simple design rather than price. MUJI undertook a transformation also in the product development process. First, MUJI abandoned the policy of having in-house designers for developing its products, and invited several high-profile Japanese designers to get help in creating a global brand. In addition, MUJI established a link with Japanese fashion company, Yohji Yamamoto Inc., which is headed by the famous fashion designer, as a part of its efforts to rejuvenate its clothing sales. Under this alliance, MUJI put its design section for clothes and accessories under the guidance of Yohji Yamamoto. MUJI reshuffled its design team, and started to work with managers dispatched from the partner. Under the managers' direction, the design team re-examined the materials being used, revamped its pattern-making methods, and came up with new products (*The Nikkei Marketing Journal* 8 May 2003). Second, the organizational structure was reformed to create a consistent brand identity. For example, the clothing and accessory division, which was previously divided into planning, production control and inventory control sections was arranged under the category manager system. In this new system, each manager for a product category was responsible for all aspects of operations from planning to inventory. MUJI tried to strengthen its brand management through such actions. By these changes greater control over the brand was established and the ratio of directly managed stores in both domestic and foreign markets was increased (see Figure 8.4). Third, MUJI established a holding company in London in 2007 to unify the financial functions for European subsidiaries in UK, France, Germany and Italy,

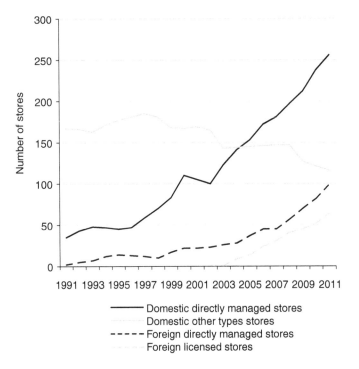

Figure 8.4 Types of store operation by MUJI (source: Ryohin Keikaku 1996–2012; Annual Securities Report 1995–2011).

and has entrusted to the holding company the management and promotion of the licensing activities in European countries (Ryohin Keikaku *News Release* 6 December 2006).

Renovation of the brand

When MUJI was launched, the brand concept was supported by the phrase 'Lower Price for a Reason'. At that time, MUJI sought comments from its customers as 'this will do, or this is good enough' rather than 'this is exactly what I want' in terms of its price and quality.

The positive evaluation for MUJI's early move into European countries was an unintended consequence. Probably, appreciation like that in foreign markets was unexpected for MUJI. Although it might be difficult to understand for Japanese people, non-Japanese people in foreign markets might have recognized MUJI as influenced by Japanese aesthetics. For example, Jasper Morrison, English product designer, stated that 'It's no surprise to find that this company's origin is Japan, a country with the strongest tradition of sensibilities in aesthetics and daily life' (Morrison *et al.* 2010: 18). This seems to correspond to a country of origin effect in international retailing. MUJI noticed its own uniqueness from the objective consumer evaluations in European markets, and decided to enhance such evaluations as an element in the brand.

While cherishing the original brand concept, MUJI made modification for it to evolve and flexed the formula. As one of the ways to embody the modification, MUJI introduced the 'World MUJI' project in 2003. In this project, MUJI started to create products through tie-ups with prestigious designers around the world. As the first trial, MUJI launched a product line of furniture collaborating with designers Enzo Mari of Italy, Sam Hecht of the UK, and Konstantin Grcic of Germany. These designers have provided MUJI with the knowledge and insights necessary to create more sophisticated products. Like all of its products, the new product line is not decorated, nor does it carry the names of the designers. The 'World MUJI' product line has played an important role in enhancing the brand recognition. At the same time, this project provides well-known designers with opportunities to get candid and anonymous evaluations for their designs. As a result, its design began to be recognized and highly credited around the world as is illustrated by gold medal awards for its product design at iF International Forum Design competition held in Germany since 2005 (Ryohin Keikaku *News Release* 11 March 2005, 4 July 2006, 10 March 2009, 11 November 2011).

In addition, MUJI has tried to embody the corporate philosophy through the 'FOUND MUJI' project since 2003. MUJI has been exploring products which are rooted in traditional local cultures around the world. That is, MUJI has tried to make use of ideas that are embedded in these products to develop its own products. This project is characterized by its attitude that tries to incorporate external existing resources rather than creating making new demands. For example, metallic tableware in Indian kitchens, hand-knitted socks in a Czech family, and a document box in French government offices have been turned into MUJI products.

Renovation of international strategy

MUJI's momentum of rapid expansion in the domestic market extended to its early international operation. MUJI tried to expand its store network without taking account of profitability. The store openings were at a cost higher than expected in many cases. MUJI had opened its stores within the premium shopping streets in foreign markets. For example, in France, it opened a European flagship store in 2000, located in an underground shopping mall at the Louvre Museum symbolizing the company's flamboyant overseas plans. The store failed to generate enough revenue to support the high rents. While the average ratio in Japan is 10 per cent, the French store had a rent-to-sales ratio of 40 per cent (*The Nikkei Marketing Journal* 18 May 2004). Although the location of stores could be an important component of the marketing communications strategies to sustain brand reputation (Moore and Doherty 2007; Moore *et al.* 2010), it placed a heavy cost burden on MUJI.

MUJI learnt from each experience and evolved to accommodate them. MUJI changed the policy on the store opening in foreign markets and expanded its store networks more cautiously to gain profitability at each store (*The Nikkei Marketing Journal* 16 May 2005); for example opening a store in Rome after making a store in Milan successful. MUJI used organic expansion as its major entry formula. This approach allows retailers to have complete control over the international venture, and helps to manage corporate identity and brand image by replicating domestic operations. However, it requires sufficient time for market research before making investment. Even after successful expansion, retailers are required to make a substantial investment to create a foundation for the business in each local market. Therefore, the international expansion of MUJI now follows a more gradual expansion process in terms of its speed and scope.

However, MUJI has employed licensing as a complementary entry mode. The company licensed in some markets (see Figure 8.5). This mode helps retailers to expand their store network and secure its presence in geographically and culturally divergent markets. Furthermore, it can give rise to economies of scale in its sourcing activity. Although retailers might run a risk of losing control, it provides retailers with the opportunity to make cross-border operations quickly without major investment. In addition, licensed stores can act as antennae for organic expansion in future. The tactical selection of entry mode has helped its wide geographical expansion (see Figure 8.6).

As of 2012, MUJI is overhauling its international store operations to create more flexible responses to the diversity of local consumers and environments. To do that, MUJI gives its foreign subsidiaries greater initiative to sell locally made products, and eliminate intermediate distribution processes from the supply chain. Formerly, its store operations in the Japanese market determined the manufacturing and shipping schedule for the foreign store operations. However, this approach could not respond to seasonal demand in each country. Timings for launching winter clothing sales in MUJI stores in the northern countries followed the timing of the Japanese store operations. This approach resulted in lost opportunities in

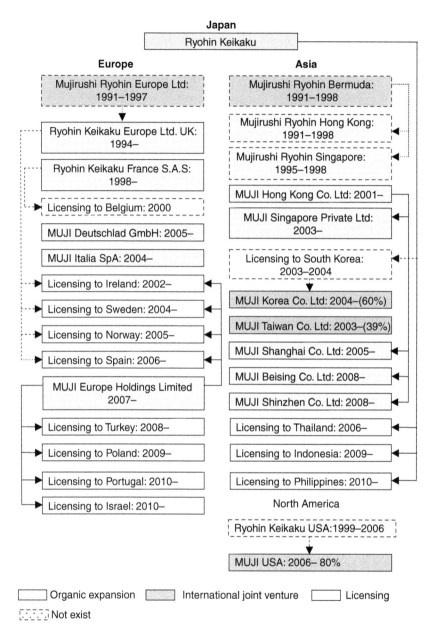

Japan

Ryohin Keikaku

Europe

Mujirushi Ryohin Europe Ltd:
1991–1997

Ryohin Keikaku Europe Ltd. UK:
1994–

Ryohin Keikaku France S.A.S:
1998–

Licensing to Belgium: 2000

MUJI Deutschlad GmbH: 2005–

MUJI Italia SpA: 2004–

Licensing to Ireland: 2002–

Licensing to Sweden: 2004–

Licensing to Norway: 2005–

Licensing to Spain: 2006–

MUJI Europe Holdings Limited
2007–

Licensing to Turkey: 2008–

Licensing to Poland: 2009–

Licensing to Portugal: 2010–

Licensing to Israel: 2010–

Asia

Mujirushi Ryohin Bermuda:
1991–1998

Mujirushi Ryohin Hong Kong:
1991–1998

Mujirushi Ryohin Singapore:
1995–1998

MUJI Hong Kong Co. Ltd: 2001–

MUJI Singapore Private Ltd:
2003–

Licensing to South Korea:
2003–2004

MUJI Korea Co. Ltd: 2004–(60%)

MUJI Taiwan Co. Ltd: 2003–(39%)

MUJI Shanghai Co. Ltd: 2005–

MUJI Beising Co. Ltd: 2008–

MUJI Shinzhen Co. Ltd: 2008–

Licensing to Thailand: 2006–

Licensing to Indonesia: 2009–

Licensing to Philippines: 2010–

North America

Ryohin Keikaku USA:1999–2006

MUJI USA: 2006– 80%

Organic expansion   International joint venture   Licensing
Not exist

Figure 8.5 Entry modes chosen for international expansion by MUJI (source: Ryohin Keikaku 1996–2012; Annual Securities Report 1995–2011).

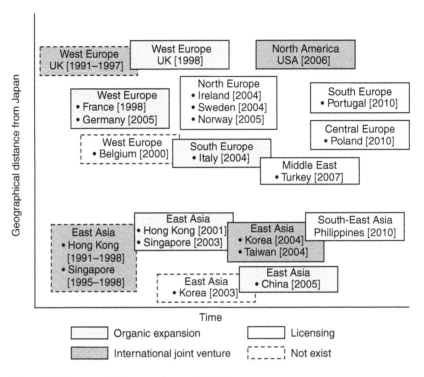

Figure 8.6 Geographical expansions of MUJI.

several countries. In order to improve the situation, MUJI started to make shipments of winter clothing earlier for the northern countries (*The Nikkei Veritas* 2011). Furthermore, MUJI also made a change in its production plan, and deliberately limited the first production order to 60–70 per cent of sales targets to make room for new items on store shelves. A transformation like this went a long way toward refreshing its stores (*The Nikkei Marketing Journal* 8 May 2003) and has broken some of the earlier rules on international standardization.

Renovation of sourcing and logistics

The sourcing and logistics system of MUJI has grown incrementally experiencing the four stages depicted in Figure 8.7. Its international distribution system was highly inefficient. Initially, all products for foreign stores passed through the main distribution centre in Japan. This increased the retail price. MUJI has tried to establish an efficient, effective, and stable global sourcing system. As the first step, this retailer founded Ryohin Keikaku Europe as a sourcing base in the UK in 1994 to invigorate its European operations by boosting local production. Its subsidiaries in Europe had been operating with losses, as heavy duties imposed on imports from China hurt their competitiveness. Since 1998, however, MUJI used several distribution centres to bolster its logistics function in China and also founded global sourcing centre in Singapore in 2006 as a strategic foothold to explore new suppliers and conduct market research. As the number of foreign stores increased, it became possible to make direct shipments from sourcing countries to stores in other countries. MUJI increased gradually its direct shipping from China to Europe without trans-shipment in Japan. Currently, MUJI procures 60 per cent of its

Phase 1. Sourcing from domestic suppliers (1980–1985)

Phase 2. Sourcing from domestic and foreign supplies (1986–1990)

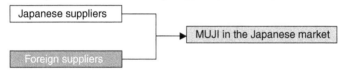

Phase 3. Shipping from Japan to foreign stores (1991–1993)

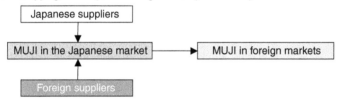

Phase 4. Shipping directly from sourcing countries to foreign stores (1994–)

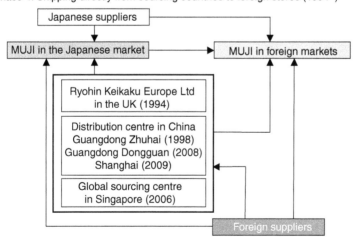

Figure 8.7 Development of global sourcing and logistics system by MUJI (source: applied from Mukoyama 1994, Figure 1, p. 33).

products from Chinese suppliers. Half of the household products sourced in China move to European markets directly. However, MUJI has a plan to reduce the number of consignment factories in China and increase its procurements from other Southeast Asian countries to cope with increased labour costs in China (*The Nihon Keizai Shimbun* 18 August 2011).

Challenges to grow by single format

MUJI is essentially a single format retailer although the formula now differs slightly from country to country and there has been considerable flexing of the base format in Japan to the extent that they are evolving into new formats. Each formula offers a unique assortment that caters to the special needs. The initial challenge started when MUJI developed a formula under the banner of 'Mujirushi Ryohin Factory Outlet' as a selling channel of dead stock in 1997. Second, MUJI opened a 'Ryohin Keikaku.com KIOSK' store at train stations by making a business link with East Japan Kiosk (later renamed JR East Retail Net) in 1999. This formula is targeted at commuters and uses an edited assortment of about 700 product items in a small store. At the end of 2011, MUJI operated nine stores around Tokyo. Third, MUJI ventured into new areas through the internet by establishing a subsidiary, Muji.net Corp. in 2000. Taking advantage of its strong name recognition among younger Japanese, its online sales are partly designed to supplement a limited product line-up at smaller stores. Fourth, MUJI developed a formula which caters to the need of travellers mainly in international airports and railway stations. MUJI named it 'MUJI to GO'. This formula made its debut at Hong Kong international Airport and John F. Kennedy International Airport in 2008. As the latest challenge, MUJI launched its first 'MUJI Beauty' store that specializes in handling cosmetics and beauty supplies in 2010 in Fukuoka prefecture in Japan. These formulae could increase the brand awareness, and also could be useful precursor channels when making further expansion in each host market in future.

Conclusion

MUJI is a unique retailer that was launched as a private label and has evolved to a corporate brand via a store brand. MUJI can be categorized as a variety store format or as a speciality store format in the sense that all items are offered under a single brand name. According to the literature on the strategy of international retailing (Salmon and Tordjman 1989; Treadgold 1990/1991; Simpson and Thorpe, 1995, 1999; Helfferich *et al.* 1997; Alexander and Myers 2000), most specialty stores take a standardization approach in their international operations. Such retailers operate in global niche markets, where consumers have similar tastes universally. There is little adaption.

The international activities of MUJI epitomize the standardization strategy. In the early stage of its internationalization process, MUJI tried to replicate the operations of its home country in a standardized manner. MUJI, after a few years, offered the unique brand on a world scale. The universal concept of MUJI gives rise to opportunities to make inroads into wide markets including homogeneous and heterogeneous markets. The internationalization process of MUJI suggests a 'Born-Global' company.

However, the current position as a global retailer was not established just by making a simple replication of the operations in home market. Its international activity began as an opportunistic action with no precise strategy. MUJI has crossed borders without having much information about target foreign markets and operated its stores under unfamiliar circumstances. Its internationalization process was almost haphazard in the early years. So this retailer had a variety of experiences, both positive and negative, in foreign markets and has learned many things heuristically. This chapter has considered the major turning points MUJI has gone through, and pointed out some crucial events that have established the growth trajectory (see Figure 8.8). MUJI has built its global strategy by accumulating learning from those rich experiences.

In summary, MUJI has introduced a unique mechanism to create products that propose a lifestyle to the world consumers by making backward integration through design and production. It is unique in that MUJI has incorporated external resources at the upper stream of its business model to nurture its brand as a

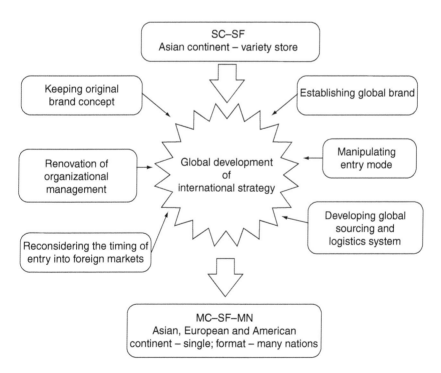

Figure 8.8 Turning points and crucial events of MUJI.

global brand. On the other hand, MUJI has tried to maintain the brand identity in the downstream activity of its business model by consistent store operations on a world scale. Its efforts to be a real global retailer are still ongoing.

References

Alexander, N. and Myers, H. (2000) The retail internationalisation process. *International Marketing Review*, 17 (4/5), 334–353.

Alexander, N. and Quinn, B. (2002) International retail divestment. *International Journal of Retail and Distribution Management*, 30(2), 112–125.

Burt, S. and Carralero-Encinas, J. (2000) The role of store image in retail internationalisation. *International Marketing Review*, 17(4/5), 433–453.

Burt, S. L. and Mavrommatis, A. (2006) The international transfer of store brand image. *International Review of Retail, Distribution and Consumer Research*, 16(4), 395–413.

Burt, S., Johansson, U. and Thelander, Å. (2011) Standardized marketing strategies in retailing? IKEA's marketing strategies in Sweden, the UK and China. *Journal of Retailing and Consumer Services*, 18(3), 183–193.

Dawson, J. A. (1994) Internationalisation of retailing operations. *Journal of Marketing Management*, 10(4), 267–282.

Dawson, J. A. and Mukoyama, M. (2006) Retail internationalisation as a process. In: J. Dawson, R. Larke and M. Mukoyama (eds) *Strategic issues in international retailing*. Abingdon: Routledge, pp. 31–50.

Helfferich, E., Hinfelaar, M. and Kasper, H. (1997) Towards a clear terminology on international retailing. *International Review of Retail, Distribution and Consumer Research*, 7(3), 287–307.

Hutchinson, K., Quinn, B. and Alexander, N. (2005) The internationalisation of small to medium-sized retail companies: towards a conceptual framework. *Journal of Marketing Management*, 21(1/2), 149–179.

Hutchinson, K., Quinn, B., Alexander, N. and Doherty, A. M. (2007) Internationalisation motives and facilitating factors: qualitative evidence from small specialist retailers. *Journal of International Marketing*, 15(1/2), 96–122.

Hutchinson, K. and Quinn, B. (2011) Identifying the characteristics of small specialist international retailers. *European Business Review*, 23(3), 314–327.

Ikeda, S. (2008) The capability of MUJI for V-shaped turnaround. *Nikkei Business*, 1450, 44–51 (in Japanese).

Jackson, P. and Sparks, L. (2005) Retail internationalisation: Marks and Spencer in Hong Kong. *International Journal of Retail and Distribution Management*, 33(10), 766–783.

Jackson, P., Mellahi, K. and Sparks, L. (2004) Shutting up shop: understanding the international exit process in retailing. *Service Industries Journal*, 25(3), 355–371.

Jonsson, A. (2010) How to maintain a process perspective on retail internationalisation: the IKEA case. *European Retail Research*, 24(1), 27–50.

Lazer, W. and Kelley, E. J. (1961) The retailing mix: planning and management. *Journal of Retailing*, 37(1), 34–41.

Metsugi, Y. (2008) Non-perfectionism and open discussions for product development in MUJI. *Nikkei Computer*, 715, 56–60 (in Japanese).

Moore, C. M. and Doherty, A. M. (2007) The international flagship stores of luxury fashion retailers. In: T. Hines and M. Bruce (eds) *Fashion marketing: Contemporary issues*. London: Butterworth Heinemann, pp. 277–296.

Moore, C. M., Doherty, A. A. and Doyle, S. A. (2010) Flagship stores as a market entry method: the perspective of luxury fashion retailing. *European Journal of Marketing*, 44(1/2), 139–161.

Morrison, J., Fukasawa, N., Hara, K. and Kanai, M. (2010) *Muji*. New York: Rizzoli.

Mujirushi Ryohin White Paper Project Team (1986) *White paper of Mujirushi Ryohin*. Tokyo: Smith Co. (in Japanese).

Mukoyama, M. (1994) Creative manufacturing and global behaviour by retailers: a case study of Ryohin Keikaku. *Japan Marketing Journal*, 54, 25–54 (in Japanese).

Mukoyama, M. (1996) *Towards the emergence of pure global*. Tokyo: Chikura Shobo (in Japanese).

Nikkei Business (1999) 27 September, p. 70.

Nikkei Inc. (2011) *Nikkei Marketing Journal resource for trend information in 2012*. Tokyo: Nikkei Publishing (in Japanese).

Owens, M. and Quinn, B. (2007) Problems encountered within international retail joint ventures: UK retailer case study evidence. *International Journal of Retail and Distribution Management*, 35(10), 758–780.

Palmer, M. (2006) International retail joint venture learning. *Service Industries Journal*, 26(2), 165–187.

Palmer, M. and Owens, M. (2006) New directions for international retail joint venture research. *International Review of Retail, Distribution and Consumer Research*, 16(2), 159–179.

Palmer, M. and Quinn, B. (2005) An exploratory framework for analyzing international retail learning. *International Review of Retail, Distribution and Consumer Research*, 15(1), 27–52.

Ryohin Keikaku (1996–2012) *Annual Securities Report 1995–2011* (in Japanese).

Ryohin Keikaku (2005–2008) *Investors' guide 2004–2009* (in Japanese).

Ryohin Keikaku (2005–2011) *News Release*, 11 March 2005, 14 July 2006, 6 December 2006, 10 March 2009, 11 November 2011 (in Japanese).

Ryohin Keikaku (2009–2012) *Data book 2010–2011* (in Japanese).

Ryohin Keikaku (2010) *MUJI*. New York: Rizzoli International Publications.

Ryohin Keikaku (2012) *Annual Report 2012* (in Japanese).

Ryutukigyou Kenkyukai (1996) *A new way of thinking for creations by MUJI*. Tokyo: OS Publishing (in Japanese).

Salmon, W. J. and Tordjman, A. (1989) Internationalisation of retailing. *International Journal of Retailing*, 4(2), 3–16.

Simpson, E. M. and Thorpe, D. I. (1995) A conceptual model of strategic considerations for international retail expansion. *Service Industries Journal*, 15(4), 16–24.

Simpson, E. M. and Thorpe, D. I. (1999) A specialty store's perspective on retail internationalisation: a case study. *Journal of Retailing and Consumer Services*, 6(1), 45–53.

The Nihon Keizai Shimbun (1984–2011) Articles on 6 September 1984, 12 January 1999, 29 March 2001, 18 August 2011 (newspaper in Japanese).

The Nikkei Marketing Journal (1986–2006) Articles on 31 July 1986, 28 January 1992, 1 October 1992, 3 April 1997, 6 October 1998, 13 February 1999, 16 January 2001, 8 May 2003, 15 May 2004, 18 May 2004, 16 May 2005, 5 June 2006 (newspaper in Japanese).

The Nikkei Sangyo Shimbun (2002) Article on 11 April 2002 (newspaper in Japanese).

The Nikkei Veritas (2011) Article on 6 November 2011 (newspaper in Japanese).

Treadgold, A. (1990/1991) The emerging internationalisation of retailing: present status and future challenges. *Irish Marketing Review*, 5(2), 11–27.

Vida, I. and Fairhurst, A. (1998) International expansion of retail firms: a theoretical approach for future investigations. *Journal of Retailing and Consumer Services*, 5(3), 143–151.

Whitehead, M. B. (1992) Internationalisation of retailing: developing new perspectives. *European Journal of Marketing*, 26 (8/9), 74–79.

Yui, T. (1991) *History of Saison: dynamism of revolution.* Tokyo: Libro Port, pp. 158–173 (in Japanese).

9   The Delhaize Group

Internationalizing the supermarket on three continents

Steve Burt

The Delhaize Group, a long-established Belgian company, was one of the first European grocery retailers to move to a multi-continent position by entering the United States in the mid-1970s. However, because of its relatively small size, which sees it ranked typically around number 31–32 in the various 'world largest retailer' lists (for example Deloitte 2013), it is often below the radar when internationalization exemplars are sought. Despite this low profile Delhaize Group is a highly internationalized company now listed on both the New York and Belgium stock exchanges, with 78 per cent of sales generated outside its Belgian homeland (Table 9.1) primarily from its extensive store network on the east coast of the USA.

In January 2013 the Delhaize Group posted 2012 sales of €22.7 billion, from 3,451 stores in 11 countries on three continents (Tables 9.2 and 9.3). Trading in both Europe and the USA has been particularly difficult in the past few years, and this is reflected in a slowing of sales growth and erosion of profit. Despite these challenging conditions, opportunities for expansion – particularly in emerging markets – continue to be pursued. The 2012 results included the incorporation of the Serbian-based Delta Maxi chain which, when acquired in July 2011, operated 450 stores with sales of around €1.4 billion from five countries in south-east Europe. This acquisition represented a new phase of geographical expansion for the Group after a number of years of consolidation within existing markets.

The Delhaize strategy has been shaped by a number of critical incidents or turning points which have influenced activities and created opportunities and barriers to the strategic direction of the group. The core competences of Delhaize are embedded in the business model supporting the supermarket format, and it is from this base that a range of format and formula adaptions have been made. In January 1999, Pierre-Olivier Beckers became the latest descendent of one of the founding families to pick up the leadership reins when he was elected to the role of CEO. The arrival of Beckers, who had spent his company apprenticeship in the American subsidiary, signalled a generation shift in leadership and heralded a focused approach on both international markets and format and formulae development.

Table 9.1 Delhaize Group – sales by geographical segment, 1980–2012 (percentages)

% sales	1980	1985	1990	1995	2000	2005	2010	2011	2012
Belgium	51.8	28.2	27.3	25.8	16.4	21.5	23.0	22.9	21.6
USA	48.2	71.8	69.6	68.1	77.4	71.5	68.0	65.4	64.4
Other	n/a	0.0	3.1	6.1	6.2	7.0	8.9	11.6	14.0

Source: compiled from data and reports available at: www.delhaizegroup.com/en/PublicationsCenter. aspx.

Table 9.2 Delhaize Group – sales and operating profit, 1990–2012 (million €)

€ million	1990	1995	2000	2005[1]	2006	2007	2008	2009	2010	2011	2012
Sales	6,598	9,134	18,168	18,628	19,215	18,943	19,024	19,938	20,850	21,119	22,737
Operating profit	311	339	740	898	946	937	904	942	1,024	812	390
%	4.7	3.7	4.1	4.8	4.9	4.9	4.8	4.7	4.9	3.8	1.7

Source: compiled from data and reports available at: www.delhaizegroup.com/en/PublicationsCenter. aspx.

Note
1 From 2003 reported under IFRS system.

The historical context: from Delhaize Frères to Delhaize Group

The history of the Delhaize Group provides the context from which the current organization has evolved (Collet 2003; Van den Eeckhout and Scholliers 2011). As a long-established and omnipresent grocery retailer in Belgium, the Group is strongly immersed in its domestic market. The historical evolution of the group over close to 150 years of operation provided an extensive grounding in neighbourhood grocery retailing (Teughels 2012) which is reflected in the formats and formula that have developed in the modern era.

The origins of the current Delhaize Group can be traced back to the 1850s and Jacques Delhaize, a wine wholesaler based in Charleroi, an industrial city in southern Belgium. Each of Jacques' four sons moved into grocery retailing and the family became instrumental in the development of chain-store retailing in Belgium. The direct lineage to the Delhaize Group is through Establisements Delhaize Frères & Cie founded in 1867, by two of the sons Jules and Edouard Delhaize and their brother-in-law, Jules Vieujant. During the 1860s a third brother, Adolphe, also started a retail business in Brussels (which was to merge with Delhaize Frères in 1950), and the fourth brother founded the Louis Delhaize chain in 1870, which is still a privately owned business operating stores in Belgium, France, Hungary and Romania

Table 9.3 Delhaize Group – number of stores, 1968–2012

Stores	Year of entry–exit	1968	1973	1978	1983	1988	1993	1998	2003	2008	2009	2010	2011	2012
Total		**717**	**460**	**382**	**631**	**995**	**1,543**	**1,905**	**2,559**	**2,673**	**2,732**	**2,800**	**3,408**	**3,451**
Europe														
Belgium[1]	1867	717	460	313	320	351	412	515	727	771	792	805	821	840
Germany	1976–1979; 2003–2009	–	–	?	–	–	–	–	1	4	–	–	–	–
Portugal	1985–1992	–	–	–	–	30	–	–	–	–	–	–	–	–
Czech Republic	1991–2006	–	–	–	–	–	8	59	94	–	–	–	–	–
Greece	1992	–	–	–	–	–	16	42	119	201	216	223	251	268
France	1994–2000	–	–	–	–	–	–	46	–	–	–	–	–	–
Slovakia	1998–2005	–	–	–	–	–	–	1	14	–	–	–	–	–
Romania	2000	–	–	–	–	–	–	–	15	40	51	72	105	193
Serbia	2011	–	–	–	–	–	–	–	–	–	–	–	366	363
Bosnia and Herzegovina	2011	–	–	–	–	–	–	–	–	–	–	–	44	41
Bulgaria	2011	–	–	–	–	–	–	–	–	–	–	–	42	43
Montenegro	2011	–	–	–	–	–	–	–	–	–	–	–	22	24
Albania	2011–2013	–	–	–	–	–	–	–	–	–	–	–	18	23
North America														
USA	1974	–	–	69	311	574	1,107	1,225	1,515	1,594	1,607	1,627	1,650	1,553
Asia														
Indonesia	1997	–	–	–	–	–	–	12	38	63	66	73	89	103
Thailand	1997–2004	–	–	–	–	–	–	5	36	–	–	–	–	–
Singapore	1999–2003	–	–	–	–	–	–	–	–	–	–	–	–	–

Source: compiled from data and reports available at: www.delhaizegroup.com/en/PublicationsCenter.aspx.

Note

1 Including Luxembourg c.40 stores.

Delhaize Frères moved from Charleroi to Brussels in 1871 and in 1883 began to develop the Ossegheim site, adjacent to the Gare de l'Ouest, where the Group is still headquartered today. Like many emerging retailing companies at the turn of the twentieth century Delhaize diversified from retailing into manufacturing to secure supplies, and by 1914 operated 23 manufacturing plants as well as 744 stores. Over this period the company adopted the 'le Lion' logo – reputedly from the royal coat of arms – as a corporate symbol for its stores and developed a low-priced private label range under the 'Derby' name. By 1939 Delhaize Frères operated 774 stores and supplied 1,500 affiliated independent retailers in Belgium and operated stores in the Belgian Congo. Dansette (1944) points to the dominant influence of Delhaize and its demonstration effect for the development of chain stores not only in grocery but across the whole of retailing in firms such as Etam and Lindor.

The Second World War inevitably signalled a period of retrenchment, and by 1945 all bar four of the manufacturing plants had closed. However, in the post-war period Delhaize emerged as the most important grocery retailer in Belgium. Merger with Adolphe Delhaize followed in 1950 and on 18 December 1957, at Place Flagey in Brussels, Delhaize opened the first self-service supermarket in Belgium. A further five supermarkets were added by 1960 and in 1962, Delhaize Frères et Cie 'le Lion' became a public company, listed on the Brussels stock exchange. At this stage the retail network consisted of 318 branches, including 14 supermarkets, and 865 affiliates. The 1960s and early 1970s was a period of consolidation and modernization of the store network, with a planned move to larger grocery store formats driven by minimum turnover criteria, and by 1980 the network had consequently shrunk to 126 company owned stores and 129 affiliates. This modernization phase also included investment in the embryonic hypermarket format, through a joint venture with Carrefour of France and two Belgian cooperatives, with the first store opening in Hornu in November 1969.

As in a number of continental European countries during the 1970s, growing concern over the expansion of large grocery stores and their competitive impact upon other forms of retailing, led to legislative restrictions on the opening of large stores. The law of 1975, commonly known as the 'Padlock Law' reinstating a name applied to earlier laws on restricting large stores that were relaxed in 1961 (Boddewyn 1971), placed severe constraints on the expansion of large food stores (Dawson 1982; Francois and Leunis 1991; Coupain 2005). This restriction, often explicitly referred to in annual reports and company documentation at the time, stimulated two distinct strategic directions for the Group. First, within Belgium, diversification into non-grocery retail markets through a range of new trading formats, and the development of clearly segmented store formulae in the grocery market, and second, a concerted investment in international markets, particularly on the east coast of the USA. The new Padlock Law of 1975 can be categorized as a critical incident in the development of Delhaize, as before the law was enacted the Group was essentially trading through a range of 'core' grocery formats in the domestic market.

The domestic market: format and formulae development in Belgium

The first move into non-grocery markets was in 1975, with the formation of the Di drugstore format. This venture expanded steadily in terms of store numbers through organic growth (and from 1998 franchising), before the 132-store-strong network was sold to a consortium consisting of NPM/CNP Group and Ackermans & Van Haaren in July 2007. Pet-food stores represented the second significant non-grocery format investment, albeit 15 years later. The Tom & Co. chain was established in 1989 through a subsidiary Aniserco, and embraced franchising early in its history. The acquisition of Amizoo (13 stores in 2000) and entry into France in 2007 have been milestones in the development of chain of 136 stores by the end of 2012. Delhaize also operated a number of petrol stations from the mid-1960s until 1985, and briefly in the 1970s a handful of restaurants, before both ventures were deemed to be non-core business and disposed of.

In the grocery sector the Padlock Law made the opening of supermarkets and hypermarkets extremely difficult. Consequently, in 1979, having acquired Carrefour's stake in the Distrimas hypermarket joint venture the previous year, Delhaize sold its 70 per cent share to Louis Delhaize. In the same year, following the introduction of similar large store planning restrictions in Germany, a minority holding in Interkaufpark, a German hypermarket joint venture company which had been formed in 1976 in partnership with Carrefour and Stussgen, was also sold. Owing to the size threshold for development introduced in the Padlock Law, supermarket development in Belgium also fell foul of the legislation – over the 15-year period from 1984 to 1999 only ten supermarkets were opened, with none opening between 1985 and 1991. The acquisition of a competitor, Cash Fresh, with 43 supermarkets in north-east Belgium in 2005 provided the first major boost to the domestic supermarket portfolio since the mid-1970s, although most of these stores were subsequently transferred to affiliates.

Constraints on the opening of larger stores thus triggered withdrawal from the hypermarket format and led to stagnation – in terms of store expansion – of the supermarket format. In this context attention was inevitably focused on the potential of smaller grocery store formats. In 1976 a limited line discount format, Dial, was launched (at the same time as Aldi entered Belgium) and grew into a 50-plus strong chain by the early 1980s. However, store numbers and sales growth slowed, and in 1998 Dial was closed with the remaining network transferred into either non-food formats or D2, a short lived 100 per cent private brand format launched in 1996 and closed five years later.

As noted above, the historical evolution of Delhaize in the post-war period provided access to a significant network of smaller grocery stores, through both company-owned stores and affiliated retailers. Although this network had been severely rationalized during the 1960s and 1970s, from the mid-1980s onwards Delhaize reversed this trend through a clear segmentation strategy, based upon a range of branded neighbourhood/convenience store formulae. The affiliated retail network, which has traded under the AD Delhaize banner since 1981, now comprises 223 outlets at the end of 2012. Three other branded formulae have also emerged in the neighbourhood/convenience format, initially based on the long established Delhaize superette network: Delhaize Proxy (from 2000); Delhaize City (from 1999); and Shop n Go which was originally developed on Q8 petrol forecourts (from 2000). Other smaller grocery store formulae piloted by the group include, in the early 2000s, Bio Square, an organic grocery format and, since 2009, Red Market – a limited assortment (6,500 SKUs), low-cost supermarket formulae operating via self-scanning checkouts. At the end of 2012 these various neighbourhood/convenience formulae comprised 306 stores, although towards the end of 2012 it was announced that Delhaize City was to be phased out with stores transferred to the Proxy formula.

Finally, in terms of format development in the domestic market, Delhaize moved into non-store retailing in 1989 through the acquisition of a majority stake (76 per cent) in Delhome, a catalogue-based home delivery operation which traded as Caddy Shop in a number of major cities. In 1998 Caddy Home started to accept internet orders, and in 2000 Delhaize acquired full ownership of the business. Alongside this home delivery business, Delhaize Direct offers a 'click and collect' service at 97 stores and was overhauled in April 2012. The emerging focus on online retailing was reinforced during 2012 with the launch at Brussels Central railway station of a shopping wall, based on QR codes with products made available at a local Delhaize store the following day, and the appointment of the first group Vice-President Digital to oversee strategy across the whole group.

In Belgium therefore the strategic approach to store development has been to maintain growth through affiliations with others, and to develop a segmented format and formulae based approach to the neighbourhood/convenience market, whilst maintaining supermarket numbers (Table 9.4). In both of these formats Delhaize have taken a clear branded formulae approach with the Delhaize trade name or (highly recognized) Lion logo to the fore. The grocery business in the domestic market is complemented by a well-established pet food store chain, whilst other diversifications (notably health and beauty) have been disposed of over time. At the end of 2011 Delhaize Group was estimated to hold a 25.8 per cent share of the Belgian grocery market through these outlets.

The USA: a mono-format, multi-branded formulae approach

A combination of the small size of the Belgian market, with its limited potential for sustained growth, and the long-signalled introduction of the restrictions within the Padlock Law, also stimulated a second strategic option – internationalization. The first move in modern times by Delhaize into international markets involved the acquisition of a 34 per cent stake in Food Town Stores in 1974. Food Town Stores was founded in 1957 in Salisbury, North Carolina by Ralph Ketner. However, by 1967 after a decade of opening and closing stores, only nine outlets were in operation. A radical reassessment led to the launch of

Table 9.4 Delhaize Group: Belgium – number of stores by formats and formula, 1968–2012

Format	Formula brand	1968	1973	1978	1983	1988	1993	1998	2003	2008	2011	2012
Total stores		**717**	**467**	**313**	**320**	**351**	**412**	**515**	**729**	**775**	**821**	**840**
Supermarkets												
	Delhaize	34	75	91	101	106	110	112	123	141	141	146
	Cash Fresh	–	–	–	–	–	–	–	–	*7*	–	–
	Red Market	–	–	–	–	–	–	–	–	–	*7*	*9*
	Delhaize 2	–	–	–	–	–	–	*13*	–	–	–	–
Discount	Dial	–	–	10	51	51	51	–	–	–	–	–
Small stores		205	71	22	2	–	–	–	–	–	–	–
C stores		–	–	–	–	–	–	–	189	276	308	326
	Proxy	–	–	–	–	–	–	–	*134*	*182*	*197*	*208*
	Delhaize City	–	–	–	–	–	–	–	*14*	*24*	*18*	*18*
	Shop N Go	–	–	–	–	–	–	–	*35*	*70*	*93*	*100*
	Other	–	–	–	–	–	–	–	*6*	–	–	–
Affiliates		472	284	149	113	144	179	237	190	215	228	223
	AD Delhaize	–	–	–	–	*64*	*98*	*142*	–	–	–	–
	Delhaize superettes	–	–	–	–	*41*	*59*	*83*	–	–	–	–
	supplied stores	–	–	–	–	*39*	*22*	*12*	–	–	–	–
Petrol stations		6	30	39	40	–	–	–	–	–	–	–
Restaurants		–	7	–	–	–	–	–	–	–	–	–
Drugstores	Di	–	–	2	13	50	66	107	134	–	–	–
Pet food	Tom & Co	–	–	–	–	–	6	46	93	136	137	136

Source: compiled from data and reports available at: www.delhaizegroup.com/en/PublicationsCenter.aspx.

the LFPINC (Lowest Food Prices in North Carolina) model which evolved into the aggressive low-price position which was to power expansion in future years. Since this initial investment, the USA has become the main international market for Delhaize and over the past 35 years the group has expanded its store network to around 1,600 stores through a combination of acquisition and format development.

Delhaize raised its stake in Food Town Stores to 52 per cent in 1976. The store network expanded steadily from 45 in 1976 to 226 in 1983, when Food Town Stores was renamed Food Lion – allegedly because inter-state expansion into Virginia was met by a court case from a company trading with the same name – and its stock was split into Class A (non-voting) and Class B (voting) shares. A further 25 stores in Tennessee were added through the acquisition of Giant Food markets in 1985, and by 1986 Food Lion operated 388 stores across five states. Marion and Nash (1983) point out that, in common with other foreign investors, network expansion was particularly focused on fast-growing metropolitan areas at this time.

Meanwhile a second venture in the US had fared less well. In 1980 Delhaize acquired Alterman Foods a 93 store chain trading as Food Giant and Big Apple. Whilst Food Lion moved from strength to strength the performance of Food Giant stagnated and losses were incurred in every year of operation until it was sold to Super Valu in 1986. This sale was part of a deal to establish a new company Super Discount Markets (SDM) to operate and expand the Cub Foods format. Cub Foods was a large-scale discount supermarket format owned by Super Valu and licensed to other operators. SDM was initially 80 per cent owned by Delhaize and 20 per cent by Super Valu, although a further 20 per cent was sold to Super Valu in 1988. Food Giant had opened a Cub store in Atlanta under licence during 1985, and this outlet plus the cash generated from the sale of the Food Giant stores was intended to underpin further expansion of the Cub format. However, expansion was slow and, despite the acquisition of a further six outlets, by 2001 SDM only traded through 21 Cub outlets and nine Save-A-Lot stores. In November 2001, SDM filed for Chapter 11, closing 19 Cub Stores and selling the Save-A-Lot stores to Super Valu. Delhaize claimed that the investment needed to be successful in the highly competitive Atlanta market could no longer be justified. As SDM struggled to expand over this period, reference was made in annual reports to the very competitive state of the Atlanta market, which had seen competition expand to support the Olympics.

In marked contrast to the trials and tribulations of Food Giant and SDM, Food Lion continued to grow spectacularly – the 388 stores of 1986 had become 1,096 located throughout 12 states by the end of 1993, although the company had by then hit a difficult trading period partly due to the fallout from an ABC *Prime-time Live* TV broadcast which questioned the quality of meat and prepared foods sold at Food Lion. Confidence in the company was rocked, as Food Lion was also involved in a long-running dispute over union recognition at the same time. Sales fell by 9.5 per cent in November and 6.2 per cent in December. An exceptional provision was made in the accounts in 1993 as Food Lion closed 47 unprofitable stores in Texas and Oklahoma, another 41 stores across south-eastern states, and paid out a \$16.2 million settlement after the company had been accused of breaking the Federal Labor Standard Act.

After this hiatus, expansion of the store network began again in the mid-1990s and the start of a multi-branded formula approach to the USA market emerged. In 1996 Food Lion acquired 11 Food Fair supermarkets in North Carolina, and more significantly purchased the Kash 'n Karry chain of 98 supermarkets and two Save 'n Pack warehouse stores in the Tampa, Florida, market, although in the following year 61 stores were closed as Food Lion withdrew from Texas, Oklahoma and Louisiana. However, the event that shaped the current configuration of Delhaize's American operation occurred in August 1999, when Hannaford, a 152-store super-market chain with sales of US\$3.3 billion trading in New England, New York and the South East was acquired. Regarded as the most profitably grocery chain in the USA, the Hannaford deal was valued at US\$3.6 billion and was concluded in July 2000, although 38 stores in Virginia and North Carolina were disposed of to satisfy the Federal Trade Commission.

At the same time Food Lion was reconfigured as Delhaize America, a holding company for the various American supermarket formulae, and listed on the New York Stock Exchange. Following this move Delhaize Group then announced their intention to buy any outstanding Delhaize America (ex-Food Lion) stock in order to fully consolidate and simplify the ownership structure of Delhaize America. Both Class A and Class B shares were purchased on the open market and in September 2000 a share exchange was put in place – with shareholders receiving 0.35 Delhaize Group shares for each Delhaize America share. Upon completion of this exchange process Delhaize Group was listed on the New York Stock Exchange in April 2001 in the form of American Depository Receipts (ADRs).

The Hannaford acquisition, plus the earlier Kash 'n Karry purchase, gave Delhaize a much wider geographical market coverage, plus a portfolio of recognizable brands (or banners, as Delhaize refers to them) with established regional reputations. This allowed a degree of realignment within the existing supermarket format portfolio. For example in 1999, 51 Food Lion stores in Florida were rebranded as Kash 'n Karry and Shop 'n Save, which were much stronger brands in this regional market. Since the turn of the century, the expansion strategy in the American market has involved further expansion of floorspace and geographical coverage through acquisition, and a focus upon new and remodelled formulae.

In-fill acquisitions included a portfolio of 28 Farmer Jack stores in Virginia in 1999 and ten stores from Winn Dixie in 2004 by Food Lion; and five Grand Union stores in 2001 and Victory Supermarkets a 19-store chain in Massachusetts and New Hampshire in 2004 by Hannaford. Larger scale acquisitions include that of a fourth regional chain – JH Harvey – for US\$26.1 million (plus US\$18 million of liabilities) in September 2003. Harveys added 43 supermarkets in central and southern Georgia, and Tallahassee, Florida to the store network, and in October 2009 a non-binding offer of US\$425 million was made for a 'substantial majority' of BI-LO's assets. BI-LO was a chain of 214 stores in North and South Carolina, Tennessee and Georgia, which had filed for Chapter 11 in March 2009.

The dynamic nature of grocery retailing and the need to renew the supermarket trading format and adapt the operational formula to regional markets within the USA has long been recognized. Hannaford had a strong quality reputation at the time of acquisition and this market position has been maintained and enhanced via the roll out of the '*festival of the senses*' programme across the chain. In the case of Food Lion and Kash 'n Karry, where sales performance had begun to flag, a more significant repositioning exercise was necessary across the store portfolio. In 2001 Food Lion opened a new prototype outlet, and the stores in the Raleigh, North Carolina, market were reinvigorated with a 'fresher' feel under a high profile 'RenewAll' programme backed with a 'take a fresh look at Food Lion' marketing campaign. Following the success of this revamp the same approach (including the closure of 41 unprofitable stores) was applied to the Charlotte, North Carolina and the Washington, DC markets, and subsequently rolled out across other regions.

In 2004, Food Lion trialled the Bloom formula (higher value added services, home meal solutions, etc.) in five stores and in 2005 launched Bottom Dollar (a 'light hearted' deep discount formula offering 'price with energy') in Florida. As the RenewAll programme was rolled out all three formulas were considered as options for the store network. Finally, between 2004 and 2007 Kash 'n Karry was rebranded as Sweetbay a formula placing a greater emphasis upon fresh food ranges and service, and following the closure of 34 stores on the east coast and in Orlando, retrenched to its core west coast of Florida market.

In response to difficult trading conditions in the US following the financial crisis, the positioning of Food Lion was again reviewed during 2011–2012. A significant number of stores were closed and a renewed emphasis was placed upon reinforcing its historical price leader position through a focus on EDLP (everyday low prices) and private brands, clean and easy to shop stores. In this environment, the more up-market Bloom formula has struggled in several markets and is to be phased out with stores closed or transferred to Food Lion and other branded formulae. At the end of 2012, the 1,553 American stores were operated under six banners: Food Lion (1,138); Bottom Dollar (56); Hannaford (181); Sweetbay (105); and Harveys (73).

The American market is now so important to Delhaize that one might question whether the group is a Belgian or American retailer. Although slightly diluted following the move into the Balkans and reflecting a tough trading year in the US, the American chains now account for 65 per cent of group revenue. Indeed since 1997 the operating review in the Annual Report has started with the American operation (Food Lion at that time), reflecting this change in emphasis across the Group.

In the US, recognition of the regional nature of the market has encouraged a series of in-fill acquisitions and formula remodelling to develop a multi-banner/branded formula approach (Table 9.5). A flexible approach to store and formula

Table 9.5 Delhaize Group: USA – number of stores by formats and formula, 1974–2012

Format	Formula brand	1974	1979	1984	1989	1994	1999	2004	2009	2010	2011	2012
Total stores		22	85	333	670	1,052	1,296	1,523	1,607	1,627	1,650	1,553
Supermarkets												
Food Lion	Food Lion	22	85	251	663	1,039	1,177	1,217	1,169	1,167	1,188	1,138
	Bloom	–	–	–	–	–	–	5	65	65	49	–
	Bottom Dollar	–	–	–	–	–	–	–	28	44	57	56
Hannaford	Hannaford	–	–	–	–	–	–	142	171	177	179	181
Kash 'n Karry	Kash 'n Karry	–	–	–	–	–	99	99	–	–	–	–
	Sweetbay	–	–	–	–	–	–	5	104	105	105	105
	Harveys	–	–	–	–	–	–	55	70	69	72	73
Food Giant	Food Giant	–	–	73	–	–	–	–	–	–	–	–
	Big Apple	–	–	9	–	–	–	–	–	–	–	–
Hypermarkets												
SDM	Cub Foods	–	–	–	7	13	20	–	–	–	–	–
	Save a Lot	–	–	–	–	–	–	–	–	–	–	–

Source: compiled from data and reports available at: www.delhaizegroup.com/en/PublicationsCenter.aspx.

presence has evolved with closures of stores and withdrawals from specific states, matched by switching between different group brands. From February 2010 all the formula banners have been supported by a single shared service organization through Delhaize America. The intention has been to 'converge and standardize what is not visible to the customer while maintaining the local and specific go-to-market strategies of our brands' (Annual Report 2010, pp. 2–3.).

Europe: format expansion and focus on developing markets

Other international ventures have been wide-ranging and varied in their level of success. Within the home continent of Europe there has been entry to and then withdrawal from a number of established markets followed by a growing focus on developing markets in south-east Europe and building a critical mass in these markets. Following the short-lived hypermarket joint venture in Germany in the mid-1970s, Delhaize returned to its core supermarket expertise to underpin its other international moves. A technical assistance agreement signed in 1981 with Jeronimo Martins of Portugal to help develop their Pingo Doce supermarket chain became a 40 per cent stake in the chain in 1985. A share issue followed in 1987 to fund the acquisition of 15 supermarkets from the Portuguese subsidiary of the Brazilian retailer Pao de Acucar reducing this stake to 38 per cent, although by 1989 the shareholding had again risen to 43.6 per cent. Despite the apparent commitment to this Portuguese venture, disagreements with Jeronimo Martins about the future strategy of Pingo Doce followed, and in 1992 Delhaize sold their stake to the Dutch retailer Ahold and withdrew from Portugal.

The early 1990s saw the shaping of the first phase of the European internationalization strategy. The withdrawal from Portugal was balanced by entry into Czechoslovakia (1991), Greece (1992) and France (1994). The Czech venture was an organic expansion based upon the formation of Delvita (75 per cent Delhaize) with the Parik brothers. Delvita expanded steadily in terms of store numbers, following the 1992 acquisition of six stores to establish the chain, and after the break-up of Czechoslovakia, also included a serendipitous entry into Slovakia in 1998. In 1999 Delhaize took full control of Delvita and acquired 50 stores (including 11 in Slovakia) from the former state-run operator Interkontakt. This acquisition gave the Delvita a critical mass of 99 stores and included some smaller neighbourhood formats, branded as Sarma, which provided an entry into convenience retailing. However Delvita never really developed from this enlarged base – store numbers failed to grow further, and whilst sales rose profitability stagnated. Attempts were made to refocus Delvita towards freshness and convenience; the private brand range was reinvigorated through a segmented brand strategy; and the store portfolio was reorganized around the Delvita supermarket, Delivta City and Delivita Proxy formulae, in a replication of the domestic format/branded formula approach. In 2005 the 11 'non-strategic' Slovakian stores were sold to the German operator Rewe for €7.7 million, followed in late 2006 by the decision to sell the remaining 97 Czech stores to Rewe – the €100 million purchase and withdrawal from the Czech Republic was concluded in May 2007.

In Greece, market entry was via the acquisition of a controlling stake of 45.98 per cent (51 per cent of the voting capital) in the established family-owned supermarket chain Alfa-Beta. Alfa-Beta Vassilopoulos was formed in 1969 with the opening of its first supermarket, although the company origins date back to 1939 when the three Vassilopoulos brothers opened their first grocery store. In 1990 the company was listed on the Athens Stock Exchange, and when Delhaize invested in 1992, the chain consisted of 15 outlets. Delhaize consistently increased its shareholding from the mid-1990s – to 50.65 per cent in 1995, to 60.6 per cent in 2005, to 65.2 per cent in 2008, and to 89.56 per cent in 2009 following a two-stage offer. In March 2010 a further offer was made for the remaining shares not controlled by Delhaize, with the intention of delisting Alfa-Beta from the Athens Stock Exchange. As in the Czech Republic, Alfa-Beta store numbers expanded steadily until 2000, when the acquisition of Trofo, the sixth largest grocery chain in Greece, doubled the size of the chain and made Alfa-Beta the second largest Greek grocery retailer. Trofo generated a turnover of €226 million through 45 Trofo supermarkets, and 12 ENA cash and carry outlets serving a further 40 supermarket franchises.

From this base further expansion has occurred. First through a replication of the domestic market segmentation approach: the City Market formula and a franchise system followed in 2002; the AB Shop N Go and AB Food Market formulae for affiliated retailers in 2005; and in 2008 a trial low-priced 'Lion Food' formula was introduced. This latter venture was rebranded as Red Market in 2010 but closed in 2011. Second, through acquisition: in 2008 Alfa-Beta completed the 'perfect in-fill acquisition' of 34 Plus Hellas stores and a distribution centre as the German retailer Tenglemann withdrew from the market – five stores were subsequently closed and the remaining 29 converted to the Alfa-Beta format – and in late 2009 the 11-store family-owned chain Koryfi was purchased for €70 million. Based in Thrace (north-eastern Greece) this move provided further geographical in-fill. By the end of 2012, the Alfa-Beta chain comprised 268 stores across four supermarket and proximity store formats, including 12 cash and carry outlets, and accounted for 19.3 per cent of the grocery market

The French investment lasted for six years from 1994 to 2000. The initial investment entailed the acquisition of a 73.8 per cent stake in PG Group, a chain of 30 supermarkets in the Nord-Pas de Calais region. The following year Delhaize introduced an affiliate system, PG Partenaires, to help store expansion, and over the next three years the Delhaize stake in PG rose to full ownership. The 1996 annual report comments on the detrimental impact of the Raffarin Act (the latest attempt to protect small shopkeepers in France) on growth, and given this context it was perhaps not surprising when in late 1997, Delhaize brought a local partner on board in the form of Comptoirs Modernes. A 50:50 joint venture was inaugurated, the French company assumed operational supervision of the chain, and the stores were converted to the Comptoirs Modernes Stoc formula. However a further complication arose in the following year, when Carrefour, who had been competing against Delhaize in Belgium since their acquisition of the GB Group in 2000, took over Comptoirs Modernes. Inevitably this arrangement did not last and in September 2000 Delhaize sold the 50 store chain (including 12 affiliates) to Carrefour.

The withdrawal from France in 2000 coincided with a new investment in the former Eastern Europe, in the shape of a controlling 51 per cent stake in the small Romanian supermarket chain, Mega Image. Founded in 1995, Mega Image had eight stores in Bucharest at the time of acquisition. Delhaize was initially to provide additional know-how whilst the original owners retained operational management. In 2002 the Delhaize stake rose to 70 per cent and full control was achieved in mid-2004. In recent years acquisition has again been used as a mechanism to accelerate the growth in store numbers. First in 2008 through La Fourmi, the operator of 14 supermarkets in Bucharest, bought for €12 million, followed by the €6 million acquisition of Prodas Holdings which also operated four supermarkets in Bucharest. Smaller-scale acquisitions have continued with the purchase of two supermarkets from Primavera (2010), and three G'Market stores from the Turkish group Gimron (2011). During 2012 Mega Image almost doubled the number of stores operated from 105 to 193. These stores included both the supermarket and the Shop N Go format. However an attempt to launch the Red Market banner in rural areas has been abandoned with the ten stores converted to the Mega Image formula to simplify advertising and merchandizing not least the expansion of private brand products.

The recent purchase of Delta M marked a new phase in Delhaize's European expansion strategy, although it represents further concentration on the 'less developed' markets of south-east Europe. Delta M was formed in Serbia in 2000 and currently offers a range of segmented formats and formula in five different markets. The formats include hypermarkets (Tempo), supermarkets (Maxi, Piccadilly, Euromax, Market 99 Plus), convenience stores (Mini Maxi, Piccadilly Express, Euromax, Market 99) and discount stores (Tempo Express). By the end of 2012 it operated around 500 stores in the Balkans: Serbia (363), Bulgaria (42), Montenegro (22), Bosnia & Herzegovina (44) and Albania (23), although the Albanian operation was to be sold during 2013.

In addition to these operating subsidiaries, Delhaize Belgium also moved into adjacent European markets. Although affiliated retailers had operated in Luxembourg since the late 1980s, in 2002 a warehouse facility was opened and in 2004 the first company-owned store opened. The previous year had also seen the Belgian supermarket chain open a pilot store in Aachen, Germany. Three other German stores were opened before all four were sold to Rewe for €7 million in 2009. Currently around 40 stores across all formats/formulae operate in Luxembourg.

In Europe a pattern has persisted of typically entering markets with a local partner, usually through a minority stake before assuming full control. Critical mass, in terms of store numbers, has been sought through in-fill acquisition and if this has not been achieved relative to competitors then withdrawal takes place – as was the case in Portugal, the Czech and Slovak Republics and France. As elsewhere, once established a segmented format/formula approach to the grocery market has been introduced, based upon the supermarket and neighbourhood/convenience formats. Local trade names have generally been retained in individual markets (e.g. Greece and Romania). Following the successful integration of various backroom services in the American operation, the inauguration from January 2012 of Delhaize Europe to manage Delhaize Belgium and SE Europe is intended to increase inter-country collaboration and leverage on a European scale.

Asia: opportunism and realignment on the third continent

As was the case for many other internationalizing European retailers, the late 1990s financial crisis in Asia opened up opportunities for Delhaize. This was noted in the 1997 annual report:

> Although 1997 was synonymous with turbulent monetary and economic times in this region, the outlook for the longer term is good. The current situation can indeed offer interesting opportunities for companies, particularly in the field of real estate. As a result of the drastic devaluation of the currencies of these countries, the original investment cost of the group could be kept down.
>
> (Annual Report 1997, p. 45)

In 1997 Delhaize formed Bel-Thai Supermarket Co. Ltd (Thailand) to 'develop large stand alone supermarkets' with local partners, the Mall Group and Saha. Delhaize was to invest US$5.4 million plus its expertise for a 45 per cent stake, whilst Mall (45 per cent) and Saha (10 per cent) provided real estate and local know-how on buying, advertising and human resources. In 1999 Delhaize bought out its partners, renamed Bel-Thai as Food Lion Fresh Market and acquired five Sunny's supermarkets from CP Group. A year later the recently formed Delhaize America formally took a 51 per cent stake in the company, but the Thai venture was terminated in August 2004 with the sale of 21 stores and the closure of the remaining 15: 'The Group concluded that the financial and HR resources required to gain a profitable presence in the Thai market would be more beneficial when invested in other areas' (Annual Report 2004, p. 26). Also in 1997, Delhaize signed a long term technical agreement with the Indonesian group, Salim, which allowed for the provision of 'technical assistance' plus the use of the Lion logo alongside the Super-Indo name on Salim's 11 existing stores. Underpinning this arrangement was the intention of Delhaize to acquire a majority stake in PT Lion Super-Indo once foreign ownership rules were relaxed in Indonesia. This occurred the following year and a debenture loan was converted into a 51 per cent stake. Expansion in Indonesia has continued, with Delhaize making continual statements about its commitment to the market, and 103 stores were operated by Super-Indo at the end of 2012. Recent emphasis has been placed upon modernizing store layouts, centralizing distribution systems, and expanding the private brand range.

The link with Salim in Indonesia also led to investment in Singapore during 1999 when QAF (a Salim subsidiary) sold a 49 per cent stake in Shop N Save to Delhaize for €11.9 million. Shop 'n Save operated 22 stores at acquisition and was the third largest grocery chain in Singapore. Shop 'n Save grew to 35 stores before Delhaize and QAF sold the business to Cold Storage, the Singapore subsidiary of Dairy Farm, in November 2003. At the time Delhaize noted that whilst they were happy with the development of Shop 'n Save: 'The attractive purchase proposal from Dairy Farm allows Delhaize Group to generate additional cash and to refocus on our two original Asian ventures' (press release 14 November 2003). The Group's Asian investments exhibit a high degree of opportunism, as Delhaize, like other European retailers capitalized on the low entry costs arising from the financial crisis. A mixture of organic development and acquisition provided the entry mechanism, but as in Europe if critical mass relative to the competition could not be achieved, market withdrawal took place.

In all the international markets a common strategy is evident. Delhaize's international endeavours are based on the supermarket format increasingly supplemented by the neighbourhood/convenience format, and their evolution into various locality-based formats. Local market adaption, characterized by the phrase 'go-to-market' formats and formulae at the customer interface is recognized in all cases (often through the retention of existing trade names/banners long after acquisition) whilst group know-how and expertise is brought to bear behind the scenes to leverage expertise in supermarket retailing. The strategic aim has been to achieve a leading position in each market or region, and if this is not achieved then market withdrawal has occurred.

Strategic focus: leveraging group synergies to support local market operations

For many years the internationalization strategy of Delhaize Group has been supported by a clear vision of the need to operate at a local level whilst creating synergies through back-room integration and standardization to leverage organizational efficiencies. This broad approach is evident in the Delhaize Group strap-line of *Group Expertise, Local Strength*. Changes over time, particularly since 2000, to the stated Group mission and values, organizational structure and commercial policies reflect this underlying philosophy and approach.

In 2002 four strategic priorities were explicitly stated: profitable top line growth; cost reduction; debt reduction; and improve functioning of the company as a group, 'whilst staying faithful to the local identities of our operations'. To support these priorities four strategic 'pillars' emerged over the 2002–2005 period:

- concept leadership – initially defined as locally adapted assortments, a value for money position and pleasant shopping experience; and at one point explicitly stated as a focus on freshness, convenience and discovery, the broad thrust of this pillar became an innovative food offer and attractive stores. However defined and articulated, this essentially meant local market differentiation through the formats and formulae;
- executional excellence – in stores, distribution systems and specific functions or activities, for example, food health and safety, technology,

purchasing etc. would lead to sales growth and increased profitability through efficiencies;

- learning company – emphasized two distinct dimensions, first employee-related commitments to training, career development, recognition and empowerment which would make Delhaize an attractive place to work, and second cross-company interaction and organizational development;
- corporate citizenship – recognizing various internal and external stakeholders with a specific emphasis on the environment, community, governance and transparency.

From 2006 the headline strategy as reported in the Annual Report was modified slightly, although the contribution of these four elements (pillars) was still visible – in effect the 'learning company' theme was subsumed into the execution theme. Three aims were specified: to generate profitable revenue growth – through concept differentiation, competitive prices, network renewal and expansion; to pursue best in class execution – in tools systems and processes, leveraging group synergies, standardization and convergence, cost management, and associate development; and to operate as a responsible corporate citizen – for associates, environment and communities (the first CSR Report was produced in 2008).

Finally, in December 2009 a new strategic plan the 'New Game Plan' (Figure 9.1) for accelerated growth was announced based upon four 'breakthrough' themes:

- operate as one group – sharing and living a common vision and set of values;
- accelerated growth – through a greater emphasis on price competitiveness and value leadership benchmarked against local competitors; maximizing the share of the wallet; building industry-leading initiatives in health and wellness; industry leadership in corporate responsibility and the use of new low-cost supermarket formats (Bottom Dollar and Red Market) and newer markets to drive store growth;
- excellence in associate development – will enable accelerated growth and be achieved by leveraging training and development programmes and business culture;
- executional excellence – will deliver increased efficiencies to fund accelerated growth and offset cost pressures.

The Group believed it had a strong base platform and faced with a challenging market environment needed to accelerate growth. The focus for store development in the immediate future was to be the new price-orientated formulae and 'newer' markets of Greece, Romania and Indonesia (which had delivered double-digit revenue growth in recent years), with a target of trebling store openings to 250 over the next three years. In addition, considerable investment was to be made in sales-building initiatives and price repositioning in response to changes in the consumer environment.

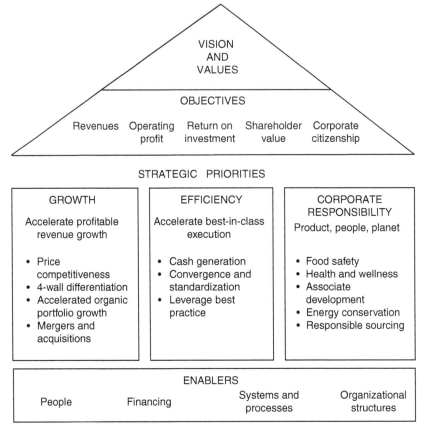

Figure 9.1 Delhaize Group: strategic plan of December 2009 (source: Annual Report 2009, p. 7).

The changing organizational structure of the Group also reflects the distinction between local ('go-to') market operations and central group support mechanisms which run as a recurrent theme throughout the Group's stated strategy. An organizational restructuring undertaken in 1998 created four geographical operational regions reflecting the home market and multi-continent presence (USA; Benelux; Europe; and Asia) supported by four Group support functions (Finance; HR; IT; and legal affairs). The stated strategic aim at this time was for all chains to be in the top three, in terms of market share, in their respective countries or regions. Changes in the country portfolio over time saw minor revisions to the composition of the geographical element. For example in 2001, Benelux and Europe were combined into a new Europe region, and in 2005 the European region was again reorganized to become Greece & Emerging Markets (Czech Republic, Thailand and Indonesia). These operational regions continued to be supported by the same central support functions until 2002, when Communication and Risk Management were added. The 2001 revision was accompanied by further statements reiterating the general approach and operating philosophy of the Group: '[the] strength of Delhaize group is built on the strength of its local banners and local management teams... DG is a federation of local companies, not a centralized monolithic structure. Therefore, the focus is on empowerment' (Annual Report 2001, pp. 2, 12).

As part of the drive to integrate Group support activities, synergy groups were set up, at both a continental level (e.g. Asia and in the USA) and at a global level to enhance knowledge transfer and organizational learning throughout the Group. As competencies in operating the supermarket business model were at the centre of the Delhaize strategy, these moves were designed to leverage skills and experience across the group. In the USA the initial aim was to leverage efficiencies in procurement, energy and risk management. Similarly, in southern and central Europe a common IT, Technology and Supply Chain department was set up to enhance operations and avoid duplication. A major drive in this area emerged in 1999 with the formation of eight working groups to explore cross-company synergies and identify best practice – in the areas of product purchasing, food safety, equipment purchasing, risk management, IT, communications and HR, and the following year 11 global projects were developed from the recommendations of these synergy groups dealing with: food safety; global knowledge centre; management development platform; equipment purchase structure; World Wide Retail Exchange; risk management; national brand modelling; purchase of products from Far East; plus three IT projects. Further examples of knowledge transfer include the introduction of cross-country benchmarking via an electronic financial reporting system in 1999, and examples of intra-group best practice transfer include the introduction of central distribution and labour management systems into the Czech Republic, category management into Thailand, and the introduction of the American inventory and margin management system into Belgium (2005).

In the USA the intra-chain linkages and support activity integration was formally consolidated at the start of 2010 when it was announced that the six formulae were to be supported by a single organizational unit, Delhaize America. The shared services represented almost every 'back office' function: supply chain, IT, finance, human resources and change management, legal and government relations, communications, strategy and research, and corporate development. Within this structure consolidation has been most prominent within buying and logistics, with the different brand/banner-based category management functions moving to a single pan-USA operation, the launch of a Preferred Broker Program which reduced the number of sales agencies permitted to contact buyers from 150 to 33, and the move to a consumer-driven supply chain by providing approved vendors with store inventory – all designed to leverage scale benefits across the different consumer facing banners. The formation of Delhaize Europe in 2012 suggests that a similar model is intended for the European operations in the future.

In a similar vein, two central aspects of commercial policy also reflect the desire to leverage Group synergies whilst responding to local market conditions – price positioning and private brand development. As the group has grown through the acquisition of different companies (particularly in the US) and new formats and branded formulae have emerged, a variety of commercial positions have formed across the group reflecting local market conditions.

In Belgium Delhaize has traditionally not been seen as the price leader in the marketplace. Various attempts have been made over the past decade to adjust this long-held market perception and make the chain more competitive on price. During the early 1990s the commercial policy of Delhaize Belgium was revised. In 1993, following a sustained campaign of price cuts on 1,500 key lines and the ending of weekly price promotions, Delhaize Belgium moved to an EDFP (Everyday *Fair* Prices) position. The distinction between 'fair prices' as opposed to 'low prices' was a subtle distinction maintained throughout the group. In broad terms, the price positioning of the Group in the early 2000s was EDLP in Food Lion and Asia, EDFP in Belgium, Alfa-Beta and Mega Image, plus in Hannaford in the USA.

However, over the past few years as recession has hit the world economy and competition in most markets has intensified with the spread of discount store formats, the Group has sought to revise and establish a clear price position. In Belgium the Excel 2008–2010 programme had as its focus a drive to generate efficiencies to improve the chains' price position, culminating in six price decreases over an 18 month period by the end of 2010. Similar efforts have been made in the US to regain the traditional competitive price position held by Food Lion, and there has been an increased focus on price-based formats and formulae such as Bottom Dollar. In recognition of a general need to remain price competitive in local markets, the New Game Plan introduced a new pricing philosophy across the Group which allowed a limited bandwidth for pricing relative to the price leader to ensure that the core banners remain competitive (if not necessarily the leader) on price.

As with most leading grocery retailers over the past 20 years the development of private brands has also been a central element of the Group's commercial strategy. Differences in the size and nature of the private brand offer across the Group again reflect the responsiveness of local markets to private brands plus the local market positioning of the various branded formulae. In 2011 the Annual Report noted that private brand accounted for 58 per cent sales in Belgium, 27 per cent in the USA and 17.5 per cent in southern Europe and south-east Asia. Over time there has been an attempt to move towards common tiers of private brands across the Group. Within Europe this was first achieved at the budget end of the range. In 2002 the EMD buying group generic brand 'Euroshopper' was introduced into all of the European supermarket chains, although two years later this was replaced by a Delhaize European-wide generic brand '365'. A pan-European general merchandise/healthcare brand 'Care' was introduced in 2007, following a successful pilot in Alfa-Beta. There are now around 300 common lines in these two ranges across the Belgian, Greek and Romanian operations.

In Belgium private brand ranges have a long history. Delhaize introduced private brands into its stores in 1979 under the 'Derby' name, a brand originally in use before the Second World War. By 1995 the 3,000 items in the Le Lion and Derby ranges accounted for 25 per cent of sales, and by 2006 close to 6,500 private brand products were on offer accounting for around 45 per cent of sales. Further segmented offers have been added over time including meal solutions and an organic range in 1999, and a 'Country of Origin' range in 2002. In 2003 the private brand range in Belgium was redesigned as the store assortment was focused on three themes: culinary delight, convenience and health. As an example of best practice and expertise transfer between the Delhaize Group chains, the 'Taste of Inspirations' brand was introduced into Delhaize Belgium from Delhaize America as the premium brand option. Most recently a 'Delhaize Kids' range has been launched for five- to ten-year-olds.

Segmentation of the private brand range has also occurred elsewhere in Europe – Alfa-Beta launched an 'eco' range and other sub-brands in 2003, and by 2006 offered a four-tier grocery brand range AB Choice (premium), AB Close to Greek Nature (regional products), AB (general food), 365 (budget) plus the Care brand in general merchandise. In Romania 'Gusturi Romanesti' ('Romanian Tastes') was launched as a segmented brand in 2009, and private brand sales in Romania reached 10 per cent by the end of 2010.

In the States the various chains had different private brand histories and experiences – reflected in the size of range of offer. Food Lion has long carried a private brand range (15 per cent of sales in 1995), whereas Kash 'n Karry (now Sweetbay) only introduced private brands in 1998 and Shop 'n Save in 2002. By 2010 in the US private brand ranges had grown to account for 27.4 per cent in Hannaford (22 per cent in 2008), and 26.7 per cent in Food Lion (19 per cent in 2008), and the stated target for private brand sales is 35 per cent by 2013. In line with its market position, Hannaford launched 'Hannaford Inspirations' as a high-end private brand in 2005, and in 2007 a policy of a three-tier private brand range – including 'Taste of Inspirations' (premium) and 'Smart Option' (budget) was introduced across all of the American chains. The 'Smart Option' budget brand was replaced by a new 'My Essentials' brand in 2011.

Conclusion

The international expansion of the Delhaize group, and its evolution in the domestic market exhibit many of the characteristics discussed in the opening chapters of this book. Whilst Delhaize has, at various times over its history, traded through a number of different formats primarily in the grocery market, it has refocused its strategy around what it believes are core competencies in the business models underpinning the supermarket and neighbourhood/convenience formats. This focus has become particularly evident under the leadership of Pierre-Olivier Beckers. The dynamic nature of the grocery market and the nuances of customer behaviour in international (and regional) markets is acknowledged in an underlying vision, organizational structure, and operating approach which standardizes 'back office' support activities, transfers 'best practice' within the Group, and which acknowledges the need for specific operational formats and branded formulae to evolve to fit their respective locational contexts.

The Delhaize Group, partly reflecting the small scale and growth potential of its domestic market is highly international. Unusually, one of its first international moves was inter-continental, entering the USA – often a graveyard for European grocery retailers – over 40 years ago. The internationalization strategy is based upon building critical mass in the markets (or parts of markets) in which it operates, through adaptive supermarket, and where appropriate neighbourhood/convenience, formats and formulae. In terms to the GPS model, from a historical starting point of small-scale grocery stores, Delhaize initially pursued a strategy of format expansion on the domestic continent, with the early transcontinental move. Over time the focus has been on formulae development and expansion within a focus group grocery formats and further in-continent and multi-continent expansion (Figure 9.2, 9.3 and 9.4).

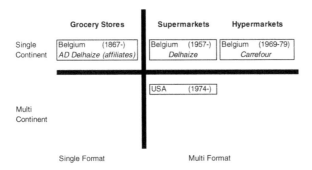

Figure 9.2 Delhaize Group: GPS map 1974 (pre-Padlock Law).

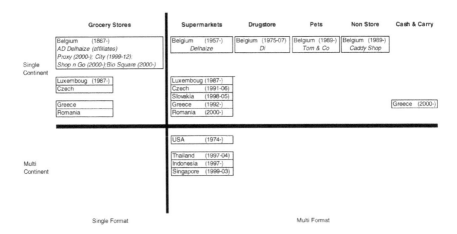

Figure 9.3 Delhaize Group: GPS map 2002 (post-Asian crisis).

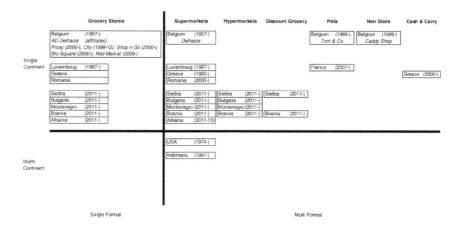

Figure 9.4 Delhaize Group: GPS map 2012.

As discussed in this chapter strategy development, particularly in respect of the approach to format, formulae and international expansion can be related to specific turning points (Figure 9.5). Whilst such narrow causality can be dangerous in a market as dynamic as retailing, there is considerable evidence – expanded upon in this chapter – to suggest that the introduction of the Padlock Law in Belgium in the mid-1970s, the Asian financial crisis at the end of the 1990s, and the arrival of Pierre-Olivier Beckers as CEO coincided with distinct changes in emphasis within the Delhaize strategy.

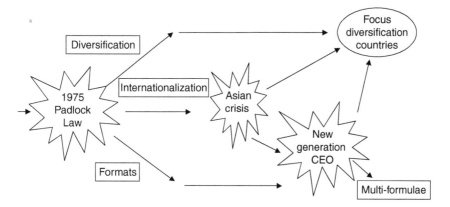

Figure 9.5 Delhaize Group: critical incidents\turning points in strategy development.

Note

www.delhaizegroup.com/en/PublicationsCenter provides access to annual reports, results presentations, press releases and other materials relevant to this chapter.

References

Boddewyn, J. J. (1971) *Belgian public policy toward retailing since 1789*. East Lansing: Michigan State University.

Collet, E. (ed.) (2003) *Delhaize Le Lion': Épiciers depuis 1867*. Bruxelles: Racine-Groupe Delhaize.

Coupain N. (2005) *La distribution en Belgium: Trente ans de mutation*. Bruxelles: Racine.

Dansette, J. J. (1944) *Les formes evoluees de la distribution*. Bruxelles: Pauli.

Dawson, J. (1982) A note on the law of 29 June 1975 to control large scale retail development in Belgium. *Environment and Planning A*, 14(3), 291–296.

Deloitte (2013) *Global powers of retailing 2013: retail beyond*. London: Deloitte Touche Tohmatsu Ltd.

Francois, P. and Leunis, J. (1991) Public policy and the establishment of large stores in Belgium. *International Review of Retail, Distribution and Consumer Research*, 1(4), 469–486.

Marion, B. W. and Nash, H. J. (1983) Foreign investment in U.S. food-retailing industry. *American Journal of Agricultural Economics*, 65(2), 413–420.

Teughels, N. (2012) Succursales partout en Belgique. Delhaize le Lion: Belgium's first food chain, its architecture and brand identity, 1867–1940. *Food and History*, 10(1), 107–140.

Van den Eeckhout, P. and Scholliers, P. (2011) The Belgian multiple food retailer Delhaize le Lion and its clientele, 1867–1914. *Essays in Economic and Business History*, 29, 87–100.

10 The Metro Group
Internationalizing the cash and carry format

Steve Burt

The Metro Group is one of a number of major European retailers that emerged from the self-service 'revolution' of the 1960s through the development of innovative retail formats. Metro is currently the fourth largest retailer by sales in the world, behind Wal-Mart, Carrefour and Tesco. In 2012 the Group generated sales of €66.7 billion from 2,243 stores operating in 32 countries with 61 per cent of sales generated by almost 1,300 international stores. During the past 40 years Metro has evolved from a family-run cash and carry business into an international retail group trading through four core retail formats and a range of well-established branded formulae.

The evolution of Metro can be charted through four phases. In the early years and the pre-floatation period, a series of acquisitions and mergers allowed Metro to transform itself from a mono-format cash and carry chain into a diversified multi-format and multi-brand operation. In contrast, during the post floatation period, the emphasis was on reducing the complexity of the organization, realigning activities and the structure of the group, and focusing on financial performance. The third period was one of consolidation, throughout which there was a further focus on the core brands and the associated internationalization of these brands, supported by cross-group synergies and organizational learning. Finally, the most recent period, can be categorized as a maturity phase, with the Metro group increasingly taking on the role of a holding company, and during which financial value was sought from the increasingly autonomous brands. This latter phase coincided with the world economic crisis resulting in difficult trading conditions across all parts of the group. The response has been a fundamental reassessment and review of the constituent parts of the Group and a retreat from less well performing markets.

The origins of the Metro Group

The early history of the Metro group is rather opaque. Typical of many privately owned German retail companies in the 1960s and 1970s the inter-locking shareholdings of the founding families kept the company from public scrutiny. It has only been since 1996 when the group went public that the requirements of financial reporting lifted the veil.

Metro was founded in 1964 by Dr Otto Beisheim. The origins of the company are firmly rooted in the cash and carry format, which first opened in the form of a 14,000 m^2 outlet at Mülheim in the Ruhr. The self-service cash and carry wholesale format, aimed at the business to business market of 'professionals' (i.e. retailers, restaurants, hotels, etc.), represented a new innovation in a sector traditionally served by home delivery wholesalers. Furthermore, the 'wholesale' designation allowed Metro to serve customers beyond the highly regulated retail trading hours operating in Germany at the time. A second store opened in Essen during 1964, and a further three were added in 1967, the year in which the Haniel and Schmidt-Ruthenbeck families became Beisheim's partners. The focus on the cash and carry format was further reinforced in 1968 through an agreement with the Dutch trading company Steenkolan Handelsvereeniging (SHV). A cross-shareholding arrangement in two subsidiaries effectively split the European cash and carry market between the two groups, with Metro Holding taking a 60 per cent share in a subsidiary which subsequently opened Metro outlets in Austria, Denmark, France and Italy, and a 40 per cent stake in Makro, which opened in the Netherlands, Spain and Portugal during the early 1970s.

During the 1970s Metro continued to grow through new cash and carry openings and also moved into large store retailing through acquisition. By 1981 Metro operated via the hypermarket format (Primus, GHZ and Meister) and in that year it took a minority 24 per cent stake in the Kaufhof department store group. It was, however, the late 1980s that saw the most significant shifts into mainstream retailing. In 1987 Metro increased its Kaufhof stake to over 50 per cent, and acquired Jorst Hurler which traded through a range of formats including hypermarkets, DIY warehouses, furniture stores and shopping centres. By the end of the decade, in addition to the Kaufhof investment, which provided access to a range of city-centre non-food retailing and service formats, the Metro empire had become a multi-format organization consisting of: the cash and carry business trading in the German grocery market as Metro, GHZ, BLV and Berolina and Office Service and Metro Deko Welt in other retail sectors; plus hypermarkets, superstores and DIY outlets trading as Huma, Hurler, Primus, BLV and Meister.

The early 1990s saw a further leap in scale through an initial agreement with, and then acquisition of, Asko. Asko had itself followed a similar growth trajectory. Originally the Saarlandes cooperative, Asko (Allegemeine Saar-Konsum) broke away from the failing Cooperative movement and went public in 1972. Under the high profile, and at times controversial, leadership of Helmut Wagner (who eventually fled to South Africa), the company grew rapidly through a series of acquisitions and had itself become a diverse multi-format retail operation trading through hypermarkets and other grocery formats; furniture stores (Mobel Unger); clothes shops (Adler) and DIY outlets (Praktiker). The initial arrangement entered into with Asko in 1990 resulted in the formation of two subsidiary companies: a new venture, MHB, a 50:50 joint venture but with Metro retaining 76 per cent of the voting rights, which combined Metro's grocery retailing formats with Asko's Massa hypermarket chain, and a second company, Deutsche

SB Kaufhaus (DSKB), originally Asko's grocery business which also became a 50:50 joint venture but this time with Asko retaining 76 per cent of the voting rights. Two years later Metro moved to a full acquisition of Asko, which was approved by the Federal Monopolies Commission subject to the disposal of some grocery, DIY and furniture stores accounting for DM1.3 billion of sales. Following this acquisition, all of the Massa and Asko DIY activities were merged under a single brand formula, Praktiker, whilst all the different group hypermarket formulae began to be converted to the Real brand.

The birth of the 'modern' Metro

In 1994, at the age of 70, the reclusive Beisheim retired from active involvement in Metro, and the reins were passed to Erwin Conradi, who had been with the company since 1970. Conradi is credited with the founding of the 'modern' Metro, which came into being with the formation of Metro AG on 1 January 1996. Metro AG emerged as part of a complex merger process from three different and legally independent companies. Essentially Asko (and its DSKB subsidiary) and Kaufhof were merged into Metro AG, and the newly formed Metro AG was listed on the stock exchange on 25 July 1996. The majority of the stock (55.1 per cent) was, however, retained by an investment vehicle, Metro Vermogensverwaltung, which was ultimately owned by Metro Holding AG, based in Baar, Switzerland, and controlled equally by the Otto Beisheim foundation, the Haniel family and the Schmidt-Ruthenbeck family, who agreed a formal pact to act in unison until 2003.

The 'new' Metro was a complex entity, comprising 14 autonomous operating divisions, covering a range of retail sectors, and trading through a number of formats via historically derived trade names (Figure 10.1). Metro AG acted as a holding company providing group support and coordinating strategy and resource allocation through a number of service companies offering purchasing, logistics, information technology and advertising support.

> As the group management, METRO AG establishes strategies and targets in conjunction with the divisions. Within its field of responsibility, it decides on the allocation of resources, globalization and how to generate synergies. It coordinates the divisions and outlet chains and is responsible for the selection and career development of qualified executives within the Group.
>
> (Annual Report 1997, p. 6)

Inevitably given the history of the group in the pre-floatation period one initial task for the new company was to rationalize the formats and formulae and to develop divisional synergies. The emerging hypermarket formula, Real, for example was derived from ten different brands: Real-Kauf; Divi; Continent; Esbella; Basar; Massa; Mass-Mobil; Meister; BLV and Huma. Each of these had their own interpretation of the hypermarket format. Not only did this require a substantial rebranding exercise but also the integration of very diverse operating and control systems to enable a uniform business model to be operated. Similar issues were faced in the furniture division, made up not only of Mobel Unger and the 49 per cent-owned Roller chain, but also containing stores trading as Massa, Divi and Mobel Busch. In the food store division the Extra supermarket format and TiP discount store format were complemented by other chains trading as Bolle, Comet and Schätzlein. A series of disposals of fringe activities commenced almost immediately. In 1996, 66 smaller Bolle supermarkets were sold to Spar Handels and 142 Schätzlein stores were sold to Tengelmann. The BLV delivery business was disposed of and the Wenz mail order business was sold to the Kingel group. The MacFash clothing chain, Mobel Unger and Massa

Operating division (formats)	Key tradenames (formula)
Wholesale cash and carry	Metro; Sigma BüroWelt
Department stores	Galeria Kaufhof; Horten; Kaufhalle
Hypermarkets	Real-
Food stores and discount food	Extra, Tip
Consumer electronics	Media Markt; Saturn
Home improvement centres	Praktiker
Furniture stores	Unger; Roller
Computer centres	Vobis; Maxdata
Clothing stores	Adler; MacFash
Footwear stores	Reno
Mail order	Oppermann; Hawkesko
Restaurants & cafeterias	Dinea
Real estate	MGV; BSV; CMG
Others	Rungis Express; Jaques Wein-Depot

Figure 10.1 Metro AG: operating divisions and key trade names, 1996.

furniture stores, Oppermann mail order business and Rungis restaurant supply business followed in 1997.

As the consolidation strategy evolved during 1996 and 1997, it was not all about divestment. The home improvement division acquired 27 Bau Spar and 59 Wirichs DIY stores, and in footwear, Reno, took a 30 per cent stake in Meyer Schuh, a high quality shoe formula, whilst the Dinea restaurant and catering division purchased 42 De Buffeteria in-store catering outlets and motorway restaurants from Schickedanz. Similarly, Peacock a wholesale/distribution operation was added to the computer store division and Kaufhalle (the variety store format originally owned by Kaufhof) was fully integrated through the purchase of the outstanding shares. Finally, the Allkauf hypermarket chain was added early in 1998.

Alongside this consolidation strategy, a second characteristic of the post-floatation period was a focus upon financial performance. The 1997–1999 business plan set financial targets of a group return of 3 per cent of sales before tax, and a return on equity of 15 per cent after tax. This was to be achieved by:

- optimizing productivity by exploring synergies across the group in purchasing, technology, etc.;
- expansion in the domestic market via selected format-based divisions and a rationalization of brands in the hypermarket (to Real), supermarket (to Extra) and department store divisions (to the Galeria concept);
- selective expansion abroad led by Metro and Real.

In effect, after a period of rapid, and at times scattergun expansion, a period of retrenchment was to occur with a focus on a narrow range of key formats and the development of core branded formula.

This business plan established the broad parameters within which the group has developed, and this strategic direction culminated in two major events during 1998 which did much to determine the future shape and approach of the group. First, Metro AG acquired the European cash and carry operations of its partner SHV. This entailed the acquisition of SHV's 60 per cent shareholding in Makro. At the time this consisted of 86 outlets in the UK, Netherlands, Spain, Portugal, Greece, Poland, the Czech Republic and Morocco. SHV's 40 per cent stake in Metro's non-domestic outlets, located in Denmark, Austria, France, Italy, Hungary and Turkey was acquired in the same exercise. These Metro outlets were already under the operational management of Metro International Management.

Second, a major reorganization took place, focusing activity around four 'core' retail divisions:

- cash and carry (Metro/Makro);
- food retail (Real/Extra);
- non-food (Media Markt and Saturn/Praktiker);
- and department stores (Galeria Kaufhof),

This established the future shape of the Metro group. Other businesses generating DM10.3 billion in sales but deemed to be 'non-core' operations were placed into a new joint venture company, Divaco, which was formed as a holding company to realize the value of these assets. Metro held a 49 per cent stake and 24.5 per cent of the voting rights in this venture, whilst a group of investors fronted by Deutsche Bank held the majority stake and assumed managerial control. Many of these operations, particularly the grocery outlets and mail order businesses were soon sold off, but disposal of other assets proved more difficult.

Despite considerable success in reconfiguring the Metro portfolio, rumours of tensions within the senior management surfaced at the turn of the century. During 1999 and early 2000, Metro was subject to intense takeover speculation. Rumours of a possible merger with a range of major international retailers including Wal-Mart, Ahold, Tesco and Kingfisher circulated. In July 2000 press stories claimed that Metro was to exchange its Real and Extra chains for around 1,000 of Wal-Mart's Sam's Club warehouse clubs. The persistence of these rumours forced a formal rebuttal from the three partner–owners, and the CEO, Edwin Conradi, resigned to be replaced by the chairman of the executive board Dr Hans-Joachim Köber.

Under Köber, the four format-based retail divisions, and their constituent brands became the basis of Metro activities for most of the next decade. Divisional financial performance and return on investment became a key focus of management with the concept of economic value added (EVA) introduced as the key monitoring mechanism from 2000. The guiding criteria for the four divisions were identified as

- ability to attain market leadership or be amongst the leaders in their respective market segments;
- an above average return on sales and long-term profitability;
- the market segment and division should be of a significant size within the portfolio;
- internationalization potential.

The extent to which each of these divisions performed in respect of sales is shown in Table 10.1. The Metro cash and carry and Media-Saturn consumer electronics divisions were consistently shown to be the best performers in terms of financial results. The performance of other divisions was more varied, and two formats DIY (Praktiker) and supermarkets (Extra) were sold in 2005. Similarly, Divaco was restructured as Divaco-neu in 2002 and the following year Metro effectively cut its losses on this venture by selling its stake in the company to the management for €1. As part of this divestment exercise Metro took back control of the Alder discount clothing business: 'with this step we are closing out the past and sharpening our profile as an international, transparent and capital-orientated, modern style trading and retailing company' (H.-J. Köber, CEO, 2002).

Table 10.1 Metro Group: net sales by division and group profit, 1999–2012

Net sales € million	1999	2000	2001	2002	2003	2004	2004r[1]	2005	2006[2]	2007	2008	2009	2010	2011[2]	2012
Metro Group sales	43,833	46,930	49,522	51,526	53,595	56,409	53,475	55,722	58,279	64,210	67,956	65,529	67,258	65,926	66,739
Sales division															
• Metro C&C	19,473	21,032	22,726	23,972	25,093	26,442	26,442	28,087	29,907	31,698	33,143	30,613	31,095	31,121	31,636
• Real	7,972	8,166	8,375	8,198	8,205	8,182	10,727	9,922	8,775	11,003	11,636	11,298	11,499	11,032	11,017
• Extra	2,940	2,921	2,980	2,835	2,773	2,545	–	–	–	–	–	–	–	–	–
• Media-Saturn	6,144	7,619	8,341	9,583	10,563	12,210	12,210	13,306	15,156	17,444	18,993	19,693	20,794	20,604	20,970
• Praktiker	2,508	2,579	2,543	2,584	2,811	2,953	–	–	–	–	–	–	–	–	–
• Kaufhof	4,001	3,941	3,971	3,900	3,819	3,768	3,768	3,575	3,609	3,556	3546	3,539	3,584	3,119	3,092
Other companies	795	672	586	454	331	309	328	832	832	509	668	386	286	50	24
EBIT	999.7	1,024.8	1,130.2	1,165.5	1,590.4	1,809.2	1,723.3	1,727.9	1,928	2,098	1988	1,681	2,211	2,113	1,391
EBT	681.0	754.1	673.3	829.7	817.5	1,344.0	1,260.1	1,358.0	1,564	1,579	1413	1,505	1,630	1,473	810
Group net income	305.0	422.5	449.0	501.9	571.4	933.4	857.6	649.0	1,079	983	560	519	936	741	101

Notes
1 2004r are the restated accounts.
2 2006 and 2011 revised to take account of disposals.

The successful repositioning and alignment of most of the core retail formula around a limited number of brands culminated in a subtle shift in the positioning of the group itself in 2002. Metro AG was reconfigured as Metro Group and a new corporate identify around the brand message *the spirit of commerce* was launched. Whilst this may on the surface appear to be little more than marketing gloss, the driver was a desire to position the *group*, not just the constituent brands, as a major player in the minds of stakeholders. It was accepted that the individual retail divisions had succeeded in developing their own brand profiles but it was now necessary to emphasize the economic and social importance of the whole group.

By 2006 it could be claimed that the third phase in the evolution of Metro had been completed. The annual report clearly articulated the group strategy as being 'to increase the company's value over the long term' (p. 3). This was to be achieved through:

*   sales growth from internationalization;
*   a group portfolio aligned with the capital markets demands, comprising profitable markets/retail segments; and
*   merchandizing concepts continuously adjusted and improved to develop distinctive retail brands.

These three objectives drove much of the development and realignment of the Metro group over the decade. The Metro Group in 2006 was a far more focused operation (Figure 10.3) than that first floated in 1996 (Figure 10.2). In August 2007, the Haniel group increased its holding to 34.24 per cent, and the Schmidt-Ruthenbeck family to 15.77 per cent. Alongside the Beisheim shareholding of 18.46 per cent, this gave the three key partners an increased controlling interest of 68.47 per cent in Metro Group.

In September 2007, there was a further change in management as Köber resigned and was succeeded by Dr Eckhard Cordes. The new management team

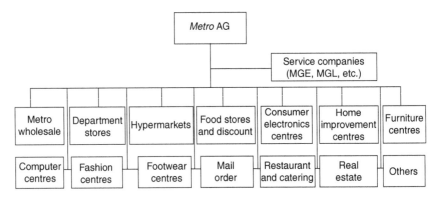

Figure 10.2 Metro AG: organizational structure, 1996.

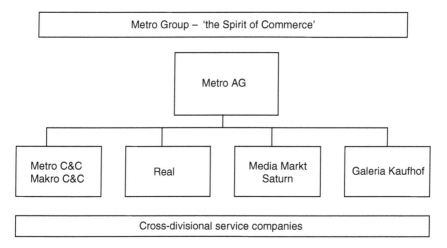

Figure 10.3 Metro Group: organizational structure, 2007.

conducted a review of the business in early 2008, which suggested that some parts of the group might be sold off to realize value. This rumour was not contradicted by Cordes: 'there will be changes, structural adjustments, portfolio changes. We will acquire companies where it makes sense ... and of course portfolio streamlining is not to be ruled out'. A growth target of 6 per cent per annum was set for 2008 and beyond. The Metro cash and carry format was to expand eastwards into 'the markets of tomorrow', whilst seeking productivity improvements in Germany and Western Europe. Real, which had continued to underperform was given two years to improve its performance. The star performer, Media-Saturn, was to pursue further expansion. However, perhaps the most significant comment revolved around the fate of Galeria Kaufhof which was no longer regarded as a 'strategic part of the portfolio'.

At the start of 2009 a new efficiency and value enhancing programme 'Shape 2012' was launched. An earnings target of €1.5 billion was set for 2012 and five pillars were identified to achieve this:

- a new leadership model which promoted customer and market centricity, which necessitated a greater degree of country-level decentralization;
- the devolution of operational responsibility to the sales divisions, who assumed management of the total value chain. Consequently the centralized cross-divisional procurement unit was dissolved with buying and supply chain responsibilities transferred to the sales divisions;
- a streamlined organizational structure with centralized finance, control and compliance functions, and an enhanced human resource function;
- the establishment of Real Estate as a fifth business unit/profit centre, from which sales division rented premises; and

- designation of clear sales and profit targets, with an emphasis on cost management and overhead efficiency.

The overarching mantra was 'as decentrally as possible, as centrally as necessary', with Cordes stating 'within the new structure, we are giving the sales divisions significantly more freedom in the operating business'. Later in the year the corporate 'Spirit of Commerce' strapline, was replaced by 'Made to Trade'. The following year five separate IT and IS units were merged into a new central unit, Metro Systems, and the new Real Estate unit decentralized its property portfolio, comprising almost 700 stores in 30 countries, across seven geographical regions.

Trading conditions in Germany and many of Metro's markets have proved to be extremely challenging during the economic crisis of the past few years., During the course of 2011 rumours of tension between Cordes and the Haniel family intensified, and stories spread that the CEO's contract would not be renewed at the end of the year. Failure to dispose of Real and Kaufhof, a highly public dispute with the founding shareholders of Media-Saturn, and a failure to meet sales targets, with a consequent fall in share price, were cited as reasons. Continual rumours led Cordes to acknowledge that there was a lack of trust between himself and the board, and he resigned when his contract expired. In November 2011 the chair of the supervisory board, Jurgen Kluge, also resigned. Franz Haniel assumed this role and Olaf Koch, the Metro CFO, was appointed CEO from 1 January 2012.

Once the fate of Cordes was known the proposed sale of Real was halted, the last known bidder Apax Partners had offered €1 billion (half of the target price), and when announcing disappointing sales figures for 2011 the incoming CEO Olaf Koch also surprised analysts by suspending the proposed sale of Kaufhof.

The internationalization of core formats

Following the rationalization of trading formats in the late 1990s, the strategic focus of Metro Group has been on four format-based divisions. Each of these has operated with a high degree of autonomy, and has formed the basis of the group's internationalization activities. In 1997 6.8 per cent of the group's sales were outside Germany. This proportion became 35.2 per cent with the Makro takeover, and had risen to 44 per cent by 2011 and reached 61 per cent by 2012.

> In the five years since the merger we have developed from a highly diversified trading organization primarily engaging the German home market into a focused, powerful and internationally orientated Group with a multicultural and decentralized management in which highly qualified people from now twenty-two countries work together. With the radical portfolio optimization we drastically reduced complexity.
>
> (Annual Report 2000, p. 3)

The impact of the internationalization strategy on the shape of the Metro group is evident from Table 10.2. The importance of Germany to the group in sales, employees, selling space and outlets has declined steadily since 1999. In all these categories, the absolute numbers have also fallen. This reflects the disposal of the supermarkets (Extra) and DIY warehouse (Praktiker) formats over the period and a general switch in expansion from Germany towards Eastern Europe and Asia.

The overarching philosophy behind the internationalization drive has been to develop a standardized format concept that can be adapted to local host market conditions, and then to roll out this concept organically. Although international-ization has been a clearly stated business objective of the whole group since the mid-1990s, international activity has always been evident in the Metro organiza-tion. The cash and carry business format was internationalized in the early 1970s as both Metro (Denmark, France, Austria) and Makro (Belgium, UK, Italy) expanded outside the domestic German and Dutch markets. Although there were no new market entries until 1990, when Metro entered Turkey and Makro moved into Portugal, by 1996 there were 125 Metro cash and carry outlets outside Germany, plus the 40 per cent stake held in SHV's Makro chain. Similarly, the involvement in both Asko and Kaufhof brought established international activities

Table 10.2 The changing shape of Metro Group

Sales (€ million)	1999	%	2005	%	2012	%
Total group	43,833	100	54,722	100	66,739	100
Germany	26,647	60.8	25,948	47.4	25,630	38.4
Western Europe (exc. Germany)	11,976	27.3	17,976	32.8	19,808	29.7
Eastern Central Europe	4,494	10.3	10,614	19.4	17,752	26.6
Other/Asia and Africa	716	1.6	184	0.3	3,548	5.3
Employees (ave FTE)						
Total group	171,440	100	214,937	100	248,637	100
Germany	115,869	67.6	102,646	47.7	89,293	35.9
Western Europe (exc. Germany)	31,975	18.7	48,801	22.7	48,090	19.3
Eastern Central Europe	20,250	11.8	52,057	24.2	90,732	36.5
Other/Asia and Africa	3,345	1.9	11,433	5.3	20,522	8.3
Selling Space ('000 m²)						
Total group	9,470	100	10,518	100	13,003	100
Germany	6,825	72.1	6,093	57.9	5,779	44.4
Western Europe (exc. Germany)	1,735	18.3	2,533	24.1	2,856	21.9
Eastern Central Europe	817	8.6	1,571	14.9	3,621	27.8
Other/Asia and Africa	93	1.0	321	3.1	748	5.7
Outlets						
Total group	2,113	100	2,171	100	2,243	100
Germany	1,716	81.2	1,427	65.7	945	42.1
Western Europe (exc. Germany)	279	13.2	477	21.9	614	27.4
Eastern Central Europe	108	5.1	224	10.3	560	30.0
Other/Asia and Africa	10	0.5	43	1.9	124	5.5

into the group. By 1996 Praktiker had 11 international DIY stores (Luxembourg, Greece, Austria), TiP had 16 discount grocery stores in Poland, Adler had 15 international discount clothing stores (Luxembourg, Austria and was in the process of entering Poland), Reno had 81 footwear stores outside of Germany (France, Switzerland, Hungary, Austria), and the Vobis computer store franchise network included over 750 outlets in ten primarily western European markets.

Since 1996 there has been a commitment to internationalization across the core retail formats (Table 10.3). A concerted move into Eastern Europe and Asia has been evident. Real moved into Poland in 1997 and has subsequently entered Turkey, Russia, Romania and Ukraine. Metro in the post-Makro period has moved into Bulgaria, Slovakia, Croatia, Russia, Ukraine, Moldova, Serbia, Montenegro and Kazakhstan plus Japan, Vietnam, India, Pakistan and Egypt. Before it was floated Praktiker added Poland, Hungary, Romania and Bulgaria. Only in the case of the consumer electronics formats, Media Markt and Saturn, has the pattern of expansion been more varied with entry into several western and established EU markets a more common feature over the same period. Finally, even the department store format moved international with entry into Belgium in 2001.

The pace of internationalization also increased over this period. The cash and carry format has expanded at a rate of approximately 25 new international outlets each year. There has tended to be a market spreading strategy, with 636 outlets now found across 28 international markets (plus 107 in Germany), typically at a rate of one new market entry per year, although there has been a clear attempt to build scale rapidly in some of the larger 'new' markets. In 2012 there were 68 outlets in Russia (entered 2001); 64 in China (1996); and 33 in the Ukraine (2003). Media-Saturn now operates 538 international stores in 15 countries (plus 404 in Germany), and whilst there has been more sedate progress in terms of the number and speed of country entry, the pace of store development increased as scale was built within most markets. Between 1999 and 2002 typically c.30 stores opened per year, this rose to c.40 per year in 2003–2006, and 50–60 per year in 2007–2010. Finally, in the case of the internationalization of Real expansion was steady, rather than spectacular, whilst the repositioning of the food chains in Germany was resolved. In 2012 Real operated 109 international stores (compared to 312 in Germany).

A common pattern, which fits with Metro's strategy of cross-divisional operational synergies is to lead with the cash and carry format. Metro acts as the market entrant, with other formats following later. In recent years this pattern is evident in the case of Russia which saw the cash and carry business enter in 2001, followed by Real in 2005, and Media-Saturn in 2006, and Romania with a sequence of cash and carry (1996), DIY warehouse (2002) and hypermarket (2006).

The cash and carry format

The Metro cash and carry format, which trades with the motto 'from professionals for professionals', has provided the backbone and growth engine of Metro Group since the foundation of the company. It is regarded within the group as

Table 10.3 Internationalization: date of entry and store network in 2012

	Metro C&C		Real		Media-Saturn		Kaufhof	
	Entry[1]	2012	Entry	2012	Entry	2012	Entry	2012
Germany		107		316		389		125
International		621		110		504		15
Denmark	1971	5	–	–	–	–	–	–
France	1971	92	–	–	1989	0[4]	–	–
China	1996	52	–	–	2010	7	–	–
Hungary	1994	13	–	–	1997	21	–	–
Romania	1996	32	2006	25	–	–	–	–
Turkey	1990	24	1998	12	2007	25	–	–
Italy	(1972)	48	–	–	(1999)[2]	110	–	–
Austria	1971	12	–	–	1989	44	–	–
Poland	(1994)	29	1997	54	1998	61	–	–
UK	(1971)	30	–	–	–	–	–	–
Czech Republic	(1997)	13	–	–	–	–	–	–
Greece	(1992)	9	–	–	2005	10	–	–
Spain	(1972)	34	–	–	1999	68	–	–
Portugal	(1990)	11	–	–	2004	10	–	–
Morocco	(1991)	0[3]	–	–	–	–	–	–
Belgium	(1970)	11	–	–	2002	21	2001	15
Netherlands	(1968)	17	–	–	1999	38	–	–
Bulgaria	1999	14	–	–	–	–	–	–
Slovakia	2000	6	–	–	–	–	–	–
Croatia	2001	7	–	–	–	–	–	–
Russia	2001	62	2005	18	2006	36	–	–
Japan	2002	9	–	–	–	–	–	–
Vietnam	2002	16	–	–	–	–	–	–
India	2003	9	–	–	–	–	–	–
Ukraine	2003	31	2009	1	–	–	–	–
Moldova	2004	3	–	–	–	–	–	–
Serbia and Montenegro	2005	9	–	–	–	–	–	–
Pakistan	2007	5	–	–	–	–	–	–
Kazakhstan	2009	6	–	–	–	–	–	–
Egypt	2010	2	–	–	–	–	–	–
Switzerland	–	–	–	–	1993	27	–	–
Sweden	–	–	–	–	2006	24	–	–
Luxembourg	–	–	–	–	2008	2	–	–

Notes
1 Dates in brackets show SHV-Makro entry date, fully owned by Metro from 1998.
2 Media-Saturn entry into Italy via acquisition from Metro.
3 Metro C&C left Morocco in 2010.
4 Media Saturn left France (34 stores) in 2011; to leave China in 2013.

the 'first mover' or 'bridgehead' into international markets, with the knowledge and experience gained then transferred to other divisions in the group. The strategy has been to enter international markets where market leadership can be achieved.

The Metro cash and carry format is based on the provision of a broad range of products with high levels of availability, supported by private brand ranges in food and non-food. The format has not remained static however, evolving over time in response to changes in the market place and reflecting different international contexts. Three core differentiated formula have traditionally underpinned international expansion:

- *Classic:* typically 10,000–16,000 m² in size. Full range units with a food and non-food focus potentially containing 17,000 food and 30,000 non-food SKUs;
- *Junior:* a smaller 7,000–9,000 m² unit, with a greater emphasis on food items;
- *Eco:* a 2,500–4,000 m² unit, with an emphasis on fresh food and primarily targeted at the HORECA (hotel/restaurant/catering) sector, typically offering 11,000 food and 1,500 non-food SKUs.

The *Eco* concept was developed in the mid-1990s and proved particularly popular in France, so it was rolled out from 2000 to other Mediterranean markets (Spain, Greece, Italy and Portugal), whilst the *Junior* format, also successful in southern Europe has been a popular format in Eastern European markets and is now being 'imported' into some German regions. None of the formulae themselves stand still and in 1999 Metro began to trial an 'outlet for tomorrow' concept with more innovative merchandizing of the non-food range and a greater emphasis on fresh food (for example via fish and bakery counters). This design has since been implemented in a number of northern and western European markets.

More recent formula adaptions have emerged from within international markets. For example, in Poland a development has been *Makro Punkt*, a 1,500 m² 'satellite' store supplied by a 'mother' store offering 2,000 SKUs focused on regional products and serving local food stores. This adapted formula is now being utilized in the eastern Europe markets of Bulgaria, Croatia, Romania, Russia, Serbia and Ukraine. In China, *Metro for HoReCa* serving hotels and restaurants in downtown areas has been developed. A version of this catering-based formula has proved successful in France, and was launched in Italy in 2012 under the La Casa dell' Horeca name. In India: *Makro Genesis*, has been created as a 5,000 m² outlet incorporating a 400 m² 'mandi' marketplace for fruit and vegetables.

In Europe, further formula adaption has included the addition of delivery and services in Germany, Austria, Czech Republic, Italy and Russia. The delivery service and expanding small retailer support programme is now seen as a core element of the format and Metro regard this adaption as an expansion of the original business model. The support for small traders has also expanded into a quasi-franchising model in some former European markets. Originating in Romania and subsequently exported to Bulgaria, Poland and Serbia, small retailers trade under a (localized) logo with marketing and range development support, retailing Metro products. In 2012 there were 1,500 ODIDO traders in Poland, 1,000 Moiat Magazin retailers in Bulgaria, and 500 La Doi Pasi stores in Romania.

The broad approach in all international markets has been to develop a 'modular' cash and carry format which can be adapted and tailored to national environments by sourcing locally with 80–90 per cent of merchandise coming from the host market. A flat organizational structure, supported by cross-market operational processes and procedures, makes it easy to extend the format into other countries through a localized formula. Whilst back-store systems, such as buying, logistics and IT systems are centralized, customer-facing decisions (e.g. assortment and pricing, advertising and promotion, location and people management) are made at the local level of country or even store. Expansion has been organic rather than through acquisition as Metro feel that this allows for greater adaption to local market conditions and avoids the integration issues commonly found with acquisition. On rare occasions however, acquisition has allowed an increase in scale, for example the 1991 acquisition of the cash and carry business of Codec in France.

Following the acquisition of the SHV shareholding in the European cash and carry business, Metro carried out further internal consolidation by purchasing the stake in the non-domestic Metro cash and carry business which had been retained by Metro Holding AG. This allowed full integration with the Makro stores under a single unified management. Individual country operations remained autonomous but were initially organized into five regions (Central Europe, Western Europe, Southern Europe, Eastern Europe and Asia) each with a chief operating officer. As internationalization continued apace, in 2001 an adapted structure was developed which allowed for entry into smaller markets to be supported by the Metro chains from larger markets. These larger partner organizations provided administrative functions (e.g. accounting services and logistics) allowing the national market team to focus on customer-facing activities.

In 2009 as part of the Shape 2012 strategy the cash and carry division was restructured into three regions: Western Europe/Middle East North Africa (MENA) based in Dusseldorf, Central and Eastern Europe based in Vienna, and Asia based in Singapore. The following year this structure was again revised into two regions reflecting the different stages of development of the retail markets: Europe/MENA, where the focus was to be on private brand development, delivery services and service enhancement to grow sales, and Asia/CIS/New, Markets which would focus on market expansion. Finally in 2011, following a successful trial in the Real grocery division, a pilot decentralized management scheme was launched for 17 stores in Germany, Greece, Slovakia, the Netherlands, Spain, Turkey, Italy and Pakistan.

Supermarket and grocery store formats

The tie up with Asko in 1990 marked a serious move into grocery retailing. The history of Asko, as a company which grew rapidly by acquisition during the 1980s, plus the consolidation processes at work in the German grocery retail sector during the 1990s provided Metro with a large multi-format and multi-formulae branded grocery business ranging from hypermarkets through supermarkets and smaller neighbourhood stores to hard discount stores. Furthermore, across this format portfolio a plethora of largely historic trade names existed. It has proved to be a considerable challenge for Metro to rationalize and reconfigure these different formats and formulae into a coherent grocery business. This challenge was made even more difficult by a stagnant domestic grocery market, which exhibited a strong price emphasis driven by a dominant discount sector in the form of Aldi, Lidl, Plus and others.

The strategy within this division was to refocus the grocery businesses on two branded formula: Real and Extra. The TiP discount store format was put up for sale via Diavco at the end of 1998, and was quickly picked up in various lots by competitors such as Plus, Norma, Netto and others in Germany, and Biedronka in Poland. In contrast, network scale and format focus in the grocery division was pursued through a series of acquisitions: Allkauf (94 stores) and Kriegbaum (38 stores) in 1998 to add scale to Real and Extra, whilst the Extra bau und hobby DIY stores were transferred to Praktiker to provide a clearer focus for the grocery division management. Although denied at the time, these grocery sector acquisitions were also seen as a defensive response to Wal-Mart's entry into Germany in late 1997.

The decision to convert the larger stores into the Real branded formula was made at the end of 1992, and this policy was pursued throughout the 1990s. Typically these stores were hypermarkets of 5,000–8,000 m^2 in size containing 70,000 SKUs with three-quarters of sales from food categories. As part of this process the Real hypermarket formula began a repositioning strategy with an emphasis on merchandise reorganization particularly in the non-food area. Product groups were themed around distinct merchandise categories, and this entailed the development of a number of shop-in-shop non-food concepts. The need to encourage customer loyalty in what proved to be a challenging domestic market environment also saw Real join the national Payback loyalty scheme. By 2002 Metro were claiming that 57 per cent of Real's customers were members of this scheme, and that their spend was 55 per cent higher than that of other customers. Other approaches to drive up productivity and return on investment saw a streamlining of the regional structure (from 15 to eight regions) in 2000, and the introduction of inventory management systems.

On the international level, in line with group strategy, Real slowly moved into other markets within Europe, with a focus on the emerging markets in eastern Europe. Poland was entered in 1997 and Turkey in 1998, followed eight years later by entry into Russia and Romania, and into Ukraine in 2009.

In contrast the Extra supermarket format consistently provided a challenge over this period. The limited potential to internationalize a mature format such as the supermarket, plus strong domestic competition from discount formats at home, created problems. In the late 1990s the positioning strategy was re-examined, with the chain perceived as a 'low price, full range' supermarket format. By 2001 a switch in marketing focus was evident. Stores of around 1,500 m^2 were remodelled with an emphasis on the ease of shopping (wider aisles, clearer layouts and larger check-out areas, etc.), whilst improvements in merchandizing display were introduced to drive up space productivity. The following year Extra was referred to in the annual report as a 'neighbourhood convenience store chain' with an emphasis on fresh produce, a comprehensive product range and the provision of expert advice within a pleasant shopping atmosphere. The portfolio of stores was continually rationalized over this period with larger stores transferred to the Real formula and smaller outlets franchised under the Comet and Bolle brands.

Until 2003 Extra operated as a separate business division within Metro, but from this date the central administrative functions such as control, accounting and logistics were merged into the Real operation, whilst advertising and category management were maintained as separate activities to maintain the brand distinctiveness of the two formats. The regional structure was also simplified to fit within the Real template. In 2004, a further reduction in the size of the Extra store network took place with the sale of 119 stores to Rewe, further transfers to Real and some store closures. This divestment left Extra with a much reduced presence, restricted to the north and west of Germany.

In 2006 further investment was made in Real through the acquisition of the German operation of Wal-Mart, which provided an additional 85 stores and sales of around €2 billion, to the existing store portfolio in Germany. Outside Germany, a second phase of international expansion began as Real acquired the Martkauf hypermarket in Moscow and in Poland purchased the Géant chain of 19 hypermarkets, with sales of €1.3 billion, from the French retailer Casino. In contrast to this investment in Real, the trials and tribulations experienced with Extra came to an end as the remaining 245 Extra supermarkets and Comet and Bolle grocery store franchises, generating €1.6 billion of sales, were sold to Rewe.

Operationally a new strategy was developed for Real in 2008. This involved three aspects: a repositioning of the brand under the strapline 'one store, you won't need more'; second, optimization of the store network, entailing some outlet rationalization; and third, cost structure readjustment. The private brand strategy was revised with phantom grocery product brands replaced by a tiered brand strategy under the Real name, whilst TiP was retained for the discount private brand. Other innovations included the introduction of an online offer in May 2010 and a 'Real Drive' store, where consumers could collect online orders, in Hannover a few months later. Although the financial performance of Real improved, the chain was placed up for sale by Cordes. Tesco was rumoured to be interested in acquiring the Romanian operation but interest in the chain did not meet expectations and Real was taken off the market in 2011.

Consumer electronics formats

Alongside the cash and carry format, the consumer electronics division of Media-Saturn has traditionally been the other star performer in the Metro portfolio. This business came into the Metro group via Kaufhof, and operates two branded formulae: Media-Markt and Saturn. Founded in Ingolstadt, Bavaria in

1963, by Walter Gunz, Erich and Helga Kellerhals and Leopold Stiefel, Media-Markt opened its first store in Munich in 1979. Originally a large consumer electronics retail format, offering up to 40,000 products, on out-of-town sites, a format was subsequently developed for shopping mall locations. Kaufhof took a 54 per cent stake in Media Markt in 1988, and Saturn was acquired in 1990. Saturn was founded in 1961 in Cologne by Anni and Fritz Wafferschmidt, as an in-town hi-fi and music store originally serving the diplomatic community before opening its doors to the general public in 1969. The emphasis on music remains with an extensive CD range increasing the items on offer to around 100,000. Metro now owns 75 per cent of the Media-Saturn business with the remainder still held by the Kellerhals and Stiefel families. Since its acquisition, Saturn has operated as a separate company under the Media-Saturn umbrella competing with Media Markt in many markets.

A distinctive feature of the Media-Saturn business is that store managers have a 10 per cent stake in individual stores in order to embed and encourage entrepreneurial behaviour. Assortment selection, selling and advertising is delegated to the store level allowing rapid response and adaption to local market conditions, particularly the promotional offers of competitors. The group also enjoys high brand recall and awareness from an eye-catching and often controversial advertising platform. Range, brands and price are central to the advertising message but are couched within unconventional straplines often portrayed around cultural and social stereotypes: 'Laast euch nicht veraschen' ('don't let them make an ass out of you') and 'Ich bin doch nicht blöd!' ('I'm not stupid!') in the case of Media Markt and 'Geiz ist geil!' ('Stinginess is cool') and 'Wir lieben Technik! Wir lassen tenev' ('We love technology! We hate expense') for Saturn.

A small number of stores were added to the consumer electronics chains by the acquisition of Multi-Media and Sound & Technik in Germany, but otherwise a largely organic expansion strategy has been pursued. Media-Saturn has been international since 1989 when Media-Markt entered France and Austria. In France the chain originally operated under a different brand, Hyper Media, but this never really worked so these stores were converted to Planete Saturn from 1999. Despite growing to a chain of 34 stores performance lagged behind expectations and Planete Saturn was sold to HTM in December 2010. Elsewhere the pace of internationalization was steady rather than spectacular with market entry into Switzerland in 1993, followed by Poland in 1998. There was then a flurry of international activity in 1999, when Media-Saturn entered the Netherlands by acquisition through a 75 per cent stake in Mega-Elshout which had two stores, and took on the 23 store-strong chain Media World, which had been developed by Metro with Italian partners.

The entrepreneurial culture engendered throughout Media-Saturn by involving store managers in the ownership of their outlets is replicated in international markets where possible. An alternative model involving a profit-sharing bonus has been employed in Italy where employee shareholding is not possible. A customer market focus is also embedded through establishing a head office in each country entered, staffed primarily by locals rather than German executives.

Since 2009, Media-Saturn has invested heavily in building a multi-channel strategy. Online offers appeared from Media Markt in the Netherlands and Austria in 2009, Switzerland in 2011, and the domestic German market at the start of 2012. Saturn's online offer was launched in Germany in late 2011, followed by Switzerland in 2012. In addition to these online shops aligned with the established store branded formulae, Media-Saturn made a number of acquisitions: 24–7 Entertainment, an established B2B operator with 41 download shops in 13 European countries in 2009; Redcoon, a pure-play online electronics retailer present in ten countries, in 2011; Ibood, which offers a heavily discounted single product for 24 hours; Rebuy, a second-hand goods retailer; in 2012 a Russian electronics e-commerce chain, 003.ru; and also in 2012 Flip-4New, a German based reseller of electronic products.

Despite the successful expansion of these formats and associated formula, major tensions developed between Metro and the founding families and minority shareholders of Media-Saturn. Although Leopold Stiefel stood down from day-to-day involvement in 2006 he remained an influential figure. In 2008 Metro considered floating Media-Saturn but this did not materialize. Relationships between the parties reached a nadir in 2011–2012, as Metro attempted to reform the shareholder voting system, which gave the Kellerhals-Stiefel bloc the right of veto. Metro introduced an advisory committee and claimed that this committee had the power to make strategic decisions on a simple majority basis. Kellerhals objected and the dispute eventually reached the courts, which found in favour of the existing arrangements in late 2011, but then in favour of Metro in 2012. An appeal by Kellerhals is in process as this chapter is written.

The department store format

The fourth discrete format remaining within the Metro Group portfolio is the department store. The Kaufhof department store chain represents one of the 'old establishment' retail businesses in Germany. Its roots can be traced back to 1879 when a Jewish merchant Leonard Tietz opened a small textile store in Stralsund. In 1905 the embryonic chain of department stores was listed as Leonard Tietz AG, and by the fiftieth anniversary in 1929 the company had grown to a 43-store chain. In 1933 the business was expropriated by the Nazi party, the Tietz family emigrated, and the business was renamed Westdeutsche Kaufhof AG. Only five stores survived the Second World War but during the post-war reconstruction period a regional network of stores was re-established. Like most European department store operators, by the end of the 1980s Kaufhof had diversified into a multi-format, multi-branded formula business based around the department and variety store (Kaufhalle) formats, mail order businesses (Hawesko, Oppermann, Wenz) and a number of footwear and fashion formats (Reno and MacFash). With the exception of Media-Saturn, which as discussed above was also originally owned by Kaufhof, the majority of these business were disposed of or found their way into Diavco soon after Metro AG was formed.

In 1994 Kaufhof took a majority stake in a rival department store chain, Horten, and adopted the 'galleria' department store formula that Horten had developed. This involved a 'modular' merchandizing strategy, based upon grouped themes (e.g. women's-world; men's-world; sports-world, etc.), which integrated leading shop-in-shop brands in an attempt to position the chain as more 'up-market' and improve the shopping experience. The conversion programme started with stores with over 7,000 m² of selling space and a sales potential of DM1.5 billion and was then steadily expanded throughout the store portfolio. In 2001 the department store format was internationalized when Kaufhof acquired the Inno chain of 15 stores in Belgium which were also converted to the Galeria concept

Kaufhof continued to reposition itself in the 2000s by 'trading up' to establish a lifestyle proposition. It now operates with the strapline *world class shopping* and has supplemented leading manufacturer brands with four quality positioned private brand ranges 'Mark Adam New York' and 'Miss H' for women, Rover & Lakes' and 'Redwood' for men. As with other Metro subsidiaries an attempt to improve customer loyalty saw the launch of a Galeria loyalty card in 2000. Part of the Payback system, this scheme had attracted 6.5 million card holders by 2003. Other operational efficiencies have been sought in stockholding and availability through various ECR initiatives involving around 400 suppliers who represent 25 per cent of sales. An online shop was opened in October 2011.

Less successful was an attempt by Kaufhof at the end of the 1990s to launch a series of lifestyle-related formats in Germany – Sport Arena (upmarket sports and leisurewear); Lust for Life (fashion, music, sport and eating 'adventures'), and Emotions (women's cosmetics, lingerie/swimwear, fashion accessories, plus hairdressing, fitness/wellbeing). Only the former appears to have survived beyond the pilot stage and evolved into a small chain of 17 outlets (some now trading as Wanderzeit), Lust for Life has disappeared from company material and Emotions was closed in 2004. In 2009, the Dinea restaurant and catering subsidiary was transferred into the Galerias Kaufhof business unit and the Axxe restaurant and motel subsidiary sold.

The future of Kaufhof within Metro has been uncertain for some time. The chain was put up for sale by Cordes in 2008, but there were few takers as the future prospects for the department store format in Germany remained difficult. Indeed, there was speculation that Kaufhof would itself bid for the Karstadt department store chain which was declared bankrupt in June 2009. There appeared to have been some progress towards divestment during 2011, with a sale to either Austrian real estate investor Rene Benko, via his Signa company (which was not helped by investigations by the Vienna authorities into allegations of money laundering, which came to nothing), or the saviour of Karstadt, the German-American investor Nicolas Berggruen, in the offing. However, following the disappointing sales figures for 2011, the new CEO Olaf Koch, announced that the sale was suspended as it was felt that Metro would be unable to realize an appropriate value from divestment in the current market conditions.

The DIY warehouse format

Although no longer part of the Metro Group portfolio, any discussion of the group's internationalization strategy requires some consideration of the DIY warehouse format. Originally founded in 1978, as a joint venture between GB Inno BM of Belgium and Asko, Praktiker became a fully owned Asko subsidiary before 25 per cent of its shares were floated on the stock exchange in the early 1990s. Following the merger Metro held a 75 per cent stake in Praktiker and the remaining shares were bought up during 1999.

In the mid-1990s Praktiker consolidated its position in the German market through a series of acquisitions. In 1996, 27 BauSpar stores were bought from Spar Handels and the Wirichs chain of 58 stores (including some in former East Germany) was added in October 1997. Internally, in January 1998, 35 stores trading as Extra Bau und Hobby were transferred to Praktiker from the grocery division, and the smaller stores franchised.

The Wirichs formula held a more-mid market family orientated position than Praktiker through a wider home décor range including garden centre products. Consequently, Prakitker and Wirichs initially operated as two separate branded formulae, but with joint purchasing. In the late 1990s the view was taken that Praktiker needed to be repositioned as the 'preferred shop of choice for all kinds of job around the house and garden'. As part of this exercise the Wirichs stores were rebranded as Praktiker, fringe consumer goods products were removed and the emphasis was placed on developing and promoting a clear price position. Internal reorganization involved a greater emphasis on marketing rather than buying in the merchandise teams, the integration of administration, logistics and import activities and the stores were grouped into four regions and 20 districts to allow for more localized marketing and merchandise adaption.

By the time Praktiker was fully integrated into Metro at the end of the 1990s, the DIY warehouse was operating in six international markets. Despite being a relatively early international entrant with the DIY warehouse format, critical mass was never achieved in any market. For example, although the first store was opened in Greece in 1993, only another six outlets were added over the following decade. There was greater investment (in terms of store numbers) in Poland and Hungary, but by the mid 2000s Praktiker still only operated 61 outlets across eight international markets. The internationalization agenda was not helped by the need to manage recovery in the faltering domestic market.

The home improvement market in Germany during the 1990s was undoubtedly tough and Praktiker continued to underperform relative to the rest of the Metro group over this period. A further review of the business led to the launch of a high profile price cutting campaign during 2002. The prices of 3000 items were permanently reduced by 10 per cent, and a 'budget' private brand range of 250 items was launched. The price emphasis was further emphasized by the launch of Key Account card for craftsmen which gave discounts of 3 per cent for a spend of €1,500, 5 per cent for €2,500, and 10 per cent for €7,500 p.a. in the form of merchandise vouchers. By the end of the year it was claimed that the scheme had

40,000 card holders and this figure had risen to 220,000 by the end of 2004. The success of the repositioning allowed the group to consider a number of future options for Praktiker, and in October 2005 it was decided to float the business. In April 2006, Metro disposed of its final 40 per cent stake in Praktiker.

Conclusion

As noted at the start of this chapter, the Metro story can be broadly split into a number of phases (Figure 10.4). Rapid growth via acquisition in the pre-floatation period created a highly diverse multi-sector, multi-format, multi-formula, multi-brand organization. A period of rationalization of the portfolio followed, with the divestment of non-core activities, and a focus on four core format-based divisions, and a clarification of strategic direction including internationalization. This change in emphasis is reflected in the GPS maps for 1997 and 2012 (Figures 10.5 and 10.6), which show a reduction in the number of in-continent formats, and an expansion in the number of international markets, involving multi-continent activity in the case of the core Cash and Carry format. More recently, management has concentrated on performance and the extraction of financial value from the constituent parts of the group.

The impact of the economic recession has been felt severely by Metro. The decision of the new CEO to suspend the sale of Kaufhof and Real has only proved to be a pause allowing a re-evaluation of activities. The relative failure of the Metro and Media-Saturn divisions to maintain their growth trajectories, prompted the need for a profit warning in late 2012 as the share price fell, resulting in Metro falling from the DAX Top 30 for the first time since the Group was formed. A review of operations, including the performance of international markets was undertaken and a series of adjustments have been put into place.

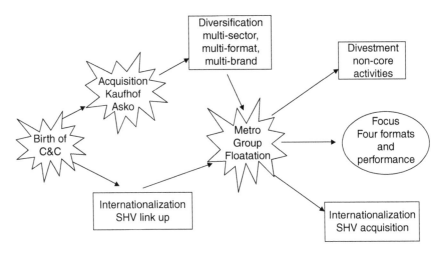

Figure 10.4 Metro Group: critical events in GPS development.

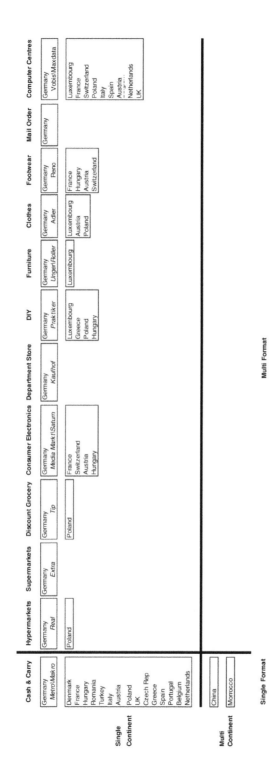

Figure 10.5 Metro Group: GPS map 1997.

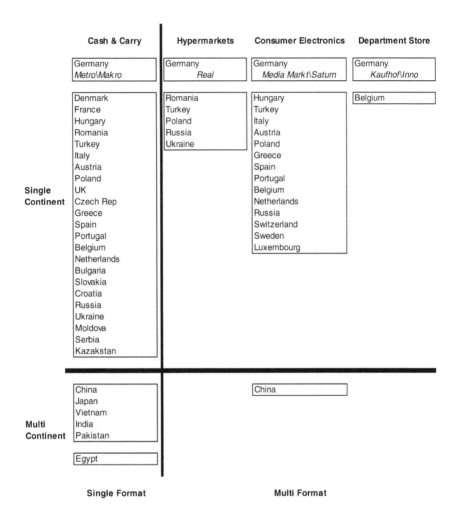

Figure 10.6 Metro Group: GPS map 2012.

At Metro Cash and Carry, the two divisions (Europe/MENA and Asia/CIS/New Markets) created in 2010 were merged and regional teams created to manage three divisions Core Markets (Germany, China, France, Italy, Poland, Spain and Turkey), Western and Eastern Europe, and Asia. Significant job cuts were announced in Germany, the Spanish and Portuguese operations were merged into a single business unit, and in May 2012 the planned entry into Indonesia was called off. In July 2012, the UK Makro chain was sold to Booker for a 9.8 per cent stake in Booker plus £15 million.

At Real, the CEO Joel Saveuse left in March 2012 and the German business was restructured from seven to three regions with more decision making devolved to store managers. At the end of the year the Central and Eastern European operation consisting of 91 stores generating €2.6 billion of sales in Poland, Romania, Russia and Ukraine was sold to Auchan of France for €1.1 billion. The Turkish operation was, however, retained. The finance raised from this deal was not to be reinvested in the business but used to reduce debt and improve ratings.

Even at the star performer, Media-Saturn, problems emerged. The continued bitter dispute with the minority shareholders over the direction and pace of the multi-channel and international strategy of the chain saw several changes in senior management during the year. The Saturn formula in particular seemed to be causing concern with the Saturn stores in Greece, Russia and Hungary transferring to the more established Media Markt formula. The planned entry of Media Markt into Norway was abandoned in June, and at the end of the year withdrawal from China was announced where, despite an initial stated goal of 100 stores by 2015, only seven stores had been opened by the end of 2012.

In this context, events at Kaufhof appeared rather uneventful. Electronics departments were phased out to be replaced with higher margin textiles and accessories, and four department stores were closed on the expiry of their leases.

The future question for Metro is to what extent it refocuses its activities to weather the storm in what are undoubtedly difficult trading conditions in western Europe in particular. Perhaps just as significant as the operational readjustments made over the past year was the announcement in November 2012 that the Haniel family was reducing their stake in Metro to 30.01 per cent. This, alongside the death of Otto Beisheim in February 2013, has cast further doubt over the long standing investment of the 'founding families' in the group they helped to shape.

Bibliography

Corporate Intelligence on Retailing (1990, 1996) *Retailing in Europe – Germany*, London: CIR.

Deutscher Industrie-und Handelstag (1983) *Konzentration im einzelhandel*, DIHT 209, Bonn: DIHT.

Kalyanam, K., Lal, R. and Wolfram, G. (2006) Future store technologies and their impact on grocery retailing. In: M. Krafft and M. K. Mantrala (eds) *Retailing in the 21st Century: current and future trends*, Berlin: Springer, pp. 95–112.

Management Horizons (1980) *Continental Retail Groups*, Kingston on Thames: MH Europe.

Management Horizons (1982, 1984, 1988) *Retail yearbook Europe: food based companies*. Kingston on Thames: MH Europe.

Management Horizons (1992, 1994–1995) *Europe's leading retailers*. Kingston on Thames: MH Europe.

Mantrala, M. K. and Kraft, M. (2010) Entrepreneurship in retailing: Leopold Stiefel's 'Big Idea' and the growth of Media Markt and Saturn. In: M. Krafft and M. K. Mantrala (eds) *Retailing in the 21st Century: current and future trends* Berlin: Springer, 2nd edition, pp. 43–60.

Metro AG (1996, 1997, 1998, 1999, 2000, 2001) *Annual Reports*. Available at: www.metrogroup.de/internet/site/metrogroup/node/29152/Len.

Metro Group (2002, 2003, 2004, 2005, 2006, 2007, 2008, 2009, 2010, 2011) *Annual Reports*. Available at: www.metrogroup.de/internet/site/metrogroup/node/29152/ Len.

Meierdorf, Z., Mantrala, M. K. and Krafft, M. (2006) Retailing in the global world: case study of Metro. In: M. Krafft and M. K. Mantrala (eds) *Retailing in the 21st Century: Current and future trends*. Berlin: Springer, pp. 27–38.

Schmekel, V. (2004) The strategic importance of retail investment in Asia and its implications for the Metro Group in Asia, *Journal of Global Marketing*, 18(1/2), 133–150.

Swoboda, B., Schwartz, S. and Hälsig, F. (2007) Towards a conceptual model of country market selection: selection process of retailers and C&C wholesalers. *International Review of Retail Distribution and Consumer Research*, 17(3), 253–282.

Zentes, J., Morschett, D. and Schramm-Klein, H. (2007) Case study: Media Markt and Saturn. In: J. Zentes, D. Morschett and H. Schramm-Klein (eds) *Strategic retail management*. Wiesbaden: Gabler, pp. 42–51.

Zentes, J., Morschett, D. and Schramm-Klein, H. (2007) Case study: Metro. In: J. Zentes, D. Morschett and H. Schramm-Klein *Strategic retail management*. Wiesbaden: Gabler, pp. 325–335.

www.metrogroup.de (corporate website, press releases).

www.planetretail.net (daily news bulletin, various).

www.answers.com (Metro AG).

11 Future directions of retailer internationalization

John Dawson and Masao Mukoyama

A characteristic of retailing in the early twenty-first century is the substantial increase of activities undertaken by retailers based in another country. National boundaries no longer act as constraints to expansion as they did in the twentieth and earlier centuries. International expansion is a feature not only of retailers based in North America and Europe. Retailers from Asian countries are expanding regionally and also are entering established and mature markets in Europe and North America (Mukoyama and Choi 2009). Firms in South America are expanding regionally as are a few East African retailers. In the Gulf States retailers who have acted as regional franchisees for retailers based outside the region have begun to seek ways to move into new markets beyond the Gulf. Whilst there is a view that 'Retail doesn't cross borders' (Corstjens and Lal 2012) the evidence points to increasing international expansion. International retailing is now a universal feature of the distribution sector.

The dominant strategic objective of a retailer is growth of sales. Economies of scale are a powerful factor in obtaining profits in the generic retail business model. Scale economies are present in many retail functions. Whilst increased sales can be generated by more intensive use of existing retail activity, creating increases in like-for-like sales, inflation adjusted growth of this type is generally small, and higher risk, compared with what can be achieved by addressing new markets. These new markets were for many years considered as markets new to the retailer but within the domestic market. Thus, retailers diversified into subsectors and created new formats and formulae to access new parts of the home market, and in a few cases as a secondary activity moved internationally. Typically the firms using this strategy in the later parts of the twentieth century were format driven, for example, Kaufhof, Tengelman, Vendex, Kingfisher, GIB, Ito Yokado, Jusco; or formula driven, for example Burtons, Next, Andre. The major strategic alternative to this domestic format and formula diversification that became widely accepted in the last decade of the twentieth century was to seek the necessary new markets outside the domestic market. Moving internationally not only increases the strength of scale-related benefits internally within the retailer but it also increases the scale of the market to which the retailer has access. The internal and external scale factors reinforce each other. Thus the opportunity arises to gain scale from multiple formats or formulae in multiple markets. Furthermore, these opportunities increase when the scope of the markets is seen as global or multi-continental with access sought to markets at different stages of the economic cycle. Whilst conceptually the strategy provides a way to increase sales and the resulting scale-related cost economies, the problems come from the mechanisms needed to manage the extended network whether multi-format/formula or international, or, as is becoming increasingly the case, both. Implementation failures have been frequent, including several of the exemplar firms mentioned above, and the requirement for new organizational structures to make the multi-format, multi-market strategy a success is now, if belatedly, widely recognized.

The GPS mapping, explored in earlier chapters, provides a framework for considering the development of an international retailer as it moves to a multi-format and multi-continent market structure. Comparative patterns of the activity of retailers can be considered with this framework. GPS is not seen as the end of some optimal progression of a firm but as a template to allow comparisons and descriptions of retailer activity. In considering the expansion and contraction in markets and formats the correspondence of key events to changes in direction of strategy can often be identified. Whilst this is useful it begs the question of why particular events, and not others, are critical in strategic change. It therefore acts as a starting point to answer questions about the nature of the internationalization process in retailing, such as:

- Are there generic factors that enable the expansion of formats in an international context?
- Are there generic capabilities that encourage entry into the countries with very different commercial cultures?
- Are there differences in the capabilities of retailers operating stores regionally and those operating on several continents?
- What factors influence, or determine, the format mix developing in a certain country?
- How is the portfolio of format mixes across countries established and evaluated?

Answers to such questions require theories that can be tested through detailed studies of a range of firms.

This concluding chapter has two aims, both of which look forwards to retailer internationalization over the next decade. First, an attempt is made to consider how retailer internationalization might develop in terms of catalysts, constraints and outcomes. Second, possible ways to theorize the internationalization process are considered as a way to develop future academic analyses.

Future directions of retailer internationalization

Reinartz *et al.* (2011) provide a useful review of elements in the business environment that are influential in retailer internationalization. They highlight the dynamism of these elements and the environment as a whole and also point to the differences in mature, emerging and less developed markets. The dynamism and with it path dependency is a feature of earlier work (Whitley 1999, 2001) that takes a more nuanced view of alternative environments and this has been taken up by Wrigley and Currah (2003) in an international retail context. More recent work by Whitley (2012) explores the increasingly dynamic institutional issues and is relevant to the future of the retail internationalization process. It is necessary, however, to consider more than the external business environment and to consider how internal management of the international retailers might direct their development. The international retailers are not simply passive agents responding to the business environment and consumers but are active in shaping the environment and the consumer culture. Gereffi and Christian (2009) point to the impacts of Wal-Mart in respect of retailer-driven demand chains but many of the points they make can be generalized to the activity of other retailers. Furthermore, retailer influence is not limited to globalized supply chains. This active role of retailers, across many aspects of social change, is one aspect of retailer internationalization that is likely to become more important and influential over the next decade.

Catalysts and constraints to internationalization

A major, possibly the most important, catalyst to any future increase in retailer internationalization is the strategic imperative to grow. Growth of sales is essential to gain scale economies and so maintain a competitive cost base, to act as a defence against unwelcome acquisition bids, show potential for welcome acquisition bids and to satisfy the requirements of a range of stakeholders. Survival of the retailer and its management often requires growth. As the retailer gets larger so the growth imperative becomes stronger. New markets have to be entered. The Wal-Mart annual report of 2010 reflects this growth imperative in stating the firm's first priority as, 'We will continue to grow around the world. We have many opportunities to grow by opening new stores, entering new markets, making acquisitions, integrating online channels, and developing new, innovative formats' (Duke 2010). A feature of the generic trend to globalization is the widening of managerial perceptions of possible markets. These perceptions coupled to the growth imperative lead inevitably to an increase in international, and multi-continental, activity.

A second major catalyst is the general increase in spending power of the global population. Whilst rates of growth are very different across markets, the opportunities presented by the markets with fast-growing spending power presently and those likely to continue with faster growth attract the retailers from the slower growth economies (see Chapter 3). The expanding markets within South and East Asia and South America are likely to be short-term targets with markets in Africa following later. As consumer spending power increases so the market for retail services increases with its catalytic effect on retail internationalization.

Technological advances, particularly in communication technologies, also act as a catalyst to more international activity. The friction of distance is lessened for the international retailer. Whilst the flow of physical goods remains affected by distance, the flow of information is not. The retailer therefore has the possibility of being able to communicate, and potentially exert managerial control, across a widely diffuse network. In respect of communication, the boundaries of national markets are not barriers, neither is the physical distance between centres of control and customer transaction places (see Chapter 2). It is claimed that mobile technologies and cloud computing, for example, reduce operating costs (Pandey *et al.* 2010) and reduce geographical constraints not only for internet-based international retailers, for example Amazon, but also for store-based retailers offering international networks or an international interactive web-based format. Jaeger, for example, in 2009 established online expansion to the USA extending its scope to be multi-continental with its online offer, which in 2009 accounted for 25 per cent of the firm's visits. With the 'cloud model, you free the business to expand, contract or reconfigure at will. Entering a new geography requires no new planning, procurement or installation of IT' (Taylor *et al.* 2011, p. 6). Cloud computing could act as a catalyst for the rapid growth of a new format of international retailing with portal operators, such as Amazon services, operating on an international basis providing a central service to retailers located in a country but with customers anywhere. The rapid evolution of communication technologies acts as a catalyst to increase the scope of international retailing as well as potentially changing some structures.

A fourth catalyst to an increase in retailer internationalization over the next decade is internal to the firms. This is the increase in knowledge and understanding of the internationalization process as a result of gaining experience from past ventures. Success generates confidence as well as establishing corporate routines and managerial capabilities that enable the international growth to be wider in scope and potentially more complex as new markets are entered. Useful knowledge is moved around the firm. Bill Simon, President and CEO of Wal-Mart US, speaking in 2010 emphasized this growth of confidence,

> We have lots of learnings around the world from Wal-Mart in small formats. Our group in Mexico and Central America, Latin America operates small formats very well and very profitably, and we are going to beg, borrow, steal and learn from them as quickly as we can, because it is important for our urban strategy [in the US].
>
> (Simon 2010, p. 6)

The growth in knowledge allows the formula creation to be designed for specific local markets and a continuous process of formula development to occur. As retailers gain more knowledge so they are able to expand internationally more quickly and with more effective formats and formulae. This accumulation of knowledge acts as a catalyst for increases in international activity in coming years.

A further catalyst to internationalization of the sector is a steady reduction in non-tariff barriers particularly in respect of investment and ownership. In a similar way to the increase in international activity following deregulation in Central Europe, the formation of the single market in Europe and NAFTA, as barriers are reduced steadily in the future, for example in in China, India, Malaysia and Indonesia, this will act as a stimulus for international retailers to enter these countries. Although the level of regulation is decreasing there remain a range of nationalistic policies that limit international retailing (Reisman and Vu 2012) but it is likely that these will be eroded steadily over the next decade.

The catalysts, however, are subjected to constraints. A number of factors will shape and possibly slow any potential explosive expansion of international activity.

The implementation of the imperative to grow has some constraints. Financing the growth becomes a constraint if sales growth falters, but whilst sales growth continues and costs are controlled then the cash-generating ability of retailing can mean that financial constraints are less important than other constraints. For the individual retailer this may be a constraint but across the sector the power of this constraint is likely to be limited. There are, for the future, likely to be two significant constraints on the speed at which the growth imperative can be implemented at sector and at firm level; both are internal to the management of retailers.

First, there is the nature of the managerial control over very large and complex network organizations. The form of large retail firms, because of their direct links with many millions of consumers and a large number of suppliers, means that several horizontal and vertical networks have to be coordinated. As the firm grows in size so the network structure becomes more complex both geographically and in terms of the variety of transaction places that are managed. The GPS discussed in this book illustrates the interlocking horizontal networks but in order to control the growing international firm the sourcing network also has to be controlled. It is far from clear if there is a maximum size that can act as a limit on the activities of a retailer. Several retailers operating stores are close to having a presence in 100 countries; Wal-Mart sales in 2012–2013 of over $466 billion are close to the total retail sales of a large country; 7&I in 2013 has over 47,000 stores in their network; Amazon has well over one billion visitors per year. How big can a retailer become and continue to have effective control systems in place? The operation of managerial control is a constraint to international growth.

A second constraint for growth is that of having executive managers who can implement the strategy. This is a constraint at firm and sector level. The studies of firms in this book show the importance of senior management in directing strategy. In many cases the executive power of a person or a small group has been instrumental in the internationalization process of these firms. In the early phases of internationalization, as pointed out in Chapter 1, the role of the individual entrepreneur is all-important. However even in later stages of internationalization, as seen in the case companies, individual executives continue to have substantial corporate power. Ensuring continuity of these key executives can become a constraint to growth. The availability of senior management is an additional human resource constraint. This is not only a quantitative constraint but also has a geographical dimension for the international retailer. Moving into new markets and expansion in those markets requires a cadre of managers who have knowledge of the rules and routines of the firm (Palmer and Quinn 2005; Jonsson and Elg 2006). Whilst some of the routines and knowledge are codified, access to tacit knowledge remains an important part of the implementation of the international growth process.

Access to knowledge of the market constitutes a third constraint to the catalysts for growth. Having knowledge of local consumers and empathy with their behaviour and demands are difficult and complex procedures to establish (Bianchi and Ostale 2006). These procedures are necessary, however, and can serve to temper the catalytic factors. There are many examples of retailers who have failed or have been less successful than expected because they have not fully understood the requirement of the local consumers in host markets. A constraint to international expansion therefore is simply the speed at which retailers, through their management, can gain the capability to adapt to local markets.

Technology developments, whilst a catalyst, are constrained by the ability of retailers to incorporate new technologies into their systems, particularly as changes in organizational structures may be necessary. Technology providers also have yet to meet the complex network requirements of large retailers. Some technology development, including cloud computing, have yet to be proven to be cost effective on a widespread basis compared to large enterprise data centres. There are also constraints associated with the reliability and security of cloud computing. Technology costs are forecast to fall and reliability and security are expected to improve as retailers work with technology providers but these issues are likely to reduce the catalytic impact of these technologies for internationalization.

A final constraint rests with the socio-economic and political institutions in the host country. Whilst there is a steady reduction in the effects of non-tariff barriers they remain an impediment to international expansion in many countries. Institutional and consumer ethnocentrism can also act as a brake on international expansion. Lobby groups and politicians can reinforce inherent consumer conservatism in some consumer cultures in order to generate campaigns against foreign retailers.

Whilst there are strong catalysts to the rapid increase of international retailing over the next decade a number of constraints can slow the process at sector and firm level. Nonetheless it seems likely that the pace of internationalization will increase with international retailers being more in evidence as providers of retail services across most countries of the world.

Possible future outcomes of internationalization in the next decade

Assuming a scenario in which international retailing becomes even more widespread what features of its form, structure and impact might be expected over the next decade?

The tendency to greater concentration of the market is widespread in almost all retail markets. In general the large international retailers take an increasing share of markets in which they are present and this is likely to continue. They also are likely to grow through merger and acquisition activity in the host markets. Cross-border acquisitions are likely to become a more common feature of the internationalization process of retailing. The growth and market concentration will increase the power of the large retailers with the effects of this power evident through their network structures and more widely into the commercial environments in which they are operating. For the very large retailers their organizational structures may need to change as they get ever larger with divisionalization or granulation becoming necessary. The creation of Supermercados Dia from a demerger with Carrefour in 2011 is illustrative of what might become more common. Dia was operated with considerable independence within Carrefour so that the demerger could be undertaken relatively easily. Whilst full demerger, as with Dia, is one possible change of structure others are possible with the granting of greater autonomy to divisions within a group corporate structure. Such moves can increase the extent of sectoral internationalization as has happened with Dia's acquisition of Schlecker and incorporation of the 1,168 Schlecker stores into Dia's European network.

The growth of the number of firms operating internationally and their increased size will almost certainly result in an increase in multi-continent operation over the next decade. The expansion of the scope of firms is likely to involve a range of different organizational arrangements with joint ventures and franchise-type arrangements probably increasing as a mechanism to satisfy the requirement for rapid growth and also as a way of meeting possible restrictions on foreign investment. Foreign retailer activity into African markets is likely to increase the multi-continent footprint of general merchandise and specialist retailers over the next decade. Whilst international retailer penetration into new markets will continue it is likely that the major investments will be into the large and growing markets in East and South Asia and South America. These investments are likely to be made not only by retailers based in Europe, North America and Japan but also by retailers based in these growing markets, following the example of Cencosud, Dairy Farm and Li & Fung, and moving into other markets in the same general region. As large firms develop in Asia, for example, some are likely to explore expansion into regional markets, including China. Therefore there is likely to be a substantial increase in multi-continental activity and also in regional retailer internationalization within East Asia and in South America. Alongside these regional international retailers new multi-continental retailers, following the example of A. S. Watson and Fast Retailing will move out of Asian markets, including Japan, to become competitors to the established firms in Europe and North America. It can be expected that over half of the largest 100 retailers will soon be operating on a multi-continental basis.

A further development in structure is likely to be an expansion of the range of formats and formulae operated by international retailers. Perceptions of increased fragmentation of consumer demand and behaviour patterns together with more sensitive adaption of formulae to local markets will result in more variety in the formula within and between the markets in which a retailer operates. More variety is likely to generate more costs but the adjustment to local demand should result in higher sales and higher margins. Maintaining standardized systems for operational procedures, for example logistics, accounting, etc. should help to offset the higher costs at the consumer interface. The increase in store-based formulae will be augmented by several new formats and formulae in e-commerce. E-commerce formats, both domestically and internationally, are at an early stage of development with several different formats gradually emerging, for example direct interactive website, a merchant services portal, membership website, in-store kiosk service, click and collect stores etc. Retailers presently are tending to operate only one of the several possible formats but this may change and different formats may be suited to some countries rather than others. Similarly there will be different formulae emerging from within these different formats. The developments in international e-retailing will add considerable variety to international format and formula development over the next decade.

These developments in international retailing over the next decade are likely to generate increased involvement by retailers in the processes of economic and societal development. This will take many forms. The international retailers will bring new styles of retailing and new distribution service offerings to consumers in response to their growing demands. They will also bring new systems and procedures for relationships with suppliers, enhancing efficiencies and enhancing quality control and its monitoring (Senauer and Reardon 2011). The network structure of retail firms has the effect of the retailer acting as an agent for the diffusion of social and economic change. The retailers, however, will not only be reactive agents but will also be more active in deliberately shaping consumer culture and effecting institutional changes in economic and political structures. This more active role in shaping social change is likely to be a major and significant outcome of the increase in retailer internationalization in the next decade.

Theorization of the internationalization process

The growth of international activity of retail firms is an important trend in the distribution sector. The internationalization process is resulting in the emergence of large multi-format, multi-continent retailers with substantial power to effect social change. It is possible to see these changes from an empirical viewpoint but it is also useful to consider if the developments can be theorized either at a broad scale in terms of social change or at the narrower scale of retail strategy.

In Chapter 1 we considered if the development of international retailing could be viewed as a Giddens structuration process in which structure and agency recursively interact to generate change in society. The internationalization process can be considered in this way with the rules and resources, internal and external to the firm, influencing and being influenced by agents who purposefully seek to create change. This generalized structuration process is evident in many aspects of internationalization and the approach could be used to theorize internationalization at a broad level. In several of the case studies the agency power of the chief executive or president is very evident but agency is influenced by external rules and internal resources. From the case studies it is also evident that experience and knowledge acquisition are important attributes of the internationalization process. This can be related to the theory of structuration with knowledge of the rules, internal and external, being important in the use of agency power to apply resources to international retail activity. For example, agent activity to adapt supplier relationships to the market results in change to structure.

There are many aspects of agency, as used in structuration theory, that are relevant to the internationalization process. Agency is both internal and external to the retailer. Agency, for example, includes the institutions and policymakers that enact rules governing foreign retailer activities. Agency is also internal to the retailer. One of the aspects of agency, if we apply structuration theory to the international retailing process, is the range of dynamic capabilities used by management as agents. There is a substantial body of research that explores the concept of dynamic capabilities as the underpinning framework for explaining competitive advantage. This is useful as we develop theory relevant to the internationalization process (Cao 2011; Cao and Dupuis 2009).

Teece *et al.* (1997) define dynamic capabilities as 'the firm's ability to integrate, build, and reconfigure internal and external competences to address rapidly changing environments' (p. 516). This definition was later clarified (Teece 2009) by disaggregating dynamic capabilities 'into the capacity: (1) to sense and shape opportunities and threats, (2) to seize opportunities, and (3) to maintain competitiveness by enhancing, combining, protecting, and when necessary, reconfiguring the business enterprise's intangible and tangible assets' (p. 4). These are clearly capabilities relevant to managerial actions in the internationalization process. Helfat *et al.* (2007) emphasize the purposive nature of dynamic capabilities, 'the processes of search and selection are inextricably connected to the creation, extension and modification of a firm's resource base. And it is managers who play a critical role in these processes.' (p. 47). This has resonance with the purposive nature of agency in structuration. The application of the concept of dynamic capabilities to international retailing within a theory of structuration enables theorization about the dynamic nature of the retail internationalization process. Sensing and seizing opportunities are clearly concerned with responding to the environment and shaping and transformational capabilities involve changing the environment. These dynamic capabilities also are relevant to internal processes, including entrepreneurial activity (Pitelis and Teece 2010) within the retail firm. They can be viewed as tools of agency within structuration. Being able to sense opportunities and threats and to seize opportunities from different commercial environments requires additional or higher order routines than are needed domestically. International dynamic capabilities revolve around rapid innovation, adaption and flexibility across multiple markets and within different consumer cultures. The dynamic capabilities, as aspects of agency, have effect when they are applied to aspects of structure.

Important aspects of structure when we apply structuration theory to international retailing are the rules and resources that generate the format and formula mix used by the retailer. The format and formula mix is central to the embeddedness of the retailer in the host market. Following Hess's (2004) view of embeddedness then structure is instrumental in establishing societal embeddedness, in effect the corporate culture of the international retailer, with format and formula the result of the rules and resources that frame the retailer's culture. Network embeddedness results from the application of agency, through dynamic capabilities, to the rules and resources that frame the relationships of format and formula with other economic and social actors. Territorial embeddedness results from the adaption of format and formula to the consumer and commercial culture of the host society. The capabilities of sensing, seizing and transforming are key to the adaption of the format and formula whilst their constant evolution requires the capabilities to be dynamic and in this way they drive the territorial embeddedness. Coe and Lee (2013) have developed the conceptualization of territorial embeddedness to emphasize the variability of adaption that takes place in internationalization into different host markets, using the term strategic localization. 'Strategic localization can be conceptualized as the specific strategies employed by TNCs to try and develop territorial embeddedness in host markets' (p. 5 doi version). We can see this approach as implemented through the dynamic capabilities exhibited by agency. These ideas of embeddedness and strategic localization can be viewed as integral parts of an overall structuration process.

Theorizing the retail internationalization as structuration allows a broader conceptualization of the process than has been used previously. As retailers become more active and directive in internationalization activity so they have more effect on societal changes. The retailer responds to the host consumer and commercial environment and also creates changes in it. Theorization needs to accommodate this two-way dynamic process. The theory of structuration also allows the approaches of dynamic capabilities and of embeddedness to be integrated into broader theory.

Conclusion

Over the next decade we can expect significantly more international activity by retailers. More retailers will become multi-format and multi-continent in their operations. The process of retailer internationalization will become more complex and more influential in shaping consumer and societal change. But within this expansion of activity a conundrum exists in retail strategy – success can result from a range of different strategies even in the same market. There is no single dominant strategy. There are, and always have been, substantial and often rapid changes in the environment in which retailing operates and to which retailers were seen as responding. As retailers now respond to the consumer and competitive environment and also shape that environment so the patterns of change become more complex. The extra complexity increases the possible ways that strategies can be designed and successfully implemented. Strategy takes on a portfolio appearance with different strategies being used for different formats and different markets within a single retailer. This results in a global portfolio approach to strategy.

The move by firms to developing a multi-format and multi-continent presence poses a number of challenges to theoretical considerations of retailer internationalization. Stages theory, push and pull, internalization theory and others do not adequately address the ways that the internationalization process is changing. Structuration theory provides a possible alternative basis for exploring the internationalization processes in the retail sector. By conceptualizing retail internationalization as resulting from the recursive interaction of structure and agency it becomes possible to incorporate new approaches to considering agency, for example through the dynamic capabilities of agents, and structure, for example through the rules and resources associated with formula and format development. The portfolio character of international retailer strategy then has a framework on which empirical case studies can be built.

References

Bianchi, C. C. and Ostale, E. (2006) Lessons learned from unsuccessful internationalization attempts: examples of multinational retailers in Chile. *Journal of Business Research*, 59(1), 140–147.

Cao, L. (2011) Dynamic capabilities in a turbulent market environment: empirical evidence from international retailers in China. *Journal of Strategic Marketing*, 19(5), 455–469.

Cao, L. L. and Dupuis, M. (2009) Core competence, strategy and performance: the case of international retailers in China. *International Review of Retail, Distribution and Consumer Research*, 19(4), 349–369.

Coe, N. M. and Lee, Y.-S. (2013) 'We've learnt how to be local': the deepening territorial embeddedness of Samsung-Tesco in South Korea. *Journal of Economic Geography* (advanced access) doi:10.1093/jeg.lbs057, now published in 13(2), 327–356.

Corstjens, M. and Lal, R. (2012) Retail doesn't cross borders. *Harvard Business Review*, April, 104–111.

Duke, M. T. (2010) CEO's letter. Available at: www.walmartstores.com/sites/ annual report/2010/ceo_letter.aspx.

Gereffi, G. and Christian, M. (2009) The impacts of Wal-Mart: the rise and consequences of the world's dominant retailer. *Annual Review of Sociology*, 35, 573–591.

Helfat, C., Finkelstein, S., Mitchell, W., Peteraf, M. A., Singh, H., Teece, D. J. and Winter, S. G. (2007) *Dynamic capabilities: understanding strategic change in organizations*. Oxford: Blackwell.

Hess, M. (2004) 'Spatial' relationships? Towards a reconceptualization of embeddedness. *Progress in Human Geography*, 28(2), 165–186.

Jonsson, A. and Elg, U. (2006) Knowledge and knowledge sharing in retail internationalization: IKEA's entry into Russia. *International Review of Retail, Distribution and Consumer Research*, 16(2), 239–256.

Mukoyama, M. and Choi, S. C. (eds) (2009) *Retail internationalisation*. Tokyo: Chuokeizai (in Japanese).

Palmer, M. and Quinn, B. (2005) An explanatory framework for analyzing international retail learning. *International Review of Retail, Distribution and Consumer Research*, 15(1), 27–52.

Pandey, A., Pandey, A., Tandon, A., Maurya, B. K., Kushwaha, U., Mishra, M. and Tiwari, V. (2010) Cloud computing: exploring the scope. Paper to *International Conference on Informatics, Cybernetics, and Computer Applications*. Available at: http://arxiv.org/ftp/arxiv/papers/1005/1005.1904.pdf.

Pitelis, C. N. and Teece, D. J. (2010) Cross-border market co-creation, dynamic capabilities and the entrepreneurial theory of the multinational enterprise. *Industrial and Corporate Change*, 19(4), 1247–1270.

Reinartz, W., Dellaert, B., Krafft, M., Kumar, V. and Varadarajan, R. (2011) Retailing innovations in a globalizing retail market environment. *Journal of Retailing*, 87S(1), S53–S66.

Reisman, M. and Vu, D. (2012) *Nontariff measures in the global retailing industry*. Working Paper ID30, Washington: US International Trade Commission.

Senauer, B. and Reardon, T. (2011) The global spread of modern food retailing. In: G. G. Hamilton, M. Petrovic and B. Senauer (eds) *The market makers: how retailers are reshaping the global economy*. Oxford: Oxford University Press, pp. 272–290.

Simon, B. (2010) Speech. Goldman Sachs Retail Conference, 15 September 2010. Thomson Reuters StreetEvents Final Transcript. Available at: http://media.corporate-ir.net/media_files/irol/11/112761/WMT-Transcript-2010-09-15T15_55.pdf.

Taylor, A., Kellett, S. and Worrall, J. (2011) *Retail retold: bringing the high street back to life with technology*. Fujitsu Services insight paper on retail. Available at: www.fujitsu.com/uk/whitepapers/retail-retold.

Teece, D. J. (2009) *Dynamic capabilities and strategic management*. Oxford: Oxford University Press.

Teece, D. J., Pisano, G. and Shuen, A. (1997) Dynamic capabilities and strategic management. *Strategic Management Journal*, 18(7), 509–533.

Whitley, R. (1999) *Divergent capitalisms: The social structuring and change of business systems*. Oxford: Oxford University Press.

Whitley, R. (2001) How and why are international firms different? The consequences of cross-border managerial coordination for firm characteristics and behaviour. In: G. Morgan, P. H. Kristensen and R. Whitley (eds) *The multinational firm: organizing across institutional and national divides*. Oxford: Oxford University Press, pp. 27–68.

Whitley, R. (2012) Internationalization and the institutional structuring of economic organization: changing authority relations in the twenty-first century. In: G. Morgan and R, Whitley (eds) *Capitalisms and capitalism*. Oxford: Oxford University Press, pp. 211–235.

Wrigley, N. and Currah, A. (2003) The stresses of retail internationalization: lessons from Royal Ahold's experience in Latin America. *International Review of Retail, Distribution and Consumer Research*, 13(3) 221–243.

Index

Page numbers in *italics* denote tables, those in **bold** denote figures.

For Product Safety Concerns and Information please contact our EU
representative GPSR@taylorandfrancis.com
Taylor & Francis Verlag GmbH, Kaufingerstraße 24, 80331 München, Germany